Northern Athabascan Survival

Winner of the 2000 North American Indian Prose Award

AWARD COMMITTEE

Gerald Vizenor, Chair, University of California at Berkeley

Diane Glancy, Macalester College

A. LaVonne Brown Ruoff, University of Illinois at Chicago

Northern
Athabascan
Survival:

Women, Community, and the Future

Phyllis Ann Fast

University of Nebraska Press

Lincoln and London

Part of chapter 3 was previously published as
"Subsistence among the Gwichin Athabascans
of Northern Alaska," *Cultural Survival* 21 (1998):
57–58, and is reprinted by permission.

Composition by Wilsted & Taylor Publishing Services
Manufactured in the United States of America
♾
Library of Congress Cataloging-in-Publication Data
Fast, Phyllis Ann, 1946–
    Northern Athabascan survival : women,
community, and the future / Phyllis Ann Fast.
        p. cm.
    Includes bibliographical references and index.
    ISBN 0-8032-2017-0 (cloth : alk. paper)
        1. Gwich'in Indians—Social conditions.
2. Gwich'in Indians—Economic conditions.
3. Athapascan Indians—Social conditions.
4. Athapascan Indians—Economic conditions.
5. Athapascan women. I. Title.
E99.K84 F37 2002
305.89′972—dc21
2002017979

"𝒩"

Contents

Tables

Acknowledgments

Many individuals and agencies contributed to my efforts in writing this study. I thank the National Science Foundation for financial support received through its fellowship program for minorities. I also thank Harvard University for its financial support through the President's Prize Fellowship for Minorities. I am deeply grateful to each of the members of my thesis committee, who spent many hours reading my drafts and helping me formulate a better study. In particular, I thank David Maybury-Lewis, who advised me in every phase of my graduate career at Harvard University. I am equally indebted to Inés Talamantez of the University of California at Santa Barbara, who insists that Native Americans have their own epistemologies, ontologies, and paradigms. I also thank Ronald Niezen of Harvard University, whose knowledge of Native Americans in Canada and the United States was of immeasurable help to me during my final year of writing this study.

Many Athabascan people in Alaska also contributed to this study in significant ways. Among these are members of my family: Esther Lee Fast, Richard Jonathan Fast, Donald A. Harper, Louise Harper Blair, Helen Connie Harper, Mary Harper Denton, Michael C. Harper, Flora Jane Harper Petri, Lawrence Haines, Jane E. Harper, and Jan Harper Haines. I am indebted to Marilyn Savage, who spent hours helping me understand the Gwich'in language, translated many documents for me, and mentored me throughout my stay in Gwich'in villages. I am particularly grateful to Marilyn for spending so much time explaining concepts of Gwich'in leadership to me. Clara R. Johnson, whose roots are also in Rampart, was one of the most determined of my mentors, as she is for other Alaska Native scholars. I thank Linda Wells for her friendship and patient support of all my academic efforts. I thank Audrey Fields for letting me burn the hamburgers and undercook the chicken in her restaurant, not to mention teaching me many of the practical facets of living in Gwich'in land. In addition, I thank Mary Fields for her great assistance in teaching me Gwich'in. I thank Carolyn Peter, who helped me in several areas of this study and befriended me and my family ever since I met her. Likewise, I am grateful to Sarah James and Lillian Garnett, who mentored me throughout this effort. In addition, I thank Clarence Alexander, who urged me to understand consensus as the Gwich'in do and reviewed early drafts of my writing. I also thank Gideon James, who instructed me about the ancient Athabascan trading partner system, the contemporary political efforts of the Venetie Tribal Government (IRA), and the complex meanings underlying the terms *vat'aii* and *dat'aii*. I thank Nancy James for her critical review of every phase of my field research. Finally, I thank the late Peter Kalifornski for his poetry and other words of inspiration. I also give thanks to Carrie Joseph, Doris Ward, Mardow Solomon, Jonathan Solomon, Martha Flitt, Ellen Bruce, Mae Wallis, Margaret Cadzow, Mary Simple, the late Julia Peter, the late Abel Zhuh Tritt, and the late Stephen Peter for their wisdom in teaching me about Athabascan life and their many other kindnesses to me.

In addition, I thank Patricia Stanley, Joyce Hughes, Hanne Bergman, Cheryl Williams and Earl Cadzow, Kathy and Richard Carroll II, Caroline and Kenneth Frank, Trimble Gilbert, Steve Ginnis, Grafton Njootli, Adeline Peter-Raboff Kari, Donald Peter, Ethel Simple, Shirley Thomas, Virginia Alexander, Phyllis Ward, and Silas and Selina Alexander. I also thank Mae Glazer and Bonnie Peter, Mardow Solomon Jr., Marybeth Solomon, Theresa Thomas, Lincoln and Aron Tritt, Phyllis White, and Dee Walters.

I thank Bernard Christopher Perley, Elizabeth Sakordie-Mensah, and Rosita Worl for reading the final drafts and befriending me through the other intricacies of achieving a Ph.D. from Harvard University. I also thank my friends Maria Williams and Ruth Kalerak for all of their advice and guidance. Finally, I give thanks to the late Barry Wallis for his mentorship and gentle guidance and to the late Wally Peter for his careful review of my work.

Shitjyaa naii Phyllis Ann Fast sharahnyaa. Aii shahan t'ee Elsie Harper Fast oozhii ts'a' shahan vahan t'ee Louise Minook Harper oozhii. Aii shitsuu vahan t'ee Martha Sport Minook ts'a' oodi' teetsii k'iidi' shitsuu vahan ts'a' yeedii khadoozhii. Hizhii gwats'a' Tanana haa vakai' John Minook quich'ii. Shitsuu Rampart hoiizhii haa vakai' Samuel Harper. Shahan Rampart gwilik, aiitł'ee Fairbanks aiitł'ee Anchorage hoiizhii haa vakai'. Shiti' t'ee Oscar Harold Fast oozhii. Shachaa Richard Jonathan Fast oozhii ts'a' shijuu Esther Lee Fast oozhii. Akwat it'ee jyaa dagwahtsii ts'a'.

This is a greeting to Gwich'in speakers in a style based on the vocabulary of the late Belle Herbert as found in the story of her life, *Shandaa* (1988), and corrected by Mary Fields of Fort Yukon, Alaska. Herbert was born around 1860. In this greeting I identify myself in a formal way to Native people:

> *My friends, my name is Phyllis Ann Fast. My mother was called Elsie Harper Fast, and my grandmother's name was Louise Minook Harper. My great grandmother was called Martha Sport Minook, and my great grandmother came from way down [the Yukon] river. She went to live in Tanana with her husband, John Minook. My grandmother went to live in Rampart with her husband, Samuel Harper. My mother was born in Rampart and then lived in Fairbanks and then Anchorage with her husband. My father was Oscar Harold Fast [a white man from Kansas]. My younger brother is Richard Jonathan Fast. My younger sister is Esther Lee Fast. That is all I am going to say.*

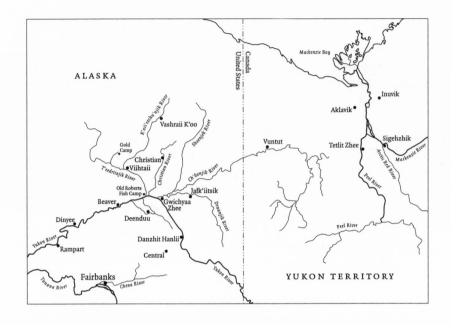

The World of the Northern Athabascans

Northern Athabascan Survival

1 Contemporary Life: *Caustic Bonds*

The lights of Gwichyaa Zhee glowed yellow below thick ice fog. The ten-passenger aircraft had already descended toward the runway four times. We had been circling for nearly an hour. My legs had long since informed me that one set of thermal underwear was insufficient, and my feet were getting cold in their Bunny boots. Terror was doing more to freeze my heart than the -50 degree temperature outside. I willed the pilot to give up and take me home. Instead, he found the signal he needed and brought us down. Ganaandaii, the brother-in-law of my friend Itree, was there to drive me to Itree's house. His old sedan was one of the few vehicles that could run in this weather. Itree was out — teaching a language class at the local university. Ganaandaii left, and the house seemed to close against me. A single wood stove warmed the four-room building, allowing a prong of ice to grow through a nearby electrical outlet. Everything seemed brighter than reality. I felt both huge and invisible, on the inside of a place that did not know me, an urban Athabascan woman entering the homeland of rural (or, in my imagination, real) Northern Athabascans. I had come to Gwichyaa Zhee partly because of the notoriety of the Arctic National Wildlife Refuge, which is north of Gwichyaa Zhee. I was also there because my friend Itree thought I should learn what it was really like to live in a village. She is Gwich'in. I am Koyukon from my mother's side.

The village of Gwichyaa Zhee lies at the confluence of the Yukon and the Ch'ôonjik Rivers in northeastern Alaska about 100 miles west of the U.S.–Canadian border and eight miles north of the Arctic Circle. Approximately 750 people claim residency in Gwichyaa Zhee year round.

They live in wooden structures, mostly single-family homes, although there are four or five multifamily houses. The Gwichyaa Zhee airstrip is the primary means of access to this community and for most outsiders constitutes the only entry and exit point to the village. There are a couple of small, privately owned buildings beside it. My luggage was tossed out of the aircraft and placed on the icy snow beside the steel-mesh fence that outlines the airstrip. A huddle of people and waiting vehicles assembled for other passengers. An emergency vehicle had brought two frostbitten men for deportation to a hospital in the nearest urban center — Fairbanks. I learned months later that the airline I used provides a van to take passengers to and from their homes in Gwichyaa Zhee. There were also a few residents who charged $3.00–5.00 for a ride in their "taxis," privately owned vehicles, one of the several cottage industries in Gwichyaa Zhee that I discuss in chapter 3.

A nearly abandoned U.S. Air Force base dominates the east side of Gwichyaa Zhee. In clear weather, four huge electromagnetic receiving structures announce the entryway to the compound. The two larger of these constructions were erected during the 1950s as part of a defensive measure to protect the United States from possible invasion from the Soviet Union. Two smaller antennae replaced the function of the older ones during the early 1980s, but the older antennae remain in place, being too expensive to dismantle. The military portion of the base closed in 1986. The U.S. Bureau of Land Management, the Civil Air Patrol, the Army National Guard, and other federal agencies maintain facilities within it. Military aircraft bring shipments into Gwichyaa Zhee for the base once or twice a month, indicating one aspect of the fiscal presence of the U.S. federal government in Gwichyaa Zhee. The goods shipped in via military aircraft include trucks and vans, visible to everyone, and probably, but invisibly, office supplies and food for the government employees who live there. These and other manifestations of outside economic interest in Northern Athabascan territory caught my eye from the first day. Like many Western institutions, the U.S. government has invested heavily in maintaining a physical presence in Gwichyaa Zhee while avoiding a corresponding amount of capital investment in the people who live there. Again, related issues appear in chapter 3.

After a preliminary visit to Gwichyaa Zhee in 1992, I returned on January 21, 1993, and resided there until August 4, 1995. Most of my research took place in Gwichyaa Zhee, but I also visited five other Northern Athabascan communities in Alaska including my mother's birthplace, Rampart. I visited several Tanana Athabascan communities, including Fairbanks, Minto, and Nenana; the southern Tuchone community of Whitehorse in Canada; and all of the Dena'ina Athabascan communities of my own birthplace, Anchorage. I focused on several Gwich'in villages, all of which are located on or near rivers: Vashraii K'oo on the K'aii'eechu'njik River; Viihtaii on the T'eedriinjik River; Beaver, Danzhit Hanlii, and Dinyee along the Yukon River; and four Northern Athabascan communities in Canada: Vuntut in Yukon, Tetlit Zhee on the Peel River, Sigehzhik on the Arctic Red River, and Inuvik (all of the latter are in the Northwest Territories). Although there is a language area and a kinship network surrounding these villages, none of them is populated exclusively by one Athabascan nation. The population base of the smaller communities is, therefore, primarily mixed Northern Athabascan, with 10–15 percent non-Native residents throughout.

In each community I spent many hours talking primarily with women about issues that affected their lives. Perhaps because most people either assumed or knew that I was employed by the university as a facilitator, the education and safety of their children factored significantly into many conversations, as did alcoholism, getting sober, and good health. Northern Athabascan women, some of whom held positions of authority within the tribes, often brought up local political issues. When I began my fieldwork I wanted to seek women's views, but I was without a formulated expectation of what I would find. In the final analysis of my field notes, I realized that if I did not present women's experiences from their perspective, much of what I had heard and witnessed would lose a significant aspect of its political and economic dimension. Northern Athabascan women tend to hold year-round jobs, while men often work for wages during the summer only. Many Northern Athabascan women function without economic support or accountability from the fathers of their children. However, they face larger problems in tackling their daily social responsibilities as Athabascan matrons, responsibilities that slither around and sometimes butt up against mainstream values and priorities.

Based on the concerns and metaphors expressed by both women and men about these issues, this study explores Northern Athabascan use of traditional techniques to undermine stereotypes about Native Americans as well as the ambiguities of federal policy administration in isolated regions where economic control is shaky. Much of the supportive information in this study concerns the Gwich'in Athabascans of northeastern Alaska and northwestern Canada. As in many parts of Indian Country, economic activity in Gwich'in Athabascan territory is enmeshed in the commerce of addictive products, addictive therapies, and their attendant financial systems. Like most Northern Athabascans, the Gwich'in make use of both traditional and adopted ideas for many reasons, one of which is to invoke new healing processes to end addictions.

Economy takes on a different image in terms of quotidian semiotic expression in Gwichyaa Zhee than it does in the mainstream United States. The artifacts of exchange representing the Northern Athabascan economy are structured around different concepts of cash, what cash does, and how it is used. Those who use and maintain bank accounts without difficulty are known and trusted by those who do not as wealthy intermediaries to the Western world. During the time I lived in Gwichyaa Zhee only a small percentage of the population used bank accounts. In 1995, I tried to help one of the chiefs of Vashraii K'oo open a savings account for his daughter. I, along with the bank official in Fairbanks, tried to explain the details, including what was supposed to happen after we walked out the door — such as putting more money into the account periodically. I still wonder if the daughter knows how to get her money out of the bank. The frustration of not speaking the same language, although all of us speak English, at that moment was enormous. The chief, whom I have designated as T'ah'in in this study, can read and comprehend Indian law far better than I do and has negotiated many complex contracts for his tribe. Despite his sophisticated knowledge of Western legal customs, he, like many Northern Athabascan people, has never internalized some of the economic patterns that mainstream Americans consider common sense.

Thus, while the categories of cash economy and subsistence living have meaning in both Northern Athabascan country and the mainstream United States, the semiotics involved in such items as currency or cash are very different in the two cultural areas. These issues are examined in greater detail in chapter 3. In brief, that chapter addresses three areas of economy: actual cash, hunting/fishing (also known as subsistence), and noncash products of the mainstream economy (which include corporate, state, and personal checks; tribal budgets; credit at local stores; and per diem travel and funding). Currency defines reality for many people in the villages: it represents one's ability to buy food and liquor, to gamble, to do laundry, and to loan money to relatives and other people in need. Most of the currency circulating through Northern Athabascan territory originates through various potentially addictive activities (such as bingo), whereas noncash products, such as payroll checks, often remain physically outside the village to pay creditors or earn interest in bank accounts. This distinction is noticed and criticized by Northern Athabascan leaders. Many Northern Athabascan people express a desire to break their economic and physical dependencies through a variety of healing methods ranging from youth programs to Alcoholics Anonymous (AA). Also, the Northern Athabascans as a whole have become increasingly successful in bringing in new sources of revenue via tourist and educational institutions. Two areas of social action are involved in their drive to move into another economic mode of existence: one is social healing, and the other is social silence. The former springs from a statewide sobriety movement among Alaska Natives and is nurtured by local projects such as public conferences and a renewed interest in traditional healing techniques. However, theoretical dissent from Christian groups and tentative ideas about what constitutes traditional Northern Athabascan healing medicine preclude anything that resembles a widespread social movement.

Social silence, something the Northern Athabascans sometimes call consensus, works both as a benefit and as a barrier to change. Some Northern Athabascan leaders use consensus as a beneficial device to claim authority to fund numerous projects in the name of Northern Athabascan traditional government. As a barrier, Northern Athabascan social silence operates by the continuous shifting of accountability and the avoidance of investing leadership authority in single entities. In this regard, the Northern Athabascans make strategic use of consensual reinterpretation of history to justify continuation of present or future events and policy without including public debate or, hence, dissent.

As an example, many Gwich'in Athabascans voice their consent or dissatisfaction in public meetings in Gwichyaa Zhee and other Gwich'in villages quite often, as they hold well-attended public meetings regularly. While consensus achieves beneficial actions for the Gwich'in, sometimes the voices of individual Gwich'in are unheard or obviated by so-called consensual decisions. *Consensus* is a term that the Gwich'in use often, with many different levels of meaning. For some it means full agreement among voting members, but most of the time *consensus* means that two or more people have agreed to do something for the benefit of a larger group and hope their decision will be unchallenged. One of the most noteworthy uses of consensus has been in the form of small-scale ethnic violence that takes the form of evictions in Gwich'in. The 1994 eviction of a non-Native family demonstrates the complexity and density of Gwich'in cultural perseverance in its aspects of silence, consensus, and violence.

Eviction of a Family

In early spring 1994 I went to a local grocery store. A family of five occupied the only park benches in Gwichyaa Zhee — inside the store. The family members filled the small space with their otherness. The dominant symbol of that difference was the flaming red hair of the mother, daughter, and older son. Sitting with eyes fixed on the air ten inches in front of them, they did not speak. It was probably enough to wait for someone to bring the key to their new abode. It was probably enough to wonder if anyone would guide them to it. They had brought three rottweilers with them, a mated pair and a puppy. A few months after their arrival the family captured community attention in almost every way — from various governmental agencies, commercial institutions, and private citizens — not simply because of the dogs but because of the family's reasons for coming to Northern Athabascan territory. I call them the Langfields, a pseudonym.

Mr. Langfield was said to be a retired carpenter who wanted to get away from civilization and thought he might do so in a remote Alaskan village. He looked to be around 55. He was a tall and lean man, and his habitual expression was a grimace. This in itself was not unusual in Gwichyaa Zhee, as most people keep their faces still and more or less devoid of expression until they encounter a friend. Mr. Langfield offended several people in Gwichyaa Zhee, and although there was never any uproar about him specifically, I heard rumors and innuendo. For one thing, he and his oldest son walked around the town together fairly often. Both tall white men, they stood out as foreigners to the people and to the landscape. Their posture and walking styles were unlike those of most Northern Athabascans such as the Gwich'in, who are generally smaller and generally walk alone, close to the sides of the road, with toes or the outer part of the foot hitting the ground first. The Langfield father and son usually strode side by side down the centers of the roads, shoulders back, heels landing first, talking with great energy to each other. When they walked their dogs, they went together, holding the dogs with four-foot lengths of heavy-gauge chain. When my friends made comments about the family excursions, they would say something like, "I saw that family today," leaving the rest of the statement an empty bubble of unspoken thoughts. Because they usually tilted their heads toward the cabin that the Langfields rented, I would supply the name and get a nod in return. Often the speaker had nothing more to say about them, so that particular kind of discourse indicated that the individuals were simply being watched. At one point I asked my friend and mentor Ch'adantł'oo what he knew about them, and he told me that Mr. Langfield had tried to acquire land in the region but was rebuffed by the Tribal Council for which Ch'adantł'oo worked. The problem centered around Mr. Langfield's belief that he had a right to buy real estate anywhere in the United States. He did not realize that much Northern Athabascan land still held in private ownership continues to be bound by federal and tribal restrictions. Few besides Alaska Natives of any given region in Alaska meet the complexity of bureaucratic requirements.

Mrs. Langfield, who was much younger than her husband, was then in her midthirties. She got a job as a grocery clerk in the store where I first saw her. Her friendly smiles became daily greetings to all customers. She told me one day that her family had never spent two years in the same state. Her two younger children, both in their teens, were enrolled in Gwichyaa Zhee's one school. I saw the daughter, Zephyr, in company with teenagers of the village once in a while. She looked very much like her mother, with long, bright hair, a visual contrast to the dark-haired Athabascan teens who befriended her. One day I watched Zephyr and her friends come into the store where her mother worked. Zephyr leaned against the wall directly opposite Mrs. Langfield, who aimed an expert eye at her daughter and left the cash register to sniff Zephyr's breath. If she said anything to the girl, it was inaudible. The group of teens soon left the store en masse. I did not know if Mrs. Langfield had been checking for dental caries or something else.

The Langfield experience came to a climax one snowy afternoon in October 1994. Since they arrived at Gwichyaa Zhee the Langfields had troubled encounters with local residents. Their rottweilers had frightened many people, including me. After a close call in March, I inspected every street for dog shapes before walking along them in fear of a second attack. In April the Langfields stopped tying the dogs outside at night or when they were not at home because of numerous threats to kill their dogs. By the end of May they stopped walking their dogs in public. In September some Gwichyaa Zhee adolescents threw a pipe bomb into the family's house. The Langfields found different lodging in Gwichyaa Zhee, and the Gwichyaa Zhee Tribal Council offered to charter a plane to help the family move out. They declined the first offer. A second opportunity soon became available:

A figure ran toward me veiled by slow-falling snowflakes. Slim legs framed long arcs — a magical stride. Her peaked hat evoked a pixie's image. The girl stopped when a woman called to her from a truck. My path took me and my thoughts in another direction. My boots plodded without grace over slippery, snow-covered hard pack. I wondered what spirit protected the young woman's stride when I could barely walk. Now it was late October. I learned *that Mr. and Mrs. Langfield had flown into Fairbanks that morning. While the children were in school someone let their adult rottweiler dogs out of the house. The dogs attacked a four-year-old girl, and within moments both dogs were dead — shot. An angered villager went to the family's house to shoot the third animal. When I saw her, Zephyr had been running from the bodies of the two older dogs to find the third. She cuddled it for hours before someone took them both to the clinic. Her puppy's misery ended there. A few days later the family accepted free transportation out of Gwichyaa Zhee.*

People in Gwichyaa Zhee expressed their feelings about the Langfields more freely in the week following the shooting than they had before or afterward. Gwazhał and his wife befriended Zephyr during the week of the shootings. Gwazhał took Zephyr to the clinic and stayed with her until the dog was destroyed. His wife, Janica (a pseudonym), a white substance abuse counselor, offered advice to the entire family and focused her professional attention on Zephyr. In addition, one of the teenaged girls in Gwichyaa Zhee jeopardized her own ties with other village teens by announcing her loyalty to Zephyr. These tender gestures did not change the outcome. The last time I saw Mrs. Langfield in Gwichyaa Zhee was a day or so before the family left. She was walking with her younger son around the village, staring at each passerby with a fixed smile. One year later I saw her in Fairbanks. Her hair had grayed to a reddish brown. She told me that she was glad they had moved because they were all able to get jobs. She was wearing a kitchen apron marked with the insignia of an Alaskan tour company.

The way in which the people of Gwichyaa Zhee removed the Langfields enacted an aspect of habitual social violence that I saw often there. There were no public discussions or meetings about the family, and there was very little gossip except in closed, primarily gender-restricted circles. Nonetheless, everyone seemed to know what was happening through a generalized murmuring of concerns. If I had not been in town on the day of the shootings, I might not have heard about them, for I, too, was an outsider. However, during the few days afterward, and because I was known as an insider to at least one gossip group, many people beyond my own gossip circle asked me if I knew about it and offered information if I asked. Closures to gossip based on one's acceptance in the community are typical in Gwichyaa Zhee, as elsewhere. However, such reluctance to gossip beyond small cliques magnifies and expedites negative aspects of silence characteristic of Northern Athabascan social action. Because they sometimes fail to take advice or complaints from the small groups, those in larger arenas have become habituated to acting for the sake of expediency. Closure to outsiders, and closure to an unpopular situation, propelled the eviction process. It is an example in a very small population of the "routinization of collective violence" that Tambiah suggests "has increasingly become a regularized mode of enacting mass politics and a central experience in the defining self-perception of collectivities and their expectations of social intercourse" (1996:323). If the Northern Athabascans numbered in the millions instead of the hundreds, this form of violence might become noticeable as a form of ethnic violence in the way that it has in other parts of the world.

Social silence was another mechanism in operation during the event. Social silence as it occurred throughout the eviction of the Langfields gives the Gwich'in a united front that is not predicated on expectations of behavioral conformity. As the eviction ensued, consensus emerged as an uneven and common but not unanimous attitude rather than as thoughts or actions originating from a single directive point or code of behaviors. This attitude did not include everyone in the village during that crisis: some people reached out to the family, especially the daughter, but most did nothing except spread the news. None of the village authorities directed all of the activities, but all of them played some part in that inexorable series of events. The village chief offered a chartered flight on behalf of the Tribal Council in September but not in October. One of the airline companies ultimately gave the family free passage. The brand new, white city manager found ways to reimburse the family for the loss of their dogs, and one family gave a puppy to them when the city government paid for it. The police chief accepted responsibility for the death of the rottweilers although she had not pulled the trigger. Whether or not everyone in Gwichyaa Zhee joined the urge to evict them, the consequences speak for themselves: the family members left involuntarily less than a year after their arrival. That is the power of silence and consensus as the Northern Athabascans engage in them. It also manifests the strength of Gwich'in Athabascan ethnicity to bind people together in a consonant silence of social resiliency. In this event and others that happened while I was in Gwich'in territory, the Gwich'in demonstrated how much time and money they could divert to resisting unwanted people by tapping into funds sanctioned for other uses in the mainstream economy. In this, the impetus and execution of the evictions reside firmly with the Gwich'in and were funded by outside entities as one of the ironies of Northern Athabascans' dependency economy.

In this sort of social action, Northern Athabascan women play many roles, including spreading information and formulating acceptable ranges of perspectives through gossip. Women also serve as mediators in alleviating some of the tensions by offering counseling and spiritual signals to each other. Spiritual behavior or signs as I witnessed them included formal and informal invocations to *vit'eegwijyaahchy'aa* or the Christian God and singing religious songs (both Christian *ch'iliks* and traditional drum songs) as well as smudging sage (an innovation from the Pan-Indian Movement). My friend Itree visited elders when she was depressed or ill and, among other things, asked them to sing to her.

Women were also active as instigators of any evictions that resulted in the improved well-being of their children. The following event is typical.

In 1993, Andrew Dakota (a pseudonym) was hired to teach one of the preschool classes. I met him shortly after he arrived when he came to the university to present Janica with a gift of introduction and I was visiting her myself. Janica was the head of the local branch of the university. Andrew told us that he had already presented the first chief of Gwichyaa Zhee with a gift, and he was trying to meet all of the key people whom he should honor. He did it with grace, and I felt insufficient, not having done so myself. Janica wished him well, and he left after a few minutes. I did not hear anything about him until midwinter, when Janica told me that he was being terminated from his contract because he was being threatened with violence by some of the local people. Despite his initial efforts to win the trust of the parents of Gwichyaa Zhee, he had angered one of the women in the village. T'iichy'aa was a young mother of two who had been hired as a teacher's aide for Andrew. One of her sons was in their classroom. The problem arose when Andrew disciplined her little boy and other students in a manner unsuitable to T'iichy'aa. T'iichy'aa was a member of the Drin family of Gwichyaa Zhee. The Drin family members supported their daughter and threatened Andrew with guns. The principal of the school recommended that Andrew take an extra month off after the Christmas break in hopes that the affair would blow over. It did only to the extent that matters did not get worse for Andrew. When he came back in February he was removed from his original teaching slot and kept on salary until the end of the school term. Because the issue did not become a village-wide matter, he was not asked to leave early.

Many of the new teachers I met suffered similar distress during their first years of teaching, and many were not given new contracts. Some, like Andrew, were told to leave with threats of violence that the state-operated school district tried to keep quiet. As in Andrew's case, the school district often helps the teachers to move efficiently in hopes of avoiding litigation. No one approaches the families for apologies or any other form of restitution. As with so many of these evictions, there are murmurings throughout the community, with no public action or debate in defense of either position. In this way, Northern Athabascan parents maintain a solid front of silent and physical or political control over their children's educations. Some parents are not silent but voice their complaints loudly at parent meetings, whereas others, like T'iichy'aa, solicit support from their families and know that public discussion is therefore not necessary. The school district thereby is left with the financial burden of removing and rehiring new teachers every year, and the Northern Athabascan parents assume tacit control over the school district's methods of teaching. The history, economic situation, and effect of Western education on Gwichyaa Zhee form a central issue of dissent among Northern Athabascan residents. As the school system is a primary advocate of healing methods, the fact that it is perceived in such a negative light by Northern Athabascan parents increases debate and hinders community development of consistent healing theory.

In the past century the Gwich'in people have had more cause to use community support as a political force against outsiders than have many other Alaska Native populations. This study picks out some of the historical factors involved in creating, nurturing, and hardening a Gwich'in self-image that differs somewhat from that of other Alaska Natives. Economic issues persist as the center of an emergent Gwich'in voice that situates its interest in money and money's power to dominate. The Gwich'in have begun developing a renewed self-confidence in themselves as a people through intermittent efforts to privilege their cultural distinctiveness in a variety of arenas, including disputes instigated by international resource development projects and healing techniques. The privileging of Gwich'in heritage and behavior over those of any other people occurs on a daily basis in private confrontations that lead to increasing efforts toward public awareness. The following pages address some pressing and interrelated issues in Gwich'in territory during the late 20th century.

Central Issues

As previously stated, I have isolated three central, interrelated issues that contribute to the burgeoning, albeit uneven, Northern Athabascan reconsideration of themselves in this colonial era. In the following chapters I discuss the implications of each of these intertwining influences on Northern Athabascan peoples. In brief, they are as follows: Northern Athabascan women in addictive conditions, Northern Athabascan leadership, and Gwich'in economy in Gwichyaa Zhee. To provide a context for these topics, I start with a summary of Gwich'in history, which is amplified in the following chapter. As one of the frequent matters operating in Northern Athabascan country during the 1990s was a loss in social cohesion associated with addiction, all of these issues are thus interconnected with terminology related to social pathology and healing. These terms are discussed differently by the Northern Athabascans than they are by mainstream agencies that deal in addictions or legal issues. One of the functions of this study is to present Northern Athabascan theories about what might be amiss with their society, as well as their own theories about how to effect acceptable changes. In this regard, the English-speaking Northern Athabascans use the term *healing* quite often. However, they speak of their "problems" or "troubles" instead of "social pathologies," which became a prevalent phrase in the social sciences of the 1990s. One of the major issues raised in chapter 6 concerns one of the primary differences in the way the Northern Athabascans conceptualize the causal factors involved in addictions and that proposed by many outsiders. Outsiders often situate cause for addiction within the minds or bodies of the afflicted, with further explanations attributed to cultural logic. While Northern Athabascans tend to situate cause within their bodies, possibly in their minds, many Gwich'in attribute cause to the political forces which brought alcohol into Gwich'in territory and the economic institutions that encourage its continuance.

Who Are Northern Athabascans?

Northern Athabascans identify themselves as people of the rivers. In Canada their rivers are the MacKenzie, the Arctic Red, the Porcupine, and the Peel. Alaskan Athabascan rivers include the Yukon, the Chandalar, the Innoko, the Tanana, the Susitna, and the Copper. The Gwich'in people of Alaska speak an Athabascan language that links them linguistically, socially (in some cases by direct kin relations), and politically to the more than two dozen Northern Athabascan languages that are or were used in Canada and Alaska. There are 11 Athabascan languages spoken in Alaska, although almost all are in a state of rapidly declining use. Some argue that there was once a political underpinning uniting all Northern Athabascans through marriage, warfare, or trade. Northern Athabascan family oral traditions often include very specific histories of marriages between regions, as well as details of bloody disputes between Athabascans of different languages. These stories often lead to habitual or expected behaviors between ethnic groups.

Since the colonial encounters began in the mid–19th century, these ancient relationships have been overlaid by new and more dominating relationships with Euro-Americans. The Alaskan Gwich'in experience of Western economic dominion began with the aid of the Episcopal Church and several Episcopal missionaries, including Trimble Rowe and Hudson Stuck (between 1895 and 1935) and Walter Hannum (during the 1950s and 1960s). Each of these men devoted part of his mission to bargaining on behalf of his Gwich'in parishioners with various federal agencies and charitable institutions. They succeeded in bringing food, Western education, and health care to the region in the 20th century, beginning approximately 50 years after Canadian and American fur traders and miners began exploiting resources on Gwich'in land. Catholic and Anglican missions had been active in Canadian Gwich'in territory since first contact, but little is known about their direct economic impact except that they bribed potential converts with tobacco (Mishler 1990). The Episcopal presence in Gwich'in country now manifests itself through a small Native ministry that Hannum implemented. As he told me in a private interview (October 31, 1992, Yale University, New Haven), he and other missionaries have always been impressed with the profound spiritual beliefs of the Gwich'in. Hannum's handful of personally trained and now aging ordained ministers still forms an influential component of Gwich'in leadership today. Most Gwich'in baptisms and funerals are held in Episcopal churches, indicating the continuing favored position of that denomination in Gwich'in society.

During the last year and a half that I lived in Gwichyaa Zhee, Episcopal church services were conducted by resident Gwich'in lay readers, as their minister had been relocated. Shortly before I left in 1995 the minister for the Assemblies of God Church was also removed, and local residents performed his services. The memberships in these two churches have remained stable with or without ordained ministers, and the local versions of these church services appear to satisfy them. While Christian missionaries maintain a strong presence in Gwichyaa Zhee, there is an equally strong resistance to Christianity in every Gwich'in village. Gwich'in people, as a whole, have retained a tradition that encourages them to appeal to the numinous to survive political and economic disruptions. Thus, while Christian missionaries may interpret Gwich'in spiritual efforts as a desire to convert, I infer that they make use of these efforts on multiple levels of meaning, one of which is to please those who pray for them. Another is to make use of a North American Native image of spirituality that is a powerful tool in negotiating with mainstream America. A third level of meaning is the cushioning or camouflaging of traditional Gwich'in codes of behavior under the guise of spirituality, which permits them to manipulate events through Christian prayer as well as to hint about traditional shamanism. In other words, Gwich'in resistance to Christianity is generally unperceived by those who might wish to see Christianity as a totalizing influence.

Besides missionary presence, three proposed resource development projects have influenced a growing awareness of all Northern Athabascan economic and political plights in contest with big money coalitions. The first of these is a failed proposal to build a hydroelectric dam that would have flooded nine Gwich'in and Koyukon Athabascan villages during the 1960s. Northern Athabascan people formed an alliance with wildlife conservation efforts to block the project and succeeded. A few years later international energy companies entered Alaska to exploit petroleum reserves on Alaska's northern coast. Because their development proposals required clear understandings of land ownership in the then-new state (Alaska became the 49th state of the United States in 1959), in 1971 the Alaska Native Claims Settlement Act (ANCSA) was passed by Congress to begin the process of isolating which lands belonged to the State of Alaska, to the U.S. government, and to the indigenous peoples of Alaska. One of the unanticipated outcomes of the act was the rift it caused between rural Alaska Natives (which includes all the Gwich'in villages) and urban Alaska Natives living in Anchorage and Fairbanks (which includes me and many Northern Athabascan people). A few Northern Athabascan villages withdrew from ANCSA to maintain their Indian Reorganization Act of 1934 reserves in fee simple title (unrestricted ownership). Statistics indicate that suicide rates among Alaska Native people (both urban and rural) skyrocketed as soon as the ANCSA debates began in the mid-1960s, and I discuss the implications of this rise in depressed behavior in chapter 4. The most recent event that has aroused Gwich'in opposition is the debate over oil exploitation in the Arctic National Wildlife Refuge (ANWR). This conflict, which began in 1976, caused a renewed partnership between Gwich'in and environmental interest groups and has given rise to a new language of ethnic identity for some Gwich'in. The resistance has been ragged but successful for over two decades, and it persists. These historic events and their bearing on Gwich'in lives are discussed in greater detail in chapter 2. The following section begins with a discussion about the complexity of Northern Athabascan lives and Northern Athabascan concepts of who they are.

Images of the Northern Athabascan Individual

Dissonance among shattered traditional ideals, political restrictions, addictions, and living experience have left the Northern Athabascans with few viable models of behavior that offer potential of pride or self-confidence. Northern Athabascan traditional theories of reality laud virtues of sharing, respect for personal autonomy, making do with little or nothing, and strength. Actual experience belies these ideals through alcoholism, child neglect and abuse, sexual abuse, displays of contempt or anger during most verbal communication, and racism or condescension from and toward outsiders. While there is a good deal of personal variation involved in how the various Northern Athabascan nations address the friction between their ideals and their actual behavior, in every case of such dissociation a third element, that of economic suppression, is involved. The mainstream political forces that have restricted Northern Athabascan autonomy are constant reminders to them that achieving traditional goals or ideals is nearly impossible. Despite all of this, the Northern Athabascans actively seek symbols of who they are, first, as Northern Athabascan people and, second, as individuals.

Northern Athabascan social poetics include theories of history, kinship or family, politics, love in all of its manifestations, and strength (personal and group). For instance, contemporary Gwich'in Athabascan tropes include the saying: "We suffer, we endure, but we continue on" as people who have learned to cope with an endless series of difficulties. Some Northern Athabascan metaphors (especially those concerning family and leadership) also reveal the systematic patterns in logic and cultural goals that lead to the formation of enduring modes of behavior in daily Northern Athabascan life. A significant underpinning to such patterns is a tacit but ubiquitous cultural ideal that demands shared resources and shared responsibility. The antithesis of this goal is expressed in mainstream American culture: the amassing of personal power and wealth. The difference between these cultural goals presents one of the many conflicts that muddy individual Northern Athabascan life choices. In chapters 3 and 4 I describe applications of the logic of Northern Athabascan power and material dispersement as it occurs in the local economy and Northern Athabascan leadership, respectively. In essence, sharing power and wealth is an ancient tradition that is met with resistance from mainstream sources in contemporary Northern Athabascan lives. Ensuing rifts between individuals compounded with political hegemony lead to many social problems and personal turmoil regarding what constitutes acceptable behavior.

Northern Athabascans have been prey to many researchers during the past century, including educators, social workers, and anthropologists. Some of the material produced by outside scholars has been received with alacrity by people who are actively seeking coherence in their lives. Osgood (1934, 1936), McKennan (1965), and the Scollons (1979) have written ethnographic monographs on the Northern Athabascans that are often recited by Northern Athabascan adults and schoolchildren as authentic explanations of who and what they are. Canadian researchers likewise have offered cognitive studies about Northern Athabascans that, though not as easily accessible to Alaskan Northern Athabascan readers, nonetheless offer insights that are similar to those of other Athabascan scholars. More general works on Native American identity, many of which are included in Northern Athabascan libraries, also serve as references for Northern Athabascans. In demonstration of this objective, the coordinator of the local branch of the University of Alaska was asked by Gwich'in students in both Gwichyaa Zhee and Vashraii K'oo to teach a course in "Indian" psychology, which she did during the 1980s. The paradigms of thought and behavior that she taught have since reinforced a generation of Northern Athabascans' concepts of themselves. Some ascriptions (primitive, drunken, spiritual, stupid, half-breed), which are applied to Native Americans throughout the continent, smack of hegemonic co-optation through mainstream stereotyping, yet many Northern Athabascan people refer to themselves with such terminology, while others resent it.

Besides these general labels, Northern Athabascans are actively pursuing a regionwide emphasis on establishing a Northern Athabascan character that distinguishes them from other ethnic groups. Some of this effort to differentiate stems from resistance to extractive economic projects that have targeted the Yukon River basin since the gold rushes of the late 19th century. Later, ANCSA (1971) required all Alaska Natives to define themselves as politically distinct from white society or risk losing their individual or group rights to the settlement. See chapter 2 for more information on this topic.

Since the mid-1970s Northern Athabascans, particularly the Gwich'in, have resisted, with the help of environmentalist nongovernmental organizations, further oil exploitation on the northern slope of Alaska because of the detrimental impact on their wildlife resources. All of these political efforts have spurred the Gwich'in to express their ethnic separateness from other Alaska Native peoples with greater frequency and to an increasingly worldwide audience. In this they have been advised and manipulated by outside forces. Several videotapes of the Gwich'in in Alaska and Canada have been produced to serve various economic or political purposes. Some have promoted tourism and thus focus on the landscape first and the Gwich'in or other Northern Athabascans secondarily. Such videos often represent Northern Athabascans as traditional Indians in traditional regalia. For example, traditional-looking costumes in synthetic fabrics for the children in Vashraii K'oo were made by the Yukon Flats School District and are therefore property belonging to the school. The children use the regalia to raise money for school projects but never wear the garments except to perform.

A series of videotapes has been arranged and funded by environmental task forces that increasingly promote images of traditional Northern Athabascans. A 1988 videotape produced by Northern Native Broadcasting Yukon (1989) and distributed by the Gwich'in Steering Committee (a public advocacy agency whose mission has been to prevent oil development in ANWR) displays no Gwich'in in traditional clothing, while a 1995 videotape (*Voice from the North: The Gwich'in People and the Arctic National Wildlife Refuge*) produced by Masako Cordray Wescott and a Hawaiian film group, and, again, distributed by the Gwich'in Steering Committee, primarily features Gwich'in in traditional garb.

These fabrications of Northern Athabascan reality are useful to commercial or environmental interest groups, but they also cheapen and vilify other Northern Athabascan people who are striving for dignity in other contexts, such as achieving sobriety, Christian piety, or economic independence through some mechanism other than tourism and politics. Images of a bygone Indian lifestyle deny the presence of the ongoing destruction of alcohol, just as images of Christian devotion actively destroy the merits of ancient Northern Athabascan religious beliefs. Discord between these varying Northern Athabascan paradigms is unwieldy in its own right, and the imbalance is rendered untenable when many Northern Athabascans themselves do not aspire to such claims on a daily basis. Children denounce the difference between the wishful thinking and the actual behavior of the adults around them as prevarication rather than idealism.

Other than these holistic, idealized images of what a traditional Northern Athabascan lifestyle might be, most of the ethnic tropes implemented by the Northern Athabascans are fragmentary. Such fragments include ideas about racial purity, such as eye color (raisin black eyes are more Northern Athabascan than brown eyes, which are more Northern Athabascan than hazel, gray, or blue eyes). In conjunction with this, the term *half-breed* is a pejorative label used by Northern Athabascans for those of mixed heritage. I heard parents use the label to their children. Language is another trope that is used as a weapon: During the early 1990s those who were not known to speak, understand, or read an Athabascan language were deemed less Athabascan than others. In this regard, the Gwandak radio station in Gwichyaa Zhee spotlights the slippery quality of assessing language as a standard of Gwich'in identity, as those few who spoke Gwich'in over the air during "Gwich'in Hour" used different dialects (some not understandable to people in other villages) or spoke Gwich'in with widely varying levels of proficiency. Finally, living in an Athabascan village year round rather than living in an urban center part of the time is a valued symbol conveying a sense of respect for one's Athabascan heritage. Each of these labels is used by Athabascans to exclude or shun each other. At best they are tools of a political armature used against outside intervention. At worst, they destroy morale and relations between family members and friends.

Most of these symbols are constructed as allusions toward an ideal that has no living model. However, one trope comes closer to a positive image of an Athabascan ideal person than do others, and this (which I explain in greater detail in chapter 4) is the term *gwintsii veegoo'aii*, for which I am grateful to Itree for taking four long days in 1992 to explain to me. Gwintsii veegoo'aii is an ideal person, a prototype of selfless energy who works tirelessly on behalf of the people and who somehow commands without making overt demands for the obedience of his or her followers. This conflictual symbol of centralized yet deflected power describes many people whom I met, almost none of whom would be seen as a leader in the mainstream political arena. Two of them were Christian ministers, a few of them were respected and valued administrators, and many of them were parents who found successful methods of raising their children in addictive conditions. None of the elected chiefs fit the model. Using gwintsii veegoo'aii as a pattern for an ideal Athabascan person, there are five essential elements that alert other Athabascans to the achievement of this status. One is selflessness (of material goods, time, and energy), second is an amorphous sense of family orientation, third is a relationship with the numinous toward accomplishing one or more missions on behalf of others, fourth is acknowledging accountability to others, and fifth is that leadership is an expected part of the role. For example, because the Gwich'in language is not in active use, the term *gwintsii veegoo'aii* is not commonly known, and hence the reinforcement by a linguistic correlate is missing. Nonetheless, the qualities of this ideal are touted as elements of what it takes to be Gwich'in, and people who fulfill all or part of the image are praised. Those (particularly leaders) who do not are denigrated for the lack of one or more of these five ideals of behavior. Those who achieve some degree of this image strive to do so consciously and with great effort.

Indigenous terms such as *gwintsii veegoo'aii* and the phrase provided at the beginning of this section, ''We suffer, we endure, but we continue on,'' illumine several of the ideal virtues of Gwich'in life, something that can be said for other Northern Athabascans as well. Another important concept is love: romantic love, family love, altruistic love, and spiritual love. A traditional Tanana Athabascan chief of Minto, Peter

John, identified spiritual love as it is used in his Lower Tanana Athabascan language as *ch'eghwtsen'*, or "the true love," love that is associated
with spiritual power. As Chief Peter John puts it, "Love is the white
man's word, but it has too many different meanings. I use *ch'eghwtsen'*
the Athabascan word for true love. Pure. It's powerful, that word is
powerful" (1996:37). John defines the term in its most altruistic, ideal-
istic potential, rather than as a tool of romantic communication. The
Gwich'in have a similar concept in *-indhan*, a verb stem that can be artic-
ulated into various spiritual nuances through infixes denoting subject,
case, tense, and modality. *Ch'eet'igwiidhan*, for instance, signifies something like "I revere that on which we depend." The verb stem *-indhan*,
used in spiritual or altruistic love, differs from the Gwich'in awareness
of interpersonal affection, such as paternal, filial, or romantic love, for
which they use the verb stem *-inchy'aa* (*yeet'inchy'aa* means "she loves
him").

Metaphors in Music

One of the most common mechanisms for conveying personal or ethnic
choices is music, and Athabascan culture is no exception. There is no
single form of Northern Athabascan music, any more than there is a single cultural type to characterize late-20th-century Athabascan people.
Athabascan musical genres can be loosely categorized as traditional
drum dancing, fiddle music, country music, soft rock, and Christian
gospel. It should be noted that most of the musical forms are somewhat
marginalized in context with mainstream music. For instance, Athabascan fiddle music (which encompasses jig dancing) does not conform to
contemporary American square dancing in rhythm, musical scoring, or
choreography and therefore represents a pocket out of time in the musical world. Mishler (1993:153) postulates that Athabascan fiddle music
can be classified as a distinctive regional and ethnic musical genre in the

same way that African American blues, Anglo-American bluegrass, Creole zydeco, and Hispanic *conjunto* are so viewed. In addition to their keen interest in fiddle music, Athabascans are also devoted fans of country music, often ascribing to only a portion of the full panoply of country music available to them (see later discussion). Athabascan traditional drum dancing has become popular again since the 1970s, although Christian disapproval nearly wiped it out at the beginning of the 20th century. Now many Athabascan children are learning to sing in one or more of the various Athabascan languages and to dance with traditional regalia for non-Native audiences in public areas. Such dancing, as some traditional dancers have expressed, is a statement of political action. Ironically, however, those who are most often enjoined to dance the drum dances are children, not adults, and political action appeals to only a minority of Athabascan children. All of those who engage in traditional dancing face peer pressure from age-mates who do not dance and who label it and the dancers as fake or foolish. Such pressure is difficult to resist or refute.

A more age-mate-acceptable statement of ethnic identity in dance is a musical genre derived from the fur trade that has become associated with the ethos of being a "traditional" Athabascan. According to Mishler (1981, 1993), French and Scottish jig dancing became popular over a century ago among Athabascan peoples. These art forms are still celebrated in contests and other gatherings in most Athabascan villages in the interior of Alaska. To "win Jig" (win a dancing contest) is a tangible symbol of success as a traditional Athabascan person, something that many village-born Athabascans learn to do as soon as they can walk. In addition, some Athabascan men and women are celebrated in Alaska Native communities for their performance of fiddle music and are invited (sometimes with pay) to play for weddings, funerals, potlatches, and spring carnival events in Alaska and Canada. Some of them also play in bars in Fairbanks as members of professional bands. These musicians have added 20th-century commercial instruments and styles to their repertoires. In addition to the fiddle music repertoire, which is distinctively Athabascan, Northern Athabascan musicians incorporate country music into their performances, leaving blurred lines of distinction between Athabascan fiddle music and country music. Although electric guitars and violins with powerful amplifiers have replaced acoustic violins as preferred instruments, fiddle music has become a commonplace marker of ethnic distinctiveness that is enjoyed as recreation by young people and provides an honorable aspect to honky-tonk country music and the alcohol that goes along with it. While in Gwichyaa Zhee, I heard many country songs and Athabascan fiddle tunes that address problems with love and marriage and render poetic "places where the whiskey drowns and the beer chases blues away."

Scholars have recently linked country music with a substratum of working-class people in America. By choosing country music as symbolic of themselves, the Athabascans demonstrate a certain awareness of the web of meaning inherent in this marked American musical form and, in a certain way, choose to align themselves with a particular socioeconomic stratum of the American working class, at least to the extent that such music glorifies pride in being poor, downtrodden, and romantically undernourished. "The Night Life Ain't No Good Life, but It's My Life" is a song that "celebrates the poor-but-proud theme" expressed by Peterson (1992:56–57) in his analysis of the working-class consciousness that country music capitalized on during the 1970s and 1980s. Sample (1996) elaborates on a theme of taste that is equally appropriate to Athabascans, although he specifies in his introduction that his analysis refers only to the white American working class and, therefore, to no other race or ethnic group. According to Sample, the loud and rowdy behaviors of the working class are expressed through and in country music in a way that emphasizes the contrast between themselves and the elite American classes in what he calls the politics of distinction in

American music. Following Bourdieu's comment that good taste is defined by that which is disgusting, Sample (1996:21) opines that the elitist disgust registered against country music in America indicates a political underpinning that those of the American working class acknowledge and disdain through the music itself. I suggest that Athabascans prefer country music for many of the same reasons suggested by these scholars: as a medium by which they can validate their poverty, political oppression, and sense of unity with each other as anything but upper class or wealthy. As an example of this mode of thought, when I complained to Itree about the frequency of country music on the Gwandak radio station, she chewed me out for my intolerance and told me that country music has a lot to offer.

Country music is written and made popular by people who generally come from the southern United States and brings many more themes into melodic awareness than poverty, resentment against elitist behaviors, and "achy breaky hearts"; however, these last are the themes that resonate with the Athabascan experience in Alaska. Songs about the South, Texas, or working "nine to five" were not played or sung very often in Athabascan territory during the early 1990s, as these songs do not reflect a genuine Athabascan experience of that time frame. For instance, very few people have full-time office jobs that require their constant supervision or time, and not many Athabascans have traveled out of Alaska. Sample (1996:21) also suggests that the practices surrounding country music have led to new criteria among the working class, which has created an informed appreciation of the music. In this as well, I suggest that Northern Athabascans have developed and reinforce an informed, critical theory about their own music. The education and reinforcement about their own music come in the form of contests, financial gain, and cultural norms that encourage antagonistic verbal exchange with each other. The annual Old Time Athabascan Fiddle Festivals, which began in 1983, serve as the largest forum in which Athabascan musicians and fans can evaluate, celebrate, and praise each other.

The fact that country music also implies "cowboy" music suggests a multiplicity of related meanings for Athabascans. Playing "cowboys and Indians" is not a game of choice among Athabascan children, although it was a favorite game among Alaska Native children in general for many years until the 1970s, when ANCSA, the influences of the American Indian Movement, and increased public awareness of American racism brought about a renewed sense of pride in being Native. One Koyukon mother told me that "they [her children] have to decide for themselves which one they are going to be: a cowboy or an Indian." Such a choice implies that the Indians are the losers and the cowboys are the winners in a game that represents a discursive reification of the colonization of North America. Awareness of hegemony and its prickly psychological impact on Athabascan people begins as soon as children make such a decision and hear themselves criticized for acting like a white man or woman. This form of rebuke occurred often in Athabascan communities of the 1990s but, according to those I asked, happened seldom before the 1970s.

Put another way, before Alaskan statehood and the Red Movement of the larger American Indian world, Athabascan children were encouraged to pass for white rather than to act out their Athabascan ethnicities, in yet another discursive hardening of a colonialist mentality. As Koyukon Athabascan and Alaska State Senator Georgianna Lincoln writes about a statement issued by former U.S. President Ronald Reagan, "Mr. Reagan was perpetuating the cowboy and Indian image; the cowboy to the rescue and the Indian doing the scalping" (1998:95). With the increasing political and economic pressures that have been brought to bear against Native American people in Alaska and elsewhere has come an expanded understanding of the causes and consequences of racism and political hegemony. (Mr. Reagan allegedly stated to Moscow State University students "that it might have been better to have forced Native Americans to enter Western culture instead of living in a 'primitive life-style' on reservations.") The effects of colonial oppression have resulted in psychological trauma for many Alaska Natives, manifested as alcoholism, suicide, and clinical depression. A quality of this trauma is expressed in country music, much of which is written about alcohol, expresses the problems of alcoholics, and is often sung in bars.

Christian gospel songs in both Gwich'in and English are also popular with Athabascans. Country music also has its influence in gospel music, and songs such as "Wings of a Dove" (1959, by Bob Ferguson, made popular by Ferlin Husky) are popular both in church and elsewhere in Athabascan communities. Most funerals include one or two of the hymns (ch'iliks) that Robert McDonald translated over a century ago. Itree, who teaches Gwich'in, began each class in 1993 by requiring her students to sing Ch'ilik 110 (sung to the tune of "The Sweet Bye and Bye") and sometimes Ch'ilik 65. Besides this, a few people in the village of Viihtaii have begun writing new hymns in their dialect of Gwich'in, as well as translating 20th-century Christian hymns such as "Amazing Grace."

Northern Athabascan Responses
to Alcoholism and Other Addictions

Are Northern Athabascans complacent in the presence of a drunk? The simple, but still equivocal, answer is no. One woman explained to me shortly after my arrival in 1993 that with respect to drinking there were three groups of people in Gwichyaa Zhee: those who did not drink, those who drank moderately, and those who drank continually. She drank moderately and made sure that she never drank in company of those who drank continually in order to preserve her reputation among the elders and other Athabascan people of authority. The people who drank continually were those who were recognized as public nuisances in public buildings, in private homes, and on the streets. Between 1993 and 1995, I witnessed several inebriated people being forcibly escorted from public buildings. Inebriates entering the two stores were greeted by watchful behaviors (stiffening necks and spines, eyes fixed on the inebriate, and quick glances at other patrons for some sort of unspoken corroboration). If the inebriate did anything other than make a quick and quiet purchase, someone usually stepped forward to remove him (in all cases that I saw, they were men) from the store. Behavior toward intoxicated people in private dwellings was a little different. Such individuals were usually members of the household who had established hierarchical and economic relationships with the other residents. For instance, one summer I was an overnight guest in a fish camp that was owned by two brothers. The older brother was drunk while I was there, and his younger brother and sister-in-law were watchful but did nothing to stop his drinking. They also avoided drinking themselves and chided him when he made unpleasant remarks to them or others. In other situations, I watched sisters, friends, or other acquaintances lock their doors while inebriates shouted through the walls and pounded on the doors. There were areas in Gwichyaa Zhee that I was warned to avoid because of the possibility of being accosted by the continual drinkers. On those occasions when I did walk by such areas, I was indeed approached by both men and women who were inebriated. One such elderly woman invited me into her home, and we chatted for a few minutes about my research. She did not recognize me the next time we met.

Many Athabascan children begin drinking alcohol in early adolescence, but the adults have not found a successful mechanism to prevent alcoholism in either children or adults. Do Athabascans accept the presence of an intoxicated child? Again, the answer is an equivocal no. Per-

haps a better question is, Do they have successful mechanisms for preventing alcoholism in themselves or children? There are three levels of
public responsibility in Athabascan villages that take action about alcoholism. The first level is the family, particularly the mother, which is the
topic of chapter 5. Athabascan families struggle for meaning in this respect. Some are successful, but during the 1990s most were not. The
second level of accountability resides in public services. For the past decade or so Athabascans have been trying to find workable solutions by
listening to counselors, social workers, AA volunteers, and church officials, who frequently situate fault and responsibility in the minds and
genetic makeup of the individual addicts. Issues of blame aside, these
solutions provide mechanisms that did not exist before by which those
suffering can express their dilemmas and receive social praise for want-
ing to change. Without that bridge into a healthier way of life, a deadly
form of social silence remains in place: a silence that has had no cultural
precedent among Athabascans or other Alaska Natives for social expression until recently.

The third level of responsibility is governmental. Athabascan-
initiated tribal solutions include prohibition of alcohol. The Gwich'in
people of Viihtaii and Vashraii K'oo have tried this in a desultory fashion for over a decade without observable success. The city government
of Gwichyaa Zhee has limited the business hours of the liquor store and
prohibited the sale of alcohol in any other business. In response to these
actions, bootleggers persist in every village. I suggest that until the economic framework that encourages and increases drug and alcohol activities in northern communities and elsewhere is removed, Athabascans will continue to have a difficult time ending addictions in their
communities.

Northern Athabascan Women's Experience

No study of Northern Athabascans would be complete without awareness of how women are involved in current social issues. Women's lives in Gwichyaa Zhee are more perilous during adolescence than at any other period in their lives. I was told that a few years ago Gwichyaa Zhee tribal officials changed the rules on the contemporary Spring Carnival Princess category to include girls of 13 and older. Many of the girls who might enter such contests have at least one child by the time they are 18, a factor that disqualifies them. Some of the men, sometimes the girls' age-mates, prey on the contestants of all ages, getting them drunk and having sex with them. Many Athabascans have ignored these situations, thereby condoning them with social silence. Others are actively trying to make changes. Some, such as Itree's sister Shroodiinyaa, have become Christian and try prayer and offer sanctuary to those in need. Others, like Itree, try abstinence and offer sanctuary to close friends who are trying to become sober. Itree's brother Vachaa tried a third method: he and his Koyukon wife, Hułyakk'atno, use their family fish camp on the Yukon River to teach their children skills in traditional hunting, fishing, and living in the wilderness. In addition, Vachaa has taught about these skills in the public school system in Fairbanks.

During my preliminary visit to Gwichyaa Zhee in 1992 I was able to learn something about each of these strategies in a direct and personal way. During that visit I stayed with Itree and helped her at Shroodiinyaa's lodge. Shroodiinyaa is ten years younger than Itree and has become a matriarch of the community because, like Itree and other Athabascan women, she provides food, money, permanent child care, and housing for many people beyond her nuclear family. Shroodiinyaa had a contract with the Gwichyaa Zhee ANCSA village corporation to operate a restaurant and lodge. She attended a summer workshop in Native business planning and was able to use all of the furnishings, bedding, kitchen appliances, and table settings originally purchased by the corporation. The business was successful in 1992, but Shroodiinyaa had to work long hours nearly every day of the week in order to cover for the absenteeism and inefficiencies of her employees, most of whom were her own relations. She was one of the few trained commercial cooks in the village. I learned to cook under her instruction during the following year, as I was one of the dependable people she knew she could count on to come in on short notice. It was a good way to meet people, as well as to learn how small business enterprises work in such extreme isolation.

Shroodiinyaa spoke to me quite frankly about her alcoholism. She said that she used to drink and play bingo without any consideration of the needs of her five biological children to the extent that often there was no food in the house for them. Five years before I met her she underwent a transformation and, with the help of the Baptist church, became sober and determined to raise her younger children in a safe home. Her husband continued to drink, although he offered her as much support at the restaurant as his alcoholism permitted. She sent the two older daughters away to a Christian school before I got to know them, but I became very fond of her three sons. Shroodiinyaa occasionally spoke up in the public forum to encourage other Athabascans to follow her example of accepting Christianity. The Baptist church in Gwichyaa Zhee has a small but devoted following (approximately 35–40 people, including children), and several Athabascans attend their meetings on an occasional basis, usually coinciding with life crises.

Women's lives in Northern Athabascan territory always work in tension with alcohol, even if they do not drink. Most of the women I met talked about it openly, most with descriptions of their successes in being sober for whatever period it might have been, and some with regrets that they had not yet succeeded. There are several mechanisms and agencies in Gwichyaa Zhee and other Northern Athabascan villages to help, including Alcoholics Anonymous, church revivals, and private theories about fortitude and abstinence. All of these mechanisms involve open discussion and sometimes public forums. A few of the women I met denied that they drank; nonetheless, they used the topic of alcohol as a conversational element. This openness is boosted by the statewide sobriety efforts among Alaskan Natives that began in the mid-1980s.

Many of the women I met spoke of linking alcoholism to the importation of cash into their economy by the 19th-century Hudson Bay Company and later exploitive enterprises, and many were resentful of white intrusion in their lives. The women I have discussed to this point each tried different solutions to end alcoholism, and each of the women in Itree's family, including Itree herself, fostered new economic ventures as one of her techniques to change her life. During the time I was in Gwichyaa Zhee, Itree was the manager of the new radio station, a position for which she had taken courses at the university in Fairbanks. Itree was one of the growing number of women in positions of Athabascan leadership, and she, like other Athabascan leaders, found her role was primarily one of mediator rather than as an exponent of power or authority.

A few days after my arrival in Gwich'in, Itree arranged to go to her family's fish camp to help her brother Vachaa close it for the season. Her brother and sister-in-law had been injured in a windstorm at the camp a week or so before and were unable to return to close it themselves. Boat fare involved buying three five-gallon tanks of gasoline ($76.00) as payment to one of the local men who took us upriver in his flat-bottomed, uncovered boat. There I huddled with Itree swathed in parkas, mittens, and hats. Itree had laughed at me about my city ways, so I kept secret the pair of long thermal underwear beneath my jeans. The air on the river is about ten degrees cooler than that of the adjacent land. With the windchill factor, the temperature on the boat was at least 25 degrees cooler than that on shore. It was around 40 degrees Fahrenheit that day on land.

The fish camp looked spent. Vachaa and his Koyukon wife, Hulyak-k'atno, had struck some of the tents before they were struck themselves by falling trees. Because of the injuries that both suffered, they were unable to do much work for the next several months. We collected the trash and put forgotten bits of family life into an overflowing box: a child's truck, a little boy's dirty jeans, Hulyakk'atno's pink and white tennis shoes. The shoelaces had been sliced away at the top of each hole. A spruce tree had fallen across Hulyakk'atno's legs, breaking both ankles. Rescuers had cut through the shoelaces to release her swollen feet.

While we were there Itree's son and nephew took a canoe upstream to get a fish net out of the water. While doing so Itree's 14-year-old son Tsee' Tsal killed his first bear. It had surprised the boys as they were putting the net away. Tsee' Tsal managed to grab his rifle just in time. Itree told her friends about her son's feat, saying, "He's a man now." That day Tsee' Tsal headed directly into Fairbanks from fish camp to get ready for school. He was to live with his non-Native father in Fairbanks that coming winter. Itree wanted to honor Tsee' Tsal with a first-kill potlatch in Gwichyaa Zhee but had to wait more than a year.

Vachaa and Hulyakk'atno offer a good example in performance of one of the strongest Athabascan cultural ideals: surviving in the harsh arctic environment by knowing how to protect themselves from wild animals and cold weather, as well as hunting and fishing. Men, women, and children learn strategies to become independent of each other in case they get stranded where they might have no choice but to do or die. At odds with this is that they also need to be able to count on each other in case of emergency. One of the Athabascan river customs is visiting night and day, even if the camp is dark. Fortunately, someone did just that after Vachaa and Hulyakk'atno had been injured and went for help.

This tautological semiotic of independence emerges from the Gwich'in language. Their words for "trust" are the same as those for "interdependence." *Yit'injyaahchy'aa* means both "he or she depends on him or her" and "she or he trusts her or him" (Athabascan third person pronouns and declensions are ungendered). The word for "supreme deity," *vit'eegwijyaahchy'aa*, is another declension of the morpheme *-aahchy'aa* (to trust, to depend on). For the Gwich'in trust means knowing that the other knows survival skills and social responsibilities with respect to physical survival. Gwich'in author Velma Wallis's 1993 novel *Two Old Women* is a contemporary written statement about the complex ideal of combined trust and interdependency. Mainstream English usually understands each concept in isolation from the other as well as with markedly different views about dependency. In the chapter on Northern Athabascan women (chapter 5), I discuss other strategies used by women to raise their children through new ideas.

Leadership Traditions

> As a chief [of Viihtaii], we're trying to get people work together [sic]. We organize that in our culture [sic] life and Whiteman's [sic] way of life, and try and translate each other. Get more people to understand what they're doing. The people will understand each other. We'll get with the Air Force. We're working on it yet, and that's all I know. [John Tritt, first chief of Viihtaii, "People, Science, Caribou" Conference, Vashraii K'oo, November 6, 1993]

This statement reveals much about the role of chief in Gwich'in Athabascan villages. Not only do Western officials and other outsiders rely on them for direction, but they see themselves as intermediaries between their Athabascan societies and the outside world, recognizing the immense differences in the use of meaning as perceived by their own people in contrast to that of white people. The chief cited previously spoke English with some difficulty as a second language and was learning to navigate the bureaucratic role of tribal leaders in Indian Country.

Athabascan people presently permit multiple strategies for social authority, many of which take the form of control through mainstream institutions such as police forces, court systems, and other federal and state enforcement agencies. Most of these entities direct individuals' activities by imperfect closure against certain behaviors rather than leading by assertion of rules. Other forms of leadership come in the form of tribal chiefs, other elected officials, and those encouraged by cultural precedent to advise, such as elders. No leaders currently have Athabascan authority to command behavior or demand obedience, even though their oral and written traditions indicate that such ideals were once cherished by Athabascans. Contemporary Athabascans often avoid obeisance to other individuals by demanding or deferring to imagined situations of consensus. Like whitewash, attributing public action to consensus can hide a multitude of discrepancies. Marked examples of Athabascan enactment of or reliance on consensus occur in the evictions discussed earlier. The Langfield family and Andrew Dakota were both evicted from Gwichyaa Zhee in 1994 with a minimum of public discussion in either event.

To many people Athabascan leaders appear to be powerless or dysfunctional. This is true of many of the Athabascan men and women who hold or have held positions of authority. By contrast, Athabascan leadership is a complex structural phenomenon that generalizes power, rather than locating it in a single authority, and functions with merciless efficiency. The use of defocused authority to accomplish a single task occurred in the eviction of the Langfields in 1994. Athabascan theories of kinship, their construction of the numinous, and their use of power and authority in the present-day economy are three key, but discordant, elements of Athabascan culture that form a basis for leadership. One enduring aspect of Gwich'in Athabascan traditions illustrates a core Northern Athabascan behavioral precept for leadership: gwintsii vee-goo'aii, an ethic that glorifies the trappings of hardship while accomplishing difficult tasks on behalf of others. Most Athabascans project this ethic in their daily routines.

Is there a single model of Northern Athabascan leadership? The simple answer is no. During the 1990s Athabascan leaders made use of one or more of the following signs or clusters of behavior: (1) they enjoined blurred acts of cohesion which some of them called consensus; (2) they acted out gwintsii veegoo'aii strategies of visual humility; (3) they enacted disunited fragments of traditional codes of valor or warrior behavior, such as grim postures of hostility or harangues testifying to the purity of their individual visions and the success of their personal and public actions; (4) they engaged in expressions of the numinous ranging from telling ghost stories to praying; and (5) they reproduced elements of mainstream models of bureaucracy. These signs often conflict with each other if they are not carefully edited by leaders. For instance, it is difficult to display poverty and argue that one's actions are successful, but many Athabascan people do so. It is common to hear people speak in terms of poverty while driving new $20,000 trucks. The first four signs (consensus, humility, valor, and sacred thought) emerge from religious theory and are impeded by kinship behaviors that presently function to fragment Athabascan society.

One of the traditional concepts that simultaneously support and neglect Athabascans in their struggle to maintain themselves as a distinct people is social silence, which encompasses an idea of psychic unity in such notions as consensus but also a reliance on avoiding direct assertions of accountability. Athabascan public action in this respect sometimes seems to function without verbal communication and at other times requires face-to-face discussion. When larger issues command Athabascans' attention they usually hold meetings to hear community opinions. In such meetings consensus emerges as a shared attitude rather than the delineation of a detailed common thought. A haze of partially remembered and recently invented rules, not to mention personality conflicts, distracts participants from goals that public debate might clarify.

For example, I witnessed this form of consensus in February 1994 in Gwichyaa Zhee during a public reading of this study. A few women came to hear me. From the negative aspects of some of them I suspected that the experience would be humbling, and it was. As it happened, two who objected to certain portions of the text were not in agreement with each other in other areas of their lives. One of them had more sway within that group than did her opponent, who is not Athabascan. When the less popular critic began a complaint at one point in my reading, the other woman directed her anger toward the first and away from me. I could feel a wave of antipathy move past me toward the first woman. After a heated debate over one sentence the meeting suddenly dissolved and people left. The group of people had come together with a common interest but not with a united awareness about the reading. That meeting brought to mind some of the ways in which consensus can mask areas of discord through aborted awareness of the matter at hand. Some one told me that through consensus Athabascans always know what is right without requiring discussion. That February afternoon left me just as bewildered as ever about the nature of consensus, and yet I witnessed it in action. Neither I nor my writing, though the reason for the meeting, was its target or the eventual prey of those in the mood to attack. The way Athabascans employ and in some instances consecrate the idea of consensus finds its parallel in many Native American communities. When and where it works, consensus is thought to supplant the need for overt leadership. As the earlier discussion of eviction reveals, consensus also contributes to a tacit awareness of Athabascan separateness.

Economic Hegemony

Western governmental, commercial, and religious institutions brought with them their essential framework of European and American political operations: their economy or, as viewed from the position of Athabascans, money. Three components of Athabascan economy are of interest in this study. The first I call the addictive system, the second is the educational system, and the third are local efforts at economic independence. The first two reflect multimillion-dollar budgets of which most of the money remains outside of Athabascan hands. The third limps along with little funding. Despite the imbalance of money and therefore power, Athabascans persist and usually succeed in resisting outsiders on a personal basis, as already mentioned in connection with evictions. Although no Athabascan agency budget ever names evictions as a line item, a sizable portion of many pools of money is diverted annually to such efforts. In effect, evictions have become a local genre of unofficial sanctioning of Athabascan resistance to mainstream authority via mainstream authority figures (some of whom are Athabascan people). An unbalanced economic framework contributes to ethnic disharmony between Athabascans and outsiders. Athabascans enhance that disharmony in events such as evictions by legally appropriating a share of the money designated for others in transactions that result in a superficial Athabascan solidarity against outsiders. None of this strife is planned for the purpose of ethnic divisiveness by anyone, but it is a long-standing feature of Athabascan behavior and one that nurtures a sense of Athabascan social capital. This section has introduced Athabascan economy and the political domination of Athabascans by the U.S. government and the larger global economy. Addiction and addictive products are the most destructive facets of that domination, as is discussed in the following section.

The Addictive System and Northern Athabascan Economy

Money motivates the complex system of addictions in Athabascan country through the direct importation from Western manufacturers of addictive products (alcohol, illegal drugs, and gambling devices). Many Athabascans battle with what some consider medical conditions: alcoholism and other addictions, violent behavior, and suicidal tendencies. Social workers and other social scientists refer to them as social pathologies. Solutions to them might be found by widening the analytical lenses to include the larger harmonies of society, referring to that complex network of institutional employment, services, and expectations pertaining to and enactments of community behavior which I term the addictive system. With respect to this study the addictive system is described in its economic aspect rather than its behavioral function.

Money determines the continued implementation of the addictive system through state, Christian, and tribal social welfare programs. Each of these entities pays many agencies and individuals for services, room, board, and transportation of people who counsel against the use of addictive products such as alcohol, drugs, and pull tabs. Each of these institutions contributes a portion of the money involved in the addictive system to Athabascan communities, but most of the money goes outside of the region. The Gwichyaa Zhee Youth Survivors organization, counseling programs, community uplift programs, and church revivals are among the welfare entities that benefit from grants or donations that fund positive aspects of the addictive system in Athabascan country. However, Athabascan residents (both Native and non-Native) spend even more money on transporting, housing, and selling addictive products and performing related negative activities. Transportation companies, liquor outlets, bootleggers, and private individuals participate in the negative monetary facet of the addictive system. It is a multimillion-dollar network of which Athabascans constitute only a small portion.

Addiction and its many attendant features dominate not only Athabascan economy but most of the time spent by Athabascan people. The educational system is sometimes regarded as having the province of curing social ills. For Athabascans, the Western educational system provides outlets for release from dependency and also, by its very fiscal presence, further undermines local Athabascan economy by taking jobs away from local residents and hiring outsiders to teach and by using outside contracts for a variety of projects and products. These issues are further explained later in the chapter, as well as in chapter 3.

Money also controls the mainstream educational system that dominates every Athabascan life. Teachers are the highest paid individuals in almost every Athabascan village. Teachers earned a beginning salary of $39,000 in 1995, while the average annual income for other Athabascan households was usually between $6,000 and $17,000. Unless the teachers become involved in the addictive system (a rare occurrence), the rest of their salaries goes out of the Athabascan region. Most teachers are non-Athabascan, and most vacation and retire in other states. The school districts in Alaska pay outside suppliers for the construction of schools and the importation of goods and teachers. While there are not many suppliers of these services and products in Northern Athabascan country, there are a few, and these individuals are resentful. The state and federal governments pay outsiders for the construction of plumbing and electrical services that are used in most villages only by the schools and schoolteachers. While all Athabascans advocate better education for their children, it should be noted that the money involved is considerable, and the bulk of its substance does not penetrate the local economy. Outside educational institutions continue to find ways to keep funds away from Athabascans.

In addition to its economic components, the nature of public education in Athabascan country is problematic. Mixed messages stemming from a combination of mainstream stereotypes about Native Americans and scattered attempts to incorporate local knowledge into the class-rooms leave students unprepared for understanding what it means to be Athabascan in a consistent, positive light. Numerous teenaged Athabas-can as well as other Alaska Native suicides during the late 20th century testify to the anomie of Alaska Native youth. These and other issues are explored in chapter 5.

Attempts at Economic Independence

There are a few economic endeavors in Athabascan territory that gener-ate revenue that remains in the region. Some families have engaged in activities related to tourism, but they have limited success, particularly because they do not have the financial resources required to advertise or update their services. In addition, many women and some men main-tain cottage industries to produce goods, such as beaded earrings and fur hats, while others offer guiding services and bed and breakfasts for the tourist market. There are no large-scale manufacturers in the area, although there are a fur trappers' cooperative and some skin-sewing cooperatives for women's products. Other Northern Athabascans, pri-marily women, participate in the mainstream economy through em-ployment with various corporations or governmental agencies. Because mainstream economic systems tend to dominate individual lives either through education, addictions, or employment, most Athabascan and non-Native people in Athabascan country agree that they are all depen-dent on the Western economy. Information pertaining to general cash usage within Athabascan communities is discussed in chapter 3.

While a good deal of the cash actually floating through Northern Athabascan villages arrives and moves through addictive behaviors and addictive therapies, Athabascans are willing to try any enterprise from bootlegging to selling health foods. There is and has been an assort-ment of guiding services, inns, flying and boating services, skin sewers, and beaders that cater to travelers. There is a variety of retailers who sell house and motor fuel, food, clothing, honey, fur, hardware, building supplies, and, of course, drugs and alcohol. There are also public and private service organizations that provide health care, education, counseling, religious activities, police, and fire control. Northern Athabascan leadership enables, or attempts to enable, Athabascans to take advantage of new economic opportunities.

Alaska's Gwich'in Athabascans are particularly worthy of study because they are supposedly a people at peace in mainstream America. So they are, unless one examines the many ways that people are tacitly found to be undesirable and, certainly not peacefully, forced to leave the region. They cannot be said to be a rebellious ethnicity because they have no uprisings, but recent city managers hired for and by the people of Gwichyaa Zhee have been forewarned by informal networking about the rough and wild Gwichyaa Zhee persona. One of the three Gwichyaa Zhee city managers between 1992 and 1995 told me that the Gwich'in need to learn control by demonstrating their competence regarding state and federal grants so that they might continue to receive them. The city manager considered it to be his job to teach them such control. People of Gwichyaa Zhee have been receiving federal and now state assistance for nearly a century with no cessation. I took that city manager's remark to be a representation of the economic expectations of a mainstream society annoyed by that which should be obeisant but is not.

Women, both Athabascan and non-Athabascan, are instrumental in every area in which economic changes are occurring in Gwichyaa Zhee and elsewhere in Athabascan territory. Women's roles have changed to a certain degree from the depictions of them in oral narrative; nonetheless, Athabascan oral traditions match contemporary images with regard to women's centrality in kin or sharing group economies. Contemporary women have extended their traditional sphere of influence to include public outreach to foreigners in Athabascan land and, as I suggest in later chapters, to making systemic changes in intergender behaviors regarding domestic violence and rape. The following chapters describe Gwichyaa Zhee's history as it pertains to the economy and the emergence of addictions, the Gwichyaa Zhee economy as Athabascans use it and speak of it, and Athabascan leadership. In later chapters I discuss the process of growing into Northern Athabascan womanhood and Athabascan theories of healing.

2 Footprints: Metaphors of Place, Mobility, and History

The word for "footprints" in some of the Northern Athabascan languages brings together concepts of community, seasonal rounds, leadership, and history. The Ahtna Athabascan word *kae* is exemplary in this semiotic complexity. *Kae* means footwear, animal or human tracks, home, or village, as well as travel by boat (Kari 1990:238). A derivative of this term, *kaskae*, brings together all of the Northern Athabascan theories of leadership: wealth, success, wealthy man or woman, leader, boss, and chief. Another derivative aligns women with the root: *t'sakae* (woman, women) and *tats'akae* (Water Woman of a traditional tale). All of these linguistic clues point toward a Northern Athabascan ontology about the nature of themselves, their social system, and the centrality of women in that world.

Northern Athabascan concepts of being are markedly different from the linear models of Euro-American traditions. In particular, Athabascans emphasize survival through epistemologies of physical and metaphysical power within the individual and public being, while Western theories of survival emerge from socially negotiated memories of sequence as factors in causation to be learned. Athabascan histories declaim fulfillment of Athabascan truths, rather than theories to be contested. Histories thus filtered through each of these cultural lenses, while meaningful and valid to the participants involved, have led to mutual unintelligibility across cultural boundaries. In establishing boundaries for the Alaska Native Claims Settlement Act of 1971 (ANCSA) village corporations, federal and state agencies insisted that Alaska Natives prove the long-standing permanence of their villages. To do so was antithetical to Northern Athabascan cultural systems, as is well demonstrated by terms such as *kae*. Now that mainstream American education dominates, Northern Athabascans have learned to tell their histories in linear mode while also telling family histories as always. One consequence of this is that younger generations are confused about the aesthetic and pragmatic values of either and sometimes learn neither.

The present chapter frames Athabascan concepts of being within both emic structures about origins and cause and Western theories of the past, which are in constant multiple tension with the former. Just as Northern Athabascans in Alaska ground their social foundations in matrilineages, women are key to traditional Athabascan epistemology: theories of knowledge, most of which have been taught through oral narratives about the environment, causal factors from the past, and theories about exchange in the present. This section presents two inherently conflictual views of history: one from an indigenous perspective, the other from a nonindigenous, colonial point of view. This chapter also evaluates the most salient aspects of Northern Athabascan history in terms of its impact on the lives of Athabascan women, economy, and leadership in the aftermath of colonial encounters.

Briefly, precolonial Northern Athabascan life comprised hunting, fishing, and trading with surrounding peoples, including the Iñupiat to the north; other Athabascans to the west, east, and south; and Tlingit traders who entered Northern Athabascan territory along the Yukon River drainages from the southeast. Athabascan legends indicate that war was common, and xenophobic behaviors are still part of Northern Athabascan customs, as the evictions described in chapter 1 indicate. During the colonial period in the 19th century traders from Canada wanted furs, which interfered with traditional religious beliefs about interactions with the environment, and introduced cash and Western material goods, including limited supplies of tobacco and alcohol. Several decades later, prospectors and Euro-American entrepreneurs took land and mineral resources without negotiating with Northern Athabascans or other indigenous peoples of Alaska except to defraud, intoxicate, and occasionally befriend them. The miners imported huge volumes of alcohol by barge through the river ways for personal consumption as well as for trade with indigenous peoples. Northern Athabascan leadership roles were transformed. Typical patterns of leadership were situational: someone, usually the male head of the kinship unit, led the group from one hunting or fishing area to another based on visionary dreams that indicated the best place to go. When they were under threat by traditional enemies, the person most involved in the conflict was expected to lead hostile efforts. With colonialism, one of the key problems for all Northern Athabascan people was epidemic disease. Their medical skills were usually insufficient to prevent the deaths, and every kin group was left with orphans, widows, and invalids. Leaders then became mentors of homeless children and women.

In traditional times Athabascan history was framed by references to kinship, legendary medicine men, and conflict. People were expected to know not only to whom they were related but the significance of those relationships in terms of social stratification and Athabascan religious traditions. In short, they were expected to learn and know Athabascan history and its customs. Nowadays, there are a few Athabascans who explain their traditions, but there are few structured opportunities to teach Athabascan history or ideology. Instead, Athabascan youth learn Christian dogma and scientific theory in churches and schools. Christian evangelists are sometimes held in contempt and sometimes revered, possibly as a result of the mixed messages that come to Athabascans through their colonial history. In addition, a few public school teachers in rural Alaska have poor grounding in science, math, and other core courses, and as a result, present-day Athabascans are unevenly educated about history of any sort. Women's lives have factored into the changes in Athabascan society in several ways. By tradition, women were expected to learn to hunt, fish, and cooperate with men in all levels of domestic management. Men were expected to learn to hunt, fish, and interact with outsiders. As colonial economies have changed, women have become more involved in relationships with outsiders through education, jobs, marriage, and politics. Several Athabascan women have become teachers, now competing with non-Natives presently in Alaskan schools. The following section in part describes some of the Northern Athabascan gender traditions in the context of Athabascan understandings of the past.

Northern Athabascan History
from an Indigenous Perspective

Athabascans construct their ideas about the past through blended notions of kinship, regional territories, religious traditions, legends of war, and Western history. The following story is one that Itree's grandmother told in 1989, when I was with them in Fairbanks for the Athabascan Fiddlers Festival. Itree's grandmother, the late Julia Peter, was called Granny or Vitsuu by her many relations. *Vitsuu* means grandmother in the Gwich'in language. Vitsuu was born in 1906 in Danzhit Hanlii along the Yukon River. Her father was born and lived most of his life in Vashraii K'oo about 150 miles north of Danzhit Hanlii. Vitsuu's mother came from Vuntut (also called Zhee Giiglit), Canada, on the upper reaches of the Ch'ôonjik River. Vitsuu's story is an example of the mobility of Athabascans and how they explain their political status with respect to the Iñupiat (Ch'eekwaii). It is also an example of how a Gwich'in Athabascan elder decides how to express her past to an outsider such as myself. Vitsuu spoke primarily in Gwich'in, and Itree translated as her grandmother spoke:

Vitsuu's father's father was a medicine man called Solomon, a strong medicine man. So was her father's older brother, who died in Minto [Tanana Athabascan territory]. When her father was a young man around Vashraii K'oo, he had three children before Vitsuu was born. Around that time her family found out Ch'eekwaii (Iñupiat) were coming to make war. Her father's father, the medicine man, went out hunting with other men, and upon returning to the hunting camp said to the others, "We're not going to sleep." So they went back to the village and told the people, "We have to go." There was cooked moose head there, and Vitsuu's grandfather had time to cut off just one moose nose, and that was all the food they could take with them. The reason he took the nose was because he was honorable [gogwanlii], and he didn't want to lose his honor. He grabbed part of the nose so he would always have his hunting skills.

They made a war house with a snare outside of it. Then they took all the women and children away. Her father's father, the medicine man, went back to the camp where they had cooked the moose. He disappeared in a cloud of smoke, using his medicine. At the camp there were just bones left. The Ch'eekwaii had eaten everything the villagers had left behind. The Ch'eekwaii were hungry. They were not very lucky in their hunting, like the Indians are. That's why Solomon took that moose nose. So that he would always have his hunting skills.

The medicine man knew that the Ch'eekwaii were all in the snare. They had no way to hunt. They were hungry, and there was nothing for them. The area behind the snare was piled with dry branches. They had left a little hole for guns. There was also an old woman outside the snare who was sick. The old woman pushed a piece of meat through the hole to the Ch'eekwaii. The medicine man knew what she was doing, but he let her continue to feed them anyway. He didn't say anything to her. Indians never tell us not to do this or do that. So that old lady kept sneaking the Ch'eekwaii food.

One time a Ch'eekwaii grabbed her hand and cut it off. When that happened, the Indians went after them. The Ch'eekwaii had no food, they were *hungry. So they went outside the snare. When that happened, the Indians killed them. Solomon grabbed one of the Ch'eekwaii and said to the others, "We're not going to kill this one." The reason he did this is so the Ch'eekwaii could go back home and tell the story.*

In this story Vitsuu told one of the many stories about Gwich'in conflicts with their neighbors to the north. Their relationship with the Iñupiat was and still is complex, involving generations of trade, mutual awareness and respect for their disparate religious traditions, marriage customs, and negotiations over resource usage. The most recent of the latter is part of an international dispute about development of the Arctic National Wildlife Refuge that is discussed later in this chapter.

One of the salient features in Vitsuu's story is the prominence of the Athabascan value of metaphysical power and medicine men. Through stories of this nature, Athabascan parents teach their children to concentrate on manipulating the present situation through whatever powers they might possess, especially those stemming from physical and metaphysical strength. Athabascan medicine men are reputedly capable of performing a number of feats. The most common such gift, and one that Vitsuu said she possessed, is the ability to dream the specific location and markings of wildlife. Other skills include healing through surgery and herbs (another of Vitsuu's well-known gifts), levitation and transportation (which her father's father did in this story), and using a variety of psychic processes. Underlying these abilities is knowledge of a complex reciprocal relationship among humans, animals, plants, and entities of the spirit world (which is controlled by an omnipotence or omniscience called *vit'eegwijyaahchy'aa*, "that on which we depend"). Her grandfather took as much of the moose meat as possible to signal respect for the species, respect for the relationship that had brought them the moose in the first place, and his awareness that not taking the meat jeopardized his rapport with the spirit world. This multifarious relationship suggests that there are variable qualities of power manifest in the Northern Athabascan world.

Also present in this story is one of the most fundamental ideas of Northern Athabascan, in this situation Gwich'in, leadership: no one tells anyone else what to do, although one of the most striking ironies of Athabascan consensual behavior is that others might call it domineering or intimidating. This complex issue is discussed in greater detail in chapter 4. Followers are expected to predict the common good of a group through common sense, observation, and consensus. Thus, the medicine man did not tell the old woman not to feed the Ch'eekwaii; he expected her to know what to do herself.

Northern Athabascan theories of religion, kinship, and origins reflect a centuries-old pattern of crafting their relationships with insiders and outsiders. Women were generally responsible for teaching children their customs until they reached age seven or eight. At that time, boys were expected to begin learning hunting and medicine skills from their male matrikin. The avunculate is still practiced by some Northern Athabascans to the extent that little boys will live with a knowledgeable male relative for a while to learn about hunting and subsistence survival techniques. However, they do not try to limit such apprenticeships to matrikin. Daughters generally remained with their mothers until marriage and sometimes afterward if the couple remained in the daughter's parents' vicinity to perform what is called bride service.

In sum, Vitsuu's story introduces all of the elements of kinship, power, and styles of leadership that are central to Gwich'in histories. The exact sequence of events in context with other Athabascan stories is not important, just as it was more important to identify the roles played by participants in terms of kinship, metaphysical power, and obedience to Athabascan social norms, rather than to specify names. In fact, some Northern Athabascan traditions declare that saying the names of the deceased will call malevolent attention from unseen forces to the speaker.

Hence, it is better to use kinship terms ("my grandfather") rather than name the individual specifically. Northern Athabascan epistemologies, therefore, tend to locate knowledge within a complexity of metaphysical boundaries that span time and generations. Athabascan memories of events are usually negotiations framed by tropes of personal power, including nonphysical powers, and social relations, rather than sequences of events. By contrast, Euro-American epistemologies tend to situate knowledge within definable, physical parameters and expect that memories and political power can be negotiated by social or legal conventions.

Northern Athabascan Kinship Theories

While most of the Northern Athabascan peoples of Canada follow bilateral kinship systems, most Athabascans in Alaska have made use of matrilineal clans. The Ahtna along the Copper River and the Dena'ina along the Susitna River drainage have complex, hierarchical clan structures that are significantly different from those of the populations along the interior river drainages. In precolonial times most Athabascans along the Yukon River drainages participated in a tripart matrilineal clan system that united them in trade, marriage, and travel. Doyon, the ANCSA corporation of the interior, celebrates this heritage through its educational and fund-raising programs. In English the three clans are known as the Caribou (symbolizing sky and the upper world), the Fish (symbolizing water and the middle world), and the Bear (symbolizing land and the underworld).

In 1947 Frederica de Laguna collected a story that delineates some basic principles of Alaskan Athabascan kinship; she published it in 1975. Miranda Wright (1995) describes the Koyukon Athabascan clan system with great elaboration, following the same structure, but Wright links matrikin group names to a three-part cosmological schema, as

well as to certain clan ascriptions. In this story three chiefs who had
been at war near Koyukuk Station in western Alaska (Koyukon Athabascan territory) made peace and engaged in a naming process. The first
man said, "I did not come from the top of the ground. I came from underground, and in coming through the ground I passed copper and all
different minerals, so I want to be called 'Copper,' Naltsina" (de Laguna
1975:119). He offered a piece of copper to reify his name. The second
man said, "I have come over a long stretch of water. I swam part of the
way, and I came by boat part of the way, so I want to be called 'From-out-
of-the-Water People,'" Tonidza Raltsitɬna (de Laguna 1975:119). He
brought out a string of dentalium shells as proof of his origin. The third
man said that he came from the caribou country, far away, so they called
his tribe "From-among-the-Caribou People," BatsIxtoxtana. De Laguna defines the Caribou People as people of the sky. According to
Wright there are those of the sky (the caribou people), those from below
the earth (the copper people), and those of the water (the dentalium
shell people). Gwich'in Athabascan matrikin names also reflect this
kind of metaphor, but the cosmology is no longer an active part of religious training. Gwich'in people refer to themselves as the Caribou
People.

De Laguna uses her story to identify the origin of Yukon River Athabascan matrilineal sibs. I suggest that the chiefs represent at least two
other foreign powers with which the Yukon River people had been at
war. The chief with the dentalium shells might have represented people
of the Northwest Coast culture area (Tlingit, Haida, or others) where
dentalium was fished and then used as a form of currency throughout
Canada and Alaska in the precolonial era. Also, they might have been
long-distance travelers or traders who had connections with the Yukon
River territory. The chief with the copper may have been from Canada,
where both the Copper Eskimo and the Yellowknife Athabascans
shaped native copper into implements for trade or personal use. The

copper chief might also represent the much nearer Ahtna Athabascan region in Alaska, where native copper was used in the same way. A noteworthy aspect of this story is that its metaphoric quality is so ambiguous that it can explain a multitude of situations. Thus, it provides a mask of unity through kinship and cosmological theories, much as present-day usage of consensus does for the Northern Athabascans.

Some contemporary Gwich'in explain kinship traditions in the following manner. At a public conference in 1993, a university-educated Gwich'in elder, whom I designate as Ch'ak'eiindak, told this version of Gwich'in history in Gwichyaa Zhee:

> First there were the Naantsaii Gwich'in [one of the matrilineal clans]. They lived in Gwich'in country long before any other people arrived. Later, there were people who came from across the water. It was so long ago that people of today do not know which water it was. These were called the Ch'itsyaa Gwich'in. They were foreigners asking to move into Gwich'in territory. The Naantsaii taught the incomers to live successfully in the harsh Gwich'in environment. The Naantsaii expected the Ch'itsyaa Gwich'in to become their servants or slaves, and the Ch'itsyaa Gwich'in complied. This has been their understanding of themselves in personality and in relationship to the Naantsaii Gwich'in ever since. [Gwichyaa Zhee Youth Survivors Conference, February 1993]

Ch'ak'eiindak, who is Ch'itsyaa himself, explained that he feels a natural urge to be helpful to others and that, in his opinion, it is an inborn tendency because of his Ch'itsyaa heritage, and he believes that being a servant gives him an advantage over others. Hence he balances an inferior traditional social status with moral ascendancy. In actual practice almost no one is aware of the former Northern Athabascan social ranking system or Ch'ak'eiindak's position in it. Rather, Ch'ak'eiindak's acknowledged status as a knowledgeable elder safeguards him from disrespect.

A custom of espousal selection arose between the two matrilineal groups that became their former rules for marriage. By this system those born to a woman who was Naantsaii would be Naantsaii as well. Those who were born to a woman who was Ch'itsyaa would become Ch'itsyaa. The children of a Teenjaaraatsyaa mother became Teenjaaraatsyaa, and they could chose a bride or groom from either of the other two groups. This system of marriage is no longer followed, and very few Gwich'in know whether they are Naantsaii, Ch'itsyaa, or Teenjaaraatsyaa. Moreover, some elders deny knowledge of the old matrilineal customs. Vitsuu is one such elder, and it is worthy of note that the story she told in 1989 cited earlier is one that emphasizes her father's father rather than her mother's mother. In other contexts she also told stories about her mother and her Vuntut Gwich'in heritage with equal emphasis. With respect to marriage customs of today, some parents encourage marriages out of rural Alaska, while others denigrate daughters and sons who move away from Athabascan country. Quite a few of the people I met either married or formed partnerships with Northern Athabascans of other parts of Alaska and Canada. One of the effects of the traditional marriage system is that it broadened trading networks. Present-day out-marriages are understood to be aspects of culture loss and not as a continuation of Northern Athabascan traditions.

Émile Petitot describes the marriage customs of the Canadian Northern Athabascans (Gwich'in, Hare, Chipewyan, and Yellowknife regions) of the mid–19th century in a slightly different manner. In the language of the eastern Gwich'in, the three groups were called Etchian-Koét (people of the right), Nattsein-Koét (people of the left), and Toendjidhaettset (people in the middle) (Petitot 1888:14–15). According to Petitot the Etchian-Koét were to select spouses from the Nattsein-Koét, and vice versa, and the Toendjidhaettset could chose from either of the other two. Petitot does not report origin stories like that discovered by de Laguna, but he does comment on the way each group was described by Gwich'in people. The Etchian were thought of as white, the Nattsein were considered black, and the Toendjidhaettset were brown (Petitot 1888:15).

While the kinship and marriage customs have been replaced, younger Northern Athabascan adults have expressed interest in reconstructing the old matrikin system. In 1994 I attended a lecture in Gwichyaa Zhee by an Athabascan woman who is Koyukon through her mother, although both mother and daughter were raised in Gwich'in Athabascan territory. She lectured on the old marriage system to elders and youth alike. Her talk was well received, and several asked for details about their family connections. She was knowledgeable about the kinship relations of nearly everyone present, which included a mixture of Gwich'in and Koyukon Athabascans. Such efforts to revitalize an obsolete tradition may fail, but they are indicative of dissatisfaction with the present systems of knowledge available to Athabascans. One reason they may fail is that at least three generations of Athabascans have now married and produced children outside of the traditional clan customs. For instance, by the old clan rules quite a few contemporary Athabascans in Gwichyaa Zhee cannot belong to Gwich'in clans because their mothers are not Gwich'in. Such conflicts give rise to a need to seek other explanations of an Athabascan past that might provide greater flexibility in determining Athabascan tribal identity.

Knowledge of traditional kinship and regional groupings has become part of private and public discourse, possibly because of the rise in anthropological literature about the Gwich'in. Tribal leaders are motivated to incorporate this knowledge into ordinary as well as legal dialogues because of increasing litigation with state and federal agencies that seem to base the truth of testimony on how well the witnesses live up to mainstream stereotypes. Proving birthright in court and the actual living of what is considered traditional life in Gwich'in villages call for two different modes of behavior and discourse. Only a few of the Gwich'in I met, none of whom were elders, are skilled at such disemic performances. In addition to kinship, there was one other common but now obsolescent institution throughout the arctic and subarctic regions: an international trading partner system, as described in the following section.

Trading Partner System

The interregional trading partner system provided a mode of alliance that extended beyond relations created by marriages. There were two sorts of Northern Athabascan trading partnerships: life partnerships within the regional group and trading partnerships with people from other areas. Trading partners were expected to maintain a tension-filled relationship, blending suspicion with trust, with each other throughout their lives. In Vashraii K'oo, the term used for "his or her partner or special friend" is *vitlee*, while the trading partner custom is called *ketmia*. Trading partnerships allowed small family units to cultivate their own diplomatic networks with foreigners. It was predicated on time-consuming modes of communication and detailed knowledge of inter-ethnic behavioral codes, including justification for murdering anyone who did not comply with these behaviors, which, as one might expect, conflicts with contemporary federal and state laws. Northern Athabascans have since systematized trade relations by using a combination of mainstream methods and traditional styles of behavior, none of which includes ritualized gift giving or murder.

To summarize, Athabascan narratives of their past are like the story told by Julia Peter, histories that combine theories of kinship, memories of border disputes with neighboring peoples, and awareness of metaphysical involvement. Vitsuu's story includes descriptions of her relationship to powerful medicine people, a war story, and an abbreviated version of her connections by kinship to several Alaskan and Canadian communities. Each of these elements of her life story is valued by her descendants, who use the information to facilitate travel between villages as well as to enhance their social capital with other people. Matrilineal kinship traditions are not sufficient to encompass all of anyone's kindred, and most Athabascans make contact with or reference to as many of their kin relations as possible, regardless of whether they are matrikin or not. Thus, the American bilateral kindred system is preferred by most Athabascans at this time.

With respect to interethnic tension, almost all Athabascans are familiar with legends of bloody battles with their northern neighbors, the Iñupiat, and these stories color present-day negotiations between Northern Athabascans and the coastal Eskimo. Policy negotiations within the Alaska Federation of Natives about oil development are often fraught with emotions mirrored in such legends that are told by Athabascans and Iñupiat people alike. These tensions may be camouflaged by the larger framework of national and international interests, but they exist and have telling implications in such arenas as the current debate over the Arctic National Wildlife Refuge. Thus, history from an indigenous perspective can provide insight into contemporary, colonial situations. Perhaps by coincidence, or perhaps because they are more interested in doing so than men are, Athabascan women have been key figures in shaping public versions of Athabascan history. Many Northern Athabascan men and women have compiled traditional narratives and supplied linguistic expertise, and some have contributed autobiographical accounts of their early lives. Some noteworthy examples are those of Belle Herbert (1988), a Gwich'in, and Katherine Peter (1992) and Poldine Carlo (1978), both Koyukon. Each of these accounts frames women's lives from the standpoint of personal hardship, penury, and traditional styles of dealing with these problems. Herbert states: "Gwintłoo tr'ootree ts'a' t'agwahtsii łaa, tr'injaa gwitr'it gwanljį. Duuyee tr'injaa k'eegwaadhat" [I feel like crying, that's how much the women worked. Women could never give the orders] (1988:149). Her descriptions of her life testify to the difficulties she encountered. In contrast to this statement, however, I heard many a Northern Athabascan woman giving orders to men and children and, indeed, saw them obeyed. The dichotomy between Herbert's account of her life and what I witnessed between 1993 and 1995 forms a central issue in chapter 5.

History from a Nonindigenous Colonial Perspective

Several landmark colonial events have shaped an emergent Gwich'in identity informed by Gwich'in theories of a traditional past. Since their initial encounters with Euro-Americans, a series of crises have drained Gwich'in resources. These include (1) devastating epidemics that reduced precolonial Gwich'in populations to less than one-half of what they were, (2) the psychological and spiritual undermining of traditional religious economies by gold miners and fur traders, (3) efforts to exploit natural resources on Northern Athabascan land by big energy conglomerates, and (4) political upheavals following Alaska's inception as a state in 1959. Athabascans have tried to counterbalance the effects of these crises in various ways. One of them has been through the U.S. Indian Reorganization Act of 1934, and another has been through coalitions with worldwide environmentalist efforts. These crises have impelled the Alaskan Athabascans toward a mode of political action that brings them to an understanding of themselves as a separate nation, although, as later chapters will show, this awareness is very generalized and primarily fills an interest in maintaining kinship ties among villages in both Alaska and Canada. The events that will be described are part of mainstream U.S. history.

While Northern Athabascan colonial history can and should be contextualized in a larger framework, the daily actions of individual Athabascans have been influenced by U.S. policy and the movements of Euro-Americans in a subtle, ubiquitous, but indirect way. Belle Herbert (1988:125), whose life spanned from the purchase of Alaska to more than a century later, remarks on the gold miners she saw from a distance. She speaks of the indigenous leaders who became Episcopal Church lay readers as if they were medicine men with significant status in both her familiar Athabascan world and the foreign world beyond Athabascans. Herbert, who was known as a medicine woman herself, was able to survive the many epidemics that ravaged Alaska during her lifetime, but neither she nor other healers were able to stop them.

Epidemics and Their Consequences

Disease from foreign bacteria and viruses decimated Northern Athabascan communities beginning in 1837 with the arrival of the Hudson Bay Company at the Great Bear Lake region of Canada. Northern Athabascan populations in Canada and Alaska were reduced by an estimated 60–80 percent within the next 50 years (Krech 1976, 1978a, 1978b). In less time than it takes a child to become an adult, families lost tradition bearers, hunters, and other skilled craftspeople, which is one of the fundamental reasons that present-day knowledge of the traditional customs is limited. Many turned to the Hudson Bay Company for help and got into unfamiliar financial debt because of it. Many surviving adults distributed orphaned children to relatives in other villages as a customary means of maintaining interdependency connections. Families that were able to take in extra children did so, and to help in this effort the Episcopal Church also opened several orphanages in Alaska. William

Loola in Gwichyaa Zhee took in many orphaned Athabascan children at the beginning of the 20th century, as did Shahnyaati', a well-known Gwich'in Athabascan chief. The colonists also suffered with the epidemics, and many tried to help the indigenous peoples as well as themselves. Canadian Athabascan communities received economic support from the Hudson Bay Company and later the Canadian government. After the United States purchased Alaska in 1867, medical supplies and food imported by the Episcopal Church after 1895 helped the Alaskan Athabascans and other Alaska Natives recover physically, if not otherwise.

There have been many census studies of Athabascans and other Native North Americans, some of which ignore the impact of disease on indigenous people. Earlier studies took the position that naturally existing environmental conditions resulted in very few indigenous residents of northeastern Alaska/northwestern Canada. Later studies, particularly those by Shepard Krech III, argue that there was once a large population that has been decimated by the epidemics of initial contact with Western Europeans. Since the late 19th century Athabascan people, like many Native Americans, have been counted in a variety of ways, and the results continue to frustrate demographers. Each tally of Athabascan people has been skewed in several ways.

A leading factor is inconsistency in identifying that which is counted: What body of people is to be counted, are the people located in a specific place, and are all of the people in one specific site to be counted? Another barrier to obtaining consistent results is that those who call themselves Athabascan live within the boundaries of two nation-states — Canada and the United States. This factor impacts both the mechanics of counting people and the way they actually live. Also, each count has been initiated for differing reasons. Potential welfare recipients are counted differently than those who are counted as voters. Many agencies seek statistical proof of a population base for funding purposes, but each so-called base differs somewhat from the others. Some enterprises have needed to determine how many customers they might have for different products and have produced tallies for those purposes.

Another very significant factor is that during the debilitating epidemics that occurred during the first 70 years of increasing contact with Euro-Americans, Athabascan birth and death rates constituted a shifting target. Most of the data are based on geographic factors, while more recent figures from the tribal governments are based on kinship affiliation rather than location. The tribal role of the Gwichyaa Zhee, for instance, includes people in many communities within the United States as well as Canada. Many researchers argue that the wider North American population losses range from 70 to 90 percent. The total North American population estimates range from as low as one million to 75 million precolonial Native North Americans (Stiffarm and Lane 1992:25). While no one disputes the devastating effects of epidemic disease among Northern Athabascans, it is impossible to ascertain how much of the aboriginal population was lost. Even today it is impractical to determine exactly how many Athabascan people live in a single community such as Gwichyaa Zhee, for so many move in and out of the community within a few months of arrival there. There appears to be a core population base of permanent residents who never seem to leave and another population of people who take the notion of wandering Athabascans to heart. Many return "home" (Gwichyaa Zhee) on such a routine basis that the permanent residents do not perceive them as being non–Gwichyaa Zhee people. Thus, counting Athabascans in any given location presents a demographic challenge. While there are many indications of population decimation, it is impossible to prove because it is futile to count a society as mobile as the Northern Athabascans.

The epidemics of the first century and a half of Euro-American occupation of Northern Athabascan land have continued with outbreaks in hepatitis B, influenza, alcoholism, diabetes, and now AIDS. Western measures were set in place to help counter epidemics in the form of a church-run hospital in the early part of this century. Eventually, all of the villages established small health clinics, some of which are run by state and federal agents. Others are managed by Tanana Chiefs Conference, a not-for-profit organization that offers medical and social services to Alaska Natives of Alaska's interior Athabascan regions. In addition, many Northern Athabascan men and women are actively seeking their own modes of healing not only physical problems but social, economic, and spiritual troubles as well.

Fur Traders and Religion

The most obvious impact of the fur traders on the Northern Athabascans from a Western perspective was economic, changing from hunting to cash. A more deleterious impact from an indigenous perspective occurred with the undermining of religious customs. Besides bringing disease and gambling, fur traders impinged on Northern Athabascan religious beliefs by persuading hunters to kill fur-bearing animals for the fur only. Many such animals, particularly bears, wolves, wolverines, and marten, are considered to be sacred with specific metaphysical roles outlined in myth. These sacred animals were hunted in precolonial days for their fur but not for meat. Hunters were taught to be aware that they were watched and judged by ever present spiritual entities who had great powers to exact revenge for killing without justification. Thus, hunting for the fur was a complete violation of the reciprocal relations among humans, animals, and the spirit world. Consequences of such violations were customarily expected to be starvation and illness, which happened with the epidemics, although Calvin Martin (1978) has challenged that perspective. Martin was reacting to the prevailing assumptions in anthropology that indigenous North Americans relinquished traditional forms of hunting practices by the mere presence of guns and steel traps. He suggests that the argument be relocated away from economic arguments of supply and demand into issues of ideology and custom.

Northern Athabascan country was first entered by French Canadian fur traders in 1837. They extended their territory quickly into the Northwest Territories of Canada, to the region near Tetlit Zheh, and then in 1847 to Alaska at the confluence of the Ch'ôonjik and Yukon Rivers. At that time they were, by their terms, encroaching on Russian territory, although no Russians ever penetrated the Alaskan interior to that distance. The Hudson Bay Company's goal was to acquire furs. In doing so it imposed hierarchies on indigenous people that ran counter to local customs. If community trading chiefs who met Hudson Bay Company needs were lacking, Hudson Bay Company personnel assigned Native "retainers" to take those roles. Sometimes the men so assigned were not of high status in these communities; some were not even part of such communities. Thus, not only did the process of hunting sacred animals undermine Athabascan religious beliefs, but the Hudson Bay Company also undermined their modes of leadership.

Hudson Bay Company personnel brought some addictive products with them to Athabascan villages, but transportation difficulties limited them to lightweight products: tobacco *(ts'eet'it)*, card games (Lagar and Mazhur), and money *(laraa)*. Athabascan people still play French card games with children in their homes, but Pan and Poker are now the gambling card games of choice. According to Mishler (1995:643) indigenous middlemen hired by the Hudson Bay Company traded tea, shells, and gunpowder for furs. One Yukon River explorer wrote of the Indians with whom he negotiated, saying that they "were only too glad to get serviceable articles of which they were utterly destitute" (Karamanski 1983:237, citing the personal journals of Robert Campbell, 1808–53). The fur traders were accompanied by missionaries who further undermined the religious practices of the Athabascans through proselytization.

Missionaries and the Impact of Christianity

Christian missionaries have transfigured Northern Athabascan philosophical views during the past 150 years. Most of them have been intent
on supplanting all indigenous beliefs, but a few have respected indigenous peoples. One such man was Émile Petitot, a French Oblate missionary who transcribed many Canadian Athabascan stories of what he
refers to as a Dene Bible (1886:ix). Petitot's attitude reflects an Oblate
19th-century policy that called for learning the languages and customs
of those whom they were to evangelize (Champagne 1949:188). They
were enjoined to publish dictionaries, grammars, and hymn- and prayer
books, as well as other materials (Champagne 1949:189). In 1862 Petitot
began service among the Slavey Athabascans for the order of Oblates of
Mary Immaculate at Fort Providence on the Great Slave Lake, Northwest
Territories, Canada. Three years later he moved to Fort Good Hope
among the Hare Athabascans. He was also able to travel among the
Tchiglit Inuit in the Northwest Territories between 1865 and 1867, and
he returned to France in 1882. Petitot wrote *Traditions Indiennes du Canada
Nord-Ouest* in French (1886) and a second version that includes his transcriptions of the original languages (1888). Some of Petitot's work has
been translated from the French into English by the Programme Development Division of the Department of Education of the Northwest Territories in Canada under the title *The Book of Dene: Containing the Traditions
and Beliefs of Chipewyan, Dogrib, Slavey, and Loucheux Peoples* (1976). Petitot's idealism went beyond these demands, and he is worthy of note
for his avant-garde support of human diversity. Petitot considered the
Athabascan oral traditions to merit a respectful and dignified acceptance in the world.

In 1862 Anglican missionary Robert McDonald, another Canadian
missionary whose impact on Northern Athabascans has been long-
standing, was sent to the Gwichyaa Zhee area. Said to be one-quarter

Ojibwa, McDonald spoke several languages including Ojibwa, Cree, and, with time, Gwich'in (Mishler 1990:123–125; Peake 1975:55–56). He married Julia Kuttug, a Gwich'in woman, and dwelt with the Gwich'in for the remainder of his life. In 1898 he published a full translation of the Bible into Takudh, a dialect of Gwich'in. He also translated a prayer book, hymnal, and other works. When the United States purchased Alaska (1867) he was required to move away from Gwichyaa Zhee to Fort McPherson in the Northwest Territories of Canada. His descendants are still active with First Nations political and economic projects in that region.

There is no evidence that McDonald was directed by the Anglican Church to translate the Bible, for translation was not a part of church policy at that time (Ian Douglas, personal communication, Episcopal Divinity School, Cambridge MA, 1992). Perhaps he devoted himself to Bible translation because he was trained at a time when there was a resurgence of interest in proselytizing Christianity by reaching potential converts through their own languages. McDonald's Takudh Bible has given the Gwich'in a sense of themselves as having a language that is just as valuable as any of the leading world languages and, by extension, has provided them with a sense of unity by identifying a dozen or so villages as speakers of the same language and, hence, potentially the same nation by some standards. McDonald's Bible is still in constant use in Gwichyaa Zhee, although almost no one there understands the words. Many people, including me, have memorized some of the Gwich'in hymns and sing them with enthusiasm. A theory posed by Africanist Lamin Sanneh in 1978 sheds some light on the matter. Sanneh points out that translation of the Bible into other languages has helped preserve cultural traditions of colonized people in at least one important way: it reinforces the value of the indigenous language within the minds of the people who speak it. In his words, "Local Christians acquired from the vernacular translations confidence in the indigenous cause.

While the colonial system represented a worldwide economic and military order, mission represented vindication for the vernacular" (1989:123). Mission in most of Alaska represented humiliation and conversion, but in Gwich'in it represented a modicum of self-respect because of this translation effort. The Takudh Bible serves as a point of distinction between the Gwich'in and other Alaska Natives who do not have books in their own languages. Many of the Gwich'in I met spoke of the "Indian Bible" with ethnocentric pride, as if it represents something more than the Bible in English does.

Many missionaries have had a beneficial impact on Northern Athabascans in Alaska after the Treaty of Cession between the United States and Russia in 1867. For instance, Jules Jetté was a French Jesuit priest who worked in Tanana and other Koyukon villages. His many word lists, descriptions, transcriptions of oral material, and drawings centralize knowledge about Koyukon traditions from the late 19th and early 20th century.

With the purchase of Alaska by the United States, Canadian citizens, including their missionaries, were required to move back to Canada. In 1895 the Anglican missionaries were replaced by American Episcopalians as federal agents for the U.S. Department of Education. The Episcopal missionaries include Peter Trimble Rowe, Hudson Stuck, and later Walter Hannum. Some of their Athabascan converts, such as John Fredson, have been influential as well. Bishop Rowe and Archdeacon Stuck were instrumental in obtaining direct financial, medical, and educational aid from the U.S. government and the Episcopal ministry. The epidemics mentioned earlier served as justification to the Episcopal Church for building a hospital, a territorial school, and a church in Gwichyaa Zhee at the beginning of the century. The Episcopalians were active participants in the Christian social reform movement of that era. The social reform movement held that "religion must concern itself intimately with the fate of all mankind and with the condition of the secu-

lar world in which men live" (Hylson-Smith 1988:209). Rowe and Stuck
were both alarmed by the health and social status of Alaska Natives.
Rowe usually included a plea for help in his annual reports to the central
church administration, and in one such statement he wrote: "In all the
legislation made for Alaska they [Alaska Natives] are not considered. So
far as the government is concerned, they are neither Indians nor citizens. They appear to have no rights. Appeal for them is in vain"
(1917:6). Stuck helped in another way by initiating Native leadership
from among promising young men. Stuck died in 1920 and therefore
did not live long enough to see this project through to completion. Only
one of his protégés succeeded in accomplishing enduring goals on
behalf of the Northern Athabascans or Stuck. That individual was
Fredson, who will be discussed later. Stuck's ambition for his acolytes
was that they join him in becoming missionaries for the Episcopal
Church. None succeeded, but all of them tried. John Fredson of Viihtaii
became successful in creating public facilities, such as schools, a medical clinic, mail service, and finally a reservation.

In 1938 Congress passed laws following the Indian Reorganization
Act that empowered the Department of the Interior to set up land reserves to "assist Native Americans to keep or regain tribal lands and
hunting grounds, to prevent the kind of destitution many of them endured" (MacKenzie 1985:160). Fredson recognized the potential of this
opportunity for his people and solicited tribal support from Gwichyaa
Zheh, Viihtaii, Vashraii K'oo, and Zheh Gwatsal. The Gwichyaa Zheh
Tribal Council failed to take action, but the others accepted Fredson's
offer to submit a joint proposal. After six years of negotiations the 1.8
million acre Venetie Reserve was officially created in 1943 (MacKenzie
1985:170). Although Fredson died two years later in 1945 of pneumonia
at the age of 50, his efforts initiated a path of thought that has separated
the people of Viihtaii and Vashraii K'oo irrevocably from the political

actions of other Gwich'in. The most significant act of separation was that tribal members of the Venetie Reserve opted out of the Alaska Native Claims Settlement Act of 1971 in order to preserve their reserve lands in fee simple title (unrestricted ownership). As a result of their separation from ANCSA corporations (explained later in this chapter), the members of the tribal councils of Venetie Reserve, now called the Venetie Tribal Government (IRA), did not receive any of the ANCSA settlement funds and continue to resist all efforts to reduce their tribal sovereignty. They also do not have conventional access to state political backing through the Alaska Federation of Natives, which coauthored ANCSA and is now composed only of delegates from the ANCSA corporations. As a result, Venetie Tribal Government (IRA) has spliced political links to federal and international nongovernmental organizations for economic assistance and protection. The Venetie Tribal Government (IRA) has since become embroiled in a series of legal disputes with the State of Alaska and the U.S. federal government which ended in a defeat for the tribal government in the U.S. Supreme Court in February 1998.

In summary, the fur trading economy brought to Northern Athabascans by the Canadians introduced three problems that undermined Athabascan religious traditions and physical resistance and introduced a discourse of economic dependency and hegemony that runs counter to the traditional Athabascan custom of living through mutual interdependence. The Christian missionaries who came into Alaska have both degraded and empowered the Athabascans. In their efforts to proselytize, they augmented a generalized Athabascan awareness of failure to conform to the mandates of their traditional reciprocal relationships with the natural and spiritual world by arguing that the Athabascan healers were unable to overcome the epidemics. The missionaries maintained that the Athabascan system failed because it was not Christian and demonstrated a putative Christian superiority through their more efficacious medical supplies and food. To add yet another burden, the missionaries and other Euro-Americans denounced Athabascans for succumbing to alcohol, a product that was a key trade item in use by the prospectors and fur traders to which a number of Athabascans have become addicted. Despite all of this, many Athabascans are devout Christians.

Northern Athabascan women, like Northern Athabascan men, were victims of disease and destitution, and many turned to their strongest men for help during epidemics. There are several accounts of heroic Athabascan men who protected widows and orphans, as mentioned earlier. Some of these men, such as Shahnyaati', were traditional medicine men and chiefs of widespread reputation. Others, such as William Loola, converted to Christianity and made use of the skimpy financial umbrella provided by Rowe and Stuck. Others simply survived in small isolated regions away from the centers of disease. Women like Belle Herbert continued to live much as they had always done in the outreaches of Athabascan territory, except that Herbert earned money for herself and her children by trapping. Rather than adopting a mainstream lifestyle, however, she preferred a traditional Athabascan lifestyle of living in remote areas. Her life story calls into question how to ascertain the nature of the impact of the fur trade on the daily lives of Athabascans during that era. The 20th century brought many resource hunters from other parts of the world to Athabascan territory besides the fur traders. The next invasion was the American prospectors, and after them came energy enterprises.

American Prospectors, Crime, Addictions, and Pollution

Prospectors for gold crowded into Alaska via the Yukon River drainages beginning in 1877 and have remained there in smaller numbers to this time. Miners and geologists have found rich gold deposits throughout

Northern Athabascan territory. Yukon River villages became mining hub communities because they provided slow but reliable access to supplies from the southern reaches of the continent. Every village population in the Yukon River drainage area was high with thousands of men during the gold rush. Some Gwich'in villages, such as Danzhit Hanlii, hosted thousands of miners for a decade or so, until the gold played out of that area. There are now only 94 year-round residents in Danzhit Hanlii, for instance, instead of several thousand a century ago. The prospectors brought crime to the villages and imported liquor by barge in great quantities. They also supplanted and exploited the Athabascan economy in many ways, not the least of which was prostitution: Native women along the Yukon River reportedly traded sex for food. The high populations of miners are now gone, but gambling, liquor, and crime remain. The crime brought U.S. federal marshals who have been replaced by Alaska state troopers and local police officers. In addition, efforts in the 1980s and 1990s have made negligible inroads toward restoring the land from the ravages of mining. Birds and land animals have dwindled in number, and the water in lakes and streams still holds contaminants from mining processes. The many U.S. environmental acts during the past few decades have caused mining to become cost prohibitive as a large-scale business, although some suggest that new techniques have been developed. After the initial gold rush at the beginning of the 20th century diminished, other energy resources stimulated economic efforts in Athabascan territory, including the hydroelectric potential of the Yukon River and oil development. The economic potential of the land stimulated formation of a state.

Statehood, Developers, ANCSA, and Environmentalists

After World War II, the United States became increasingly aware of the value of Alaska as a strategic defense zone not only because of its proximity to Europe and Asia regarding flight planning but also because it effectively bordered the former Soviet Union. This corresponds to a global trend delineated by Maybury-Lewis in which countries located in areas remote from centers of power during the Cold War "were endowed with strategic significance" that many have lost in the post–Cold War era (1997:138–139). Maybury-Lewis posits that those that have not lost their strategic significance have maintained it by remaining stockyards of armaments. Gwichyaa Zhee is not officially one of these areas; however, the traffic of monthly U.S. Air Force freight-carrying aircraft into the village (not to mention over its airspace) suggests that the federal government has a continued investment of some form in this remote area.

Because of this and other national movements, Alaska has seen increased federal involvement in numerous areas, including Native education and health. For instance, the first Alaska Native hospital opened in 1954 in Anchorage. Alaska became the 49th state in 1959 at the urging of entrepreneurs who wanted to ensure that some of the money derived from mineral resources would stay in Alaska. A major development project had already been introduced into Congress as a potential hydroelectric dam project during the 1950s. In addition, during the 1950s and 1960s energy companies began exploratory drilling in all of Alaska's coastal areas. The oil discovered in south-central Alaska (approximately 500 miles south of Gwichyaa Zheh) has been pumped out of the state for more than three decades. One of the major issues originally blocking development of the oil reserves was land title. Who owned the land? According to the 1959 state charter, ownership of Alaska's public land was to be negotiated among the state, Alaska Natives, and the U.S. federal government. Until these issues were settled, the oil companies could not pursue negotiations for exploitation of the Yukon River for hydroelectric engineering.

Rampart Hydroelectric Dam and the Three Gs

The Rampart Dam project constituted a major crisis in Alaskan Northern Athabascan history because of the threat of permanent flooding. The proposal, which failed, was a hydroelectric dam project that was first submitted to Congress in the 1950s and was rejected for the last time a decade later. In the 1950s hydroelectric entrepreneurs studied the Yukon River as a potential source of national electricity. If constructed the dam would have flooded nine million acres along the river's upper region. Nine Athabascan villages would have been completely submerged. The dam would have displaced approximately 1,500 people and would have destroyed nesting and feeding grounds for many bird and animal species. The project engineers included the cost of relocating village residents in their proposal but failed to consider cultural values or individual preferences. Wildlife conservation efforts proved strong enough to prevent the passage of the bill. Many villagers in each of the affected areas raised objections to dam construction, although some wanted the dam as a source of public revenue. The bill died in Congress after years of fierce debate in Alaska and other states.

One of the positive outcomes of the Rampart Dam fight was the formal organization of a now defunct, but still celebrated, Gwich'in Athabascan committee to protest the dam construction. On February 2, 1964, one group of Gwich'in opponents organized Gwitchya Gwitchin Ginkhye (the Yukon Flats People Speak), which they now call the Three Gs. It was the first active coalition of Gwich'in villages in the colonial era. Most of the people who took office in the Three Gs have continued to take leadership roles on subsequent issues that could impact the Gwich'in. For example, Jonathan Solomon, who was sent to Congress as a Three Gs delegate in 1964, was appointed the Upper Yukon River Basin User Community Representative to the International Porcupine Caribou Herd Board in 1993. The board was established by the authority of an international agreement between Canada and the United States on July 17, 1987. Solomon remains one of the most active participants with the Gwich'in Steering Committee as well as in matters pertaining to the preservation of Athabascan resources, including the Porcupine Caribou Herd. Perhaps because his father's father is the same heroic medicine man mentioned at the beginning of this chapter, Solomon's efforts are now closer to Vashraii K'oo and the Venetie Tribal Government (IRA) in the northern reaches of Athabascan territory from which his grandfather came. Solomon lives, however, in Gwichyaa Zheh, about 100 miles to the south. Solomon has also been active in voicing rural opinions about ANCSA.

In 1966 Alaska Natives responded to the urging of state leaders to come to a settlement agreement by forming the Alaska Federation of Natives (AFN). AFN continues to the present time to be the largest and most influential body of indigenous peoples in the state. Its formation, then and now, has problematized Native identity in the following ways. First, its constituents and staff are primarily urban-dwelling Alaska Natives and not people of the villages. This point was raised with force in 1984 when Canadian Justice Thomas Berger was commissioned to investigate Alaska Natives' response to ANCSA. Berger (1985) recorded testimony in most of the villages throughout the state and repeatedly heard the same message: rural Natives were left out of the decision to implement ANCSA. Few in Alaska hear alternative voices about Native issues besides that of the urban-based AFN. Those Alaska Native villages or tribal governments (such as the Venetie Tribal Government [IRA]) that have opted out of ANCSA or AFN have to find other avenues to receive financial aid. AFN's well-funded lobby is influential in the State of Alaska as well as in Washington DC. The relationships thus formed do not permit the small Alaska Native population (approximately 60,000) to elaborate a concerted political action that meets the broadest spectrum of their needs to include rural Natives. Thus, AFN, constituting the largest political face of Alaska Natives, does not meet rural Athabascan needs either as their ANCSA representation or as a representative of those Athabascans who do not affiliate with ANCSA, such as Viihtaii and Vashraii K'oo. In other words, those Alaska Natives who identify with their cultural traditions sometimes are not brought into political activities if they are also rural residents. However, following the example of many disenfranchised or otherwise enterprising groups throughout the United States, rural Natives have introduced lobbyists to the convention halls of the AFN and thereby have achieved a measure of support for their initiatives.

In 1969 a large petroleum reserve was discovered off the north slope of Alaska. It was significant enough to have ensured the investments of major energy companies in that area for the next three decades. The efforts already initiated by AFN to create ANCSA were stepped up after this discovery. President Richard M. Nixon signed the Alaska Native Claims Settlement Act into law on December 17, 1971. By the terms of that settlement Alaska Natives received $962.5 million to be distributed to 12 regional corporations, which in turn disbursed a portion of that sum to village corporations and individual shareholders. Villages that opted out of ANCSA, such as those under the Venetie Tribal Government (IRA), received none of that money. The settlement also entitled Alaska Natives to select 44 million acres of land to be held in trust by the U.S. federal government. The tribal government received fee simple title to its 1.8 million acre reserve (part of the 44 million acre ANCSA settlement) in lieu of cash because it opted out of ANCSA. Most other Athabascan villages in Alaska have received the money and ANCSA lands that are held in a land bank trust agreement with the federal government.

ANCSA has proven problematic to many Alaska Natives for a variety of reasons, as mentioned earlier. Besides public issues, it also affects conceptions of personal identity. Owning shares is not a birthright as tribal membership can be. ANCSA excludes any who do not own shares. Shares can be inherited but not sold, so many Athabascans have been excluded from ANCSA but included in village tribal rolls. This situation leads to different kinds of trouble depending on the primary residence of the person involved and the federal status of the tribe to which she or he might belong. An urban Athabascan youth may not seek or be sought for tribal enrollment and may not be a shareholder by the terms of ANCSA. Those youths often suffer racial discrimination without agency support of any kind. On the other hand, a village-dwelling Athabascan youth may suffer from racial discrimination, poverty, and joblessness but might have moral and occasional financial support from his or her tribal government. These and related issues are discussed in chapter 5.

Women like Sarah James of Vashraii K'oo are among those who are pursuing different avenues to help the Athabascans emerge from the implications of ANCSA. She is one of the principal spokespersons for the Gwich'in Steering Committee (see the following section) and routinely encourages Athabascan youths to understand their roots. In this capacity, she teaches traditional drumming, speaks out on behalf of her people on every possible occasion, and collaborates with environmentalist nongovernmental organizations.

Northern Athabascan leaders have protested ANCSA on several points. One of them is that ANCSA was created in concert with Alaska Natives who represented profit-making corporations: "They made sure that these [representatives] are going to be corporate-minded people and [a] profit-making branch of the Native people" (Gideon James, personal communication, August 14, 1994). Gideon James, who was then president of the Venetie Tribal Government (IRA), also took exception to the many nonprofit corporations representing Alaska Native interests that have sprung up in Alaska since ANCSA. Some of these entities have attempted to establish federal recognition as tribes with federal agencies. James and other Athabascan leaders object to this practice on the grounds that it unfairly takes the few federal funds reserved for Indian tribes: "Further on it weakens the tribal status in Alaska when these things happen, and it goes on every day" (James, personal communication, August 14, 1994). James and others like him have resisted attempts to subsume their tribal authorities under ANCSA corporations or the State of Alaska because doing so erodes their nation-to-nation status with the U.S. federal government.

Environmental Efforts

After their initial involvement with the Three Gs during the 1960s, conservationists remained active in Athabascan territory. Stories of visits by activist celebrities such as the late John Denver and Jane Fonda slide into conversation at opportune moments. In the mid-1980s environmentalists helped the Venetie Tribal Government (IRA) to organize and host the first Gwich'in Gathering in 1988. The Gwich'in Steering Committee was formed and has been informed by the Gwich'in Gatherings. The committee was created in the mid-1980s by Bob Childers, a white man whose allegiances have been divided between environmental issues and those of Koyukon and Gwich'in Athabascans. He brought about the first Gwich'in Gathering in Viihtaii by successfully applying for hundreds of thousands of dollars in direct donations from conservation agencies and in-kind service contributions from air transportation companies.

The objectives of some northern Athabascans, particularly the Gwich'in of northeastern Alaska, and various environmentalist agencies are linked to the preservation of the calving grounds of the Porcupine Caribou Herd on the Arctic National Wildlife Refuge (ANWR) in the United States. Northern Athabascans are not unified on this topic. In fact, some Northern Athabascan individuals, agencies, and businesses are intent on continuing oil drilling in Alaska's north slope. However, there are quite a few politically active Northern Athabascans who work closely with environmental agencies to block big energy development efforts. Those Athabascans who object to development voice their objectives in preserving the caribou herd as an aspect of an ancient belief in their reciprocal relationship with the caribou as well as the separate but conjoined reciprocal relationship between humans and the spirit world (subsumed within the term *vit'eegwijyaahchy'aa*). Jonathan Solomon (mentioned earlier with respect to Rampart Dam) maintains that the Gwich'in have a spiritual commitment to protect the Porcupine Caribou Herd. Likewise, Gwich'in activist Sarah James quit her salaried position at the Vashraii K'oo health clinic to join the environmental effort, and because of this, she lives in constant poverty. There are many Athabascans who disagree with the premises of the Gwich'in Steering Committee for a number of reasons, including disputes among kinfolk, family members who work for oil companies, or the fact that they do not live in the caribou region. The Alaskan villages most concerned with the Porcupine Caribou Herd are Vashraii K'oo and Viihtaii, which have traditionally depended on the migration of the herd, as have Canadian Gwich'in in Tetlit Zheh and Vuntut. By contrast, residents of Gwichyaa Zhee, Beaver, Danzhit Hanlii, Deenduu, Dinyee, and Jałk'iitsik traditionally hunt moose, fish, and trade for dried caribou meat with relations in Vashraii K'oo and Viihtaii. While residents of these latter villages may not actively support the Northern Athabascan communities, they also do nothing to impede their political efforts.

The environmentalists who support Athabascans represent an alternative to welfare programs offered by state and federal governments by offering some cash, a means to achieve ethnic pride, and travel. Moreover, environmentalists have helped the Gwich'in establish a worldwide reputation as environmental activists. Some Athabascans have adopted much of the rhetoric used in environmental efforts and seem willing to support other worldwide issues. The villagers of Vashraii K'oo, for instance, hosted an international scientific conference in 1993 called

"People, Science, and Caribou.'' Because there are neither hotels nor restaurants in Vashraii K'oo, this conference entailed a considerable amount of personal effort on the part of private Gwich'in citizens to house and feed 50 guests in a community whose normal population is around 150.

Environmentalists such as Childers have tried to adhere to Athabascan religious and social traditions as much as possible. Under the circumstances, this has involved extracting and implementing information from the elders that is new to younger Athabascans. This occurred in the planning stages of the first Gwich'in Gathering in 1988. Childers wanted to hold a gathering to garner support from the Gwich'in and other Alaska Native people for a unified effort to protect the ANWR from oil development. He also wanted it done in the Gwich'in way and asked about the regional gatherings that were mentioned by Osgood and Mc-Kennan in the 1930s but had not been held for decades. There were some who remembered going to such events, and they insisted that the only way to hold such a gathering was through consensus, which presented a significant barrier between two cultural theories of order. By Athabascan standards, consensus meant that there was to be no one obviously in charge of the affair. By contrast, mainstream logic's view was that the expense of creating the first Gwich'in Gathering necessitated that someone be in charge. Childers was extremely sensitive to the liminality of his position as the administrative organizer, chief fund-raiser, guiding light to inspire people to want to come to this event, and the man who wanted more than anything for this to be an Athabascan event that those who came would understand was accomplished by Athabascan standards of consensual behavior (personal communication, January 1993). He succeeded to the extent that only a few of the people whom I asked in subsequent years knew about his involvement in the gatherings. Most of them spoke of the gatherings as events that simply happened but required a lot of work on the part of themselves or their relatives. However, Childers failed to convince his backers that there was any point to the event, for the Gwich'in failed to follow the provided agenda or any advice. Many of the agencies declined to fund subsequent events. The Gwich'in Gatherings have become biennial events. Numerous Athabascans maintain, as if they had known this all of their lives, that these were held all the time a century ago.

Conservation agencies have evaluated the commitment of Athabascans by reducing some of the funding made available to them. Less environmental money has been obligated to hosting subsequent Gwich'in Gatherings, which Childers said were frustratingly disorganized to the handful of funding agents and activists who attended (personal communication, January 1993). Increased funding has been found, however, to bring small groups of Canadian and Alaskan Athabascans to Congress and the United Nations to arouse public awareness about the ANWR. For their part, the Athabascans who support environmentalists find themselves speaking on issues that do not resolve day-to-day hegemonies. Northern Athabascan addictions and unemployment are seldom addressed or reduced by conservation arguments. Childers and many environmentalists who support indigenous peoples employ a model of ethics that is somewhat informed by Native American theologies but primarily patterned on Christian models that divide the world into the Saved and the Unsaved or, in the environmentalist model, the Enlightened and the Unenlightened. Enlightened human beings, like their missionary predecessors, cast themselves into the role of guardians of the earth, protecting it from the unenlightened. While many of them respect Northern Athabascan religious traditions, their model differs in where to locate power and assert control. The Athabascan traditional model situates power in the spirit world (subsumed within vit'eegwijyaahchy'aa) and reciprocal relationships between that world and the human world as well as the natural world. The environmental action groups that have been supporting Alaska Natives appear to be not only supporting the Gwich'in but engineering a quasi-politic identity by manipulating publicity about putative traditional markers: praying to the animals and other elements of the earth,[1] drum dancing, and wearing traditional regalia. However, environmentalist support has fallen short of actually endorsing one of the most difficult court battles in which Alaska Native peoples have engaged. In 1997 the U.S. Supreme Court agreed to review a case between the State of Alaska and the Native Village of Venetie Tribal Government (IRA). Many governmental and nongovernmental entities offered letters of support on behalf of Venetie, except for the environmental lobby groups. The Supreme Court ruled against Venetie in February 1998 (Rosita Worl, personal communication, February 1998). The efforts of environmentalists, hence, display a clear priority to maintain the status quo regarding nation-states while stratifactorily boosting images of Athabascan ethnicity. When asked to demonstrate support of Athabascan sovereignty, environmental action groups back away.

1. See Masako Cordray Wescott's 1995 videotape, *Voice from the North: The Gwich'in People and the Arctic National Wildlife Refuge* (Maui Video Company, available from the Gwich'in Steering Committee, P.O. Box 202768, Anchorage).

3 Rural Economy: *Whose Addict Now?*

The foregoing chapter presents two methods of explaining a Northern Athabascan past, one from an elder's perspective, the other a chronological record that contextualizes Northern Athabascan history within a global framework. This chapter approaches the complex Athabascan economies from multiple viewpoints as well. One vantage point is from the intimacy of making a living in Athabascan land, while another frames the local economies within a worldwide spectrum to which they are connected via aircraft, telephones, and satellites. A third analyzes the semiotics of Athabascan sharing in context or contest with cash usage. The local economies of Gwichyaa Zhee in the 1990s included hunting and fishing, accelerated cash usage, and extensive sharing. As mentioned in chapter 1, there are several facets of the Athabascan economy implicated in a larger network that perpetuates addictions. The most salient factor of this addictive economy is that it replicates the extraction or profiteering model of other Euro-American enterprises. The contemporary economic milieu among the Athabascans is motivated by fragmented principles of ancient codes of behavior that are intertwined with often misunderstood ethics of mainstream cash culture and dominated by both the positive and the negative forces of the addictive economy. This chapter is divided into segments that discuss the local Northern Athabascan economy, the semiotics of sharing, and the addictive system. Within each I discuss the implications of these factors for Athabascan women and Athabascan leadership roles. The colonial history of Northern Athabascan people has caused a complete upheaval in traditional economies. In addition to healing their personal and social problems, Athabascans also face healing economic wounds that have left them impoverished. As mentioned in the first chapter, one of the issues regarding healing is discovering what Athabascans themselves consider to be social pathologies and what they include in the rubric of healing.

Most of the data for this section derive from Gwichyaa Zhee from 1993 to 1995. Gwichyaa Zhee is the largest Alaskan Gwich'in community. It perches at the confluence of the Yukon and the Ch'ôonjik Rivers in northeastern Alaska, east of the T'eedriinjik River. It is about 100 miles west of the U.S.–Canadian border. In 1994 approximately 730 people lived in Gwichyaa Zhee, and of those about 175 worked for wage-paying jobs, earning approximately $4 million that year (see Table 1). Out of 200 active households, over three-quarters were occupied by at least one employed person. In addition to paychecks, roughly $1 million per year came to over 50 households in various forms of welfare, such as Aid to Families with Dependent Children and General Assistance. During the years I was in Gwichyaa Zhee, 1993–95, many people expressed concern over impending loss of welfare funding.

Gwichyaa Zhee was once a traditional gathering place for Northern Athabascan people, and most (90 percent) of the residents are Athabascans. However, outsiders have imposed vigorous symbols of their occupation on this key land resource, such as the four huge radar antennas that dominate the Gwichyaa Zhee landscape for miles. With three rivers draining toward it, Gwichyaa Zhee remains a center of trade for a region of over 40,000 square miles and nine villages. Its airstrip is acknowledged as the regional hub by most of the local airlines. Although outsiders may not find living in Athabascan country a welcoming experience, its economic utility provides incentive to maintain far more than a symbolic or visual presence in Gwichyaa Zhee. Table 2 shows the estimated volume in pounds of goods that entered Gwichyaa Zhee in 1994. The information was gathered from nine air cargo companies and does not include military cargo flights or the river barges that bring motor-

Table 1. Sources of Primary Annual Revenue, Gwichyaa Zhee

Source of Annual Income	Number of People	Estimated Annual Income
State and derivative agencies	41	$539,070
Yukon Flats School District	40	$1,600,000
Tribal entities	19	$341,411
Conglomerate under the Council of Athabascan Tribal Governments	35	$628,915
Federal agencies	10	$53,907
Private enterprises	28	$503,132
Elders of Gwichyaa Zhee employees	4	$50,000
Cottage industries	100	$250,000
Retirees	50	$898,450
Aid to Families with Dependent Children	32	$579,008
Other financial aid	20	$400,000

Source: Data derived in part from Alaska Department of Community and Regional Affairs community profiles (1994), based on the 1990 census and related information gathered by the author.

ized vehicles and other products into the villages along the Yukon River. Also not included are the shipments made by privately owned riverboats. The monetary investment of the goods shipped represents millions of dollars brought in by merchandisers and freight carriers and an equal amount leaving Gwichyaa Zhee pocketbooks.

Northern Athabascan colonial history has brought several layers of extraction to Athabascan territory. The fur traders took animal resources, the prospectors extracted mineral ores, and oil companies want easy access to the remaining petroleum reserves in northern Alaska. Less visible extractors include myself and other academic researchers who have appropriated Native peoples' words (narratives, songs, and language) to develop personal careers. Public institutions also fit into this category as agencies that use public monies to pay local people and outsiders alike to fund projects both in and out of Athabascan land. The money from these projects usually leaves the region as soon as the checks are written to pay outside vendors. Athabascan leaders have begun combating this process in a variety of ways. One of these is to monitor all proposal activity as closely as possible, so that the leaders remain informed of cash flow. Another method is to write and execute funding proposals of their own, whereby they implement as much local control as possible. The Council of Athabascan Tribal Governments, which will be discussed shortly, is one of the leading exponents of this agenda, and there are several others.

Rural Northern Athabascan Economy

No one knows exactly what the traditional Northern Athabascan cultures were like 150 years ago, but many have ideas about what it was and incorporate part or all of those ideas into ordinary discourse. This section describes how Athabascans act out a traditional or subsistence lifestyle. Activities that fall into this realm are sharing networks, trading networks, gift exchanges, and life event celebrations. All of these are linked with hunting, fishing, and harvesting plant materials. In the local economy, no object has a uniform value over time and space or across social boundaries. What may have significant value between two people today may have no exchange value to anyone else.

Athabascan communities were small in precolonial times, and now they are somewhat larger. Numerous Athabascan war stories, as exemplified in the previous chapter, indicate that their systems of mutual

Table 2. Community Profiles of Alaskan Athabascan Villages, 1990

Village	Population	Number of Houses in Use	Type of Heating	% of Houses with Plumbing	Median Household Income
Vashraii K'oo	113	36	94.1% wood	none	$9,661
Beaver	103	43	100% wood	none	$9,661
Deenduu	42	15	100% wood	none	$5,032
Jałk'iitsik	83	33	80.6% wood	none	$12,750
Central	48	27	56.5% fuel oil	11.4	$28,036
Danzhit Hanlii	95	23	79.2% wood	12.5	$17,083
Gwichyaa Zhee	729	205	42.8% fuel oil	47.6	$17,969
Dinyee	93	37	100% wood	none	$10,000
Viihtaii	231	50	78.4% wood	none	$14,688
Combined estimated totals	1,537	469	—	—	$135,532

Source: Data derived from Alaska Department of Community and Regional Affairs community profiles (1994), which are based on the 1990 census and related information gathered by the department. These figures differ significantly from those compiled from the same database (1990 U.S. Census) by the Institute of Social and Economic Research.

Note: All of the villages have a community water system, but only a few houses have plumbing, and even fewer have sewer or septic systems attached to the houses. Where water is not plumbed into the houses, individuals must have it hauled (usually by four-wheeler or snow machine) to the house.

respect often failed. Now there are few remaining traditional cultural devices to guide the Athabascan in forgiving delinquent behavior. Traditional religious practices no longer provide mutually understood mechanisms to cleanse or strengthen social bonds. Likewise, as mentioned in the previous chapter, the system of matrilineal kinship has been superseded by the mainstream mode of bilateral kindred, and few Athabascan people know how the former matrilineal clans used to interact with other facets of daily life. However, the traditional economy is one of the cultural complexes that continue to ameliorate social injuries successfully. Its multiple aspects create and nurture many of the social bonds between kinfolk and other residents. For instance, sharing game meat is one of the best mechanisms in this region for soothing damaged relationships:

> Late one February night well after sport hunting season was closed, Ts'ivii pulled up to Itree's house on a snow machine. The trailer behind it was laden with freshly killed moose meat. He brought one large section of it that weighed approximately 30 pounds into her house. It filled her entire sink and countertop. Itree hummed as she cleaned and cut the section into four or five smaller pieces while Ts'ivii chatted with his brother-in-law. She put some of the meat into a pan to cook and wrapped the rest. When she was ready, her husband threw the wrapped parcels onto the roof of the house where her dogs could not reach it and where it would soon freeze. Itree is the oldest sister in residence of Ts'ivii's wife, Shroodiinyaa. Itree is normally very critical of her brother-in-law; however, on this occasion, she chatted pleasantly with him instead of treating him with her more usual silent contempt. Later that night Ts'ivii delivered pieces of meat to their grandmother, Vitsuu, and others in his sharing network.

Hunting in Alaska is enshrouded with cryptic regulations about sport hunting and subsistence hunting, regulations that involve continuing tensions between the state government of Alaska and the U.S. federal government over which controls resources. Subsistence hunting is a category permitted to rural hunters on designated federal lands. Athabascan hunters hunt year round and are mindful of the presence of state and federal game wardens. Some of them get official subsistence hunting permits; others proclaim their independence of such rules and refuse. Ts'ivii and most other hunters use a good deal of discretion about the timing when they hunt. The rules they follow most closely are the traditional laws about harvesting the entire animal, rather than leaving the meat in order to have a pelt or antlers, and sharing the meat within their sharing networks. When asked, many hunters will explain that these are the ancient traditions of their people and that failure to respect the animals killed for food by harvesting all of the meat jeopardizes their future hunting luck or relationship with the spirit world.

The Semiotics of Sharing

The Northern Athabascan local economy is founded on a principle of sharing everything from food to other material goods with others in social circles that are crafted along traditional meaning codes. Sharing is antithetical to the American profiteering motive. Besides serving as a means to keep all people at the same level in terms of social and material capital, the sharing process is akin to the consensual process that underlies Athabascan leadership and decision-making styles. The basic elements of the subsistence economy involve fishing for salmon in the summer, hunting for moose or caribou during the fall and winter, and then trapping muskrats and hunting geese and ducks in the spring. Each traditional hunter learns to distribute his or her wildlife harvest to specific individuals, which always includes at least one related elder. A hunter's closer ties get several pounds of meat or fish delivered to their homes every year. Close kin, like Itree, receive most of the meat and do a lot of the cooking. The senior active member of a hunter's sharing network (usually a woman but not always) usually receives the moose head and is expected to skin it and prepare the brains, eyes, tongue, and nose in a prescribed way. In chapter 1 I mention that Shroodiinyaa had a moose head in her stainless steel restaurant that Ts'ivii had brought her. At one time the person receiving the head would have prepared the head of the first moose killed in the season as part of a ceremonial ritual to honor the spirit of the moose or other game animal, but that custom has not been practiced by Athabascans for many decades. If the woman is a skin sewer, she might prepare and keep the skins for use in a variety of products. If not, the skins are given to someone who does that kind of work, or else they are discarded. Some women also keep the skin of hearts and other entrails for sewing purposes, but usually those products are simply consumed. A favorite treat is the marrow of uncooked leg bones, which has a buttery consistency and flavor. Parts of some animals are considered medicinal. For some households the food gathered this way supplies more than half, and sometimes all, of the family's annual protein intake. Other households supplement their diets with purchased groceries.

As a single person with few connections to the village, I eventually became a fringe beneficiary to one or two sharing networks. This meant that I was welcome at public potlatches (approximately once a month) and was invited to share meals once in a while. A few people gave me a fish or a portion of meat if I happened to visit at the appropriate moment. Those who want to be involved in subsistence lifestyles devote a great deal of time, physical labor, and money to maintain them. Money pays for gasoline for boats, four-wheelers, and snow machines; hardware for fish wheels; fish wheel permits; smokehouses; and guns, ammunition, and traps. Some also acquire commercial fishing licenses. Entire families come to the fish camps where there is no running water, electricity, telephone, or medical help. People make a point of stopping by nearly every active fish camp to visit their neighbors when they travel to or from their own camps. This promotes communication and gives some comfort in case of emergency, as happened with Vachaa's family mentioned in chapter 1.

Hunting trips often involve the entire family in the fall. Hunting entails following wildlife by boat or four-wheeler vehicles, as well as a lot of heavy labor to cut the meat and haul it back to town. Moose weigh between 800 and 1,200 pounds. The Athabascans try to take all parts of the animals, which is not an easy task. The secretary at the local branch of the University of Alaska, Neeyahshii Dagoo, gloated about the success of their fall moose hunt: the moose did not run into a bog when it was shot but, rather, stayed on dry ground. Neeyahshii said that even when the moose fall into the water she and her husband have to do the butchering. The moose of the year before fell halfway into deep muddy water, and it was too heavy to pull out. So she and her husband had to stand in the water to get all the meat. By contrast, caribou are much lighter, between 200 and 400 pounds, and are easy enough for one or two people to lift onto a carrier. Hunters often bring the entire caribou back in a carryall to butcher and dry the meat in smokehouses near their permanent dwellings.

Midwinter hunts are usually done by men alone or with a partner. Some hunters maintain the avunculate custom of teaching a younger male relative how and where to hunt. Occasionally alcohol aborts or precludes a hunting trip, but that does not happen often. Bringing in large wildlife pleases so many people that most men look forward to such opportunities for social praise. They are always rewarded in that way. Athabascan men are rarely rewarded for jobs well done in the office or other mainstream employment, and they are therefore encouraged to go hunting by their social networks if they have the skill and sobriety to do so. Some young Athabascan men are given first-kill potlatches as a traditional way of marking a level of manhood. Some of these potlatches are public or publicized. Other potlatches have been masqueraded as something else.

Ts'ivii's oldest son killed his first moose in 1993. He was nine. It was June, and state and federal regulations prohibit hunting moose at that time of the year. Ts'ivii and Shroodiinyaa told their son that he would have a potlatch in the fall during the official hunting season. Because his birthday is also in the fall, they used his birthday as the logical opportunity. I attended and was admonished before I arrived not to mention the moose. In fact, no one mentioned it. The boy complained to Shroodiinyaa that no one praised him about his moose. However, in consolation he got more presents at that birthday party than any other child I know.

By swearing everyone to secrecy about the out-of-season moose, the masqueraded potlatch also added to the way in which Northern Athabascan people reinforce their boundaries against outsiders. However, this double coding was confusing to me, as it may have been to Ts'ivii's son as well. The regulations and ensuing debate are blurry to those who are involved in the system, and their ambiguity is mystifying to people like me who are on the periphery. Despite his son's confusion about the potlatch ceremony, Ts'ivii made a good deal of social capital in telling the near-legend of his son's first kill, and the boy received many more presents than he usually got.

Contemporary Northern Athabascan men and women make few of their own garments out of skin products, and those skin garments that are made are usually for the tourist market. People make fur hats, gloves, boots of several styles, slippers, and many ornaments. The skills for crafting these items faded in the 1950s and 1960s, but they have been revived by special projects funded by the State of Alaska and the U.S. National Endowment for the Arts. The Council of Athabascan Tribal Governments administered several such grants to bring women from affiliated villages into Gwichyaa Zhee for two-week workshops in skin sewing in the past two decades. Gwichyaa Zhee was selected as the workshop site because of its central location in the region. The skin sewing workshops were a popular means by which skilled skin sewers (people — mostly Athabascan women — who know how to construct garments and trade goods from animal fur and hide, beads, and other decorative elements) could mentor and teach children and less informed younger women techniques for saleable products. The skin sewers also traded ideas about which products had the highest sales potential, problems with techniques, sales outlets (retail stores, office buildings, and craft fairs), and how to sell their goods. The workshops were also a vehicle by which standards of excellence were maintained or improved by the women telling each other which indexes they used to analyze the durability of their own or someone else's work. In Table 3, I have listed some of the prices Athabascan women placed on their merchandise. Those women (approximately 12 in Gwichyaa Zhee during the time I lived there) could make a modest living through the sale of goods in the two or three village sales outlets (one of the lodges and one of the stores are preferred souvenir stops for the several hundred tourists who visit Gwichyaa Zhee annually). While skin sewing is a trade that is fraught with negative ascriptions (women's work, domestic [hence, not "real" work], Indian [hence, primitive or not as good as mainstream goods]), those women who become attractive foci of cash in their sharing networks recognize the prestige and material value of such work in Athabascan communities.

While I lived in Gwichyaa Zhee, from 1993 through July 1995, the Council of Athabascan Tribal Governments (CATG) progressed through a remarkable change in size and financial status. CATG emerged as a formal entity in the early 1980s following a casual conversation between two village chiefs. CATG was organized several years ago when a chief in Tsee', Alaska, asked Chief Clarence Alexander how he thought Native people were going to stop putting their hands out, waiting for help from

Table 3. Cost of Goods in Gwichyaa Zhee, 1994

Goods		Cost
Housing	Rent (prices varied considerably)	$250–$500/month
and Utilities	Electricity	$30/month
	Fuel oil for heating homes (delivered)	$2/gallon
	Propane for hot water/stove	$75/100 pounds
	Water	$29/month
	Septic tank haulage	$25/haul
	Wood, cord, uncut	$120
Transportation	Airfare, one way, Fairbanks–Gwichyaa Zhee	$75
	Airfare, one way, Fairbanks–Vashraii K'oo	$115
	Airfare, one way, Gwichyaa Zhee–Viihtaii	$45
	Airfare, one way, Gwichyaa Zhee–Vashraii K'oo	$85
	Chartered single-engine aircraft to Vuntut	$600
	Riverboat, one way, Gwichyaa Zhee–Danzhit Hanlii	$75
	Snow machine, new	$4,000
	Four-wheeler all-terrain vehicle, used	$1,500
	Pickup truck, used	$500
	Gasoline	$2/gallon
	Twin-engine aircraft	$80,000–$125,000*
Clothing	Thermal-lined jacket	$35
	Handmade moose-hide slippers	$50–$100
	Handmade moose-hide mittens	$50–$150
	Handmade caribou-hide boots	$175–$250
	Handmade fur hats	$150–$250
	Dancing boots	$250–$500
Miscellaneous	Rice (for dog food)	$22/50 pounds
	Tallow (for dogs)	$26/5 gallons
	Hay bale (for dogs)	$15
	Commercial fishing license	$15,000
	Fishwheel license (from State of Alaska)	$11,000
	University of Alaska course	$81/credit
	Laundromat	$4/load
	Shower	$3/5 minutes

*With an estimated annual operating cost of $10,000–$15,000 based on $70–$100 per hour for fuel, insurance, and maintenance.

Source: Information gathered by the author between 1993 and 1995.

outsiders. The subsequent debate led to the formation of CATG, a non-profit organization that includes several Athabascan communities in the Yukon Flats area. The two contacted chiefs and leaders from seven other villages eventually created a coalition of nine villages in Alaska. CATG's foundation is economic, and there is a similar effort by the Gwich'in Tribal Council in the Northwest Territories of Canada that has a more governmental approach. Both entities seek ways to achieve economic independence from the governmental agencies that have dominated Athabascan lives for the past century.

Understanding cash usage in Athabascan society involves decoding or at least intuiting a variety of local and global meaning webs that are connected to cash. The traditional Athabascan economy of sharing networks and trading alliances works in contradistinction to mainstream capitalism and emphasis on profit. The traditional Athabascan economy worked through sharing networks and trading alliances that are still, just as oral tradition maintains they were in bygone times, gendered. Women maintain sharing networks through women's gossip circles, marketing networks, educational facilities (public schools and universities), their own kin, and the public service spectra. Men maintain sharing networks through men's gossip circles, business partnerships (which sometimes intersect women's marketing networks), public service entities, and to a lesser extent than women, educational facilities (more women than men work with schoolchildren or researchers).

Trading partnership, introduced in the previous chapter, was a male-dominated system of trade, political alliances, and partnership. It does not function in the cash-based economy that neutralizes communication through the use of the dollar as sign. The intricate political and social nuances signaled in gift giving and other trading partner expectations are not possible or needed at the cash register. The American tipping customs that negotiate short-lived relationships between waiters and customers are a thin echo that is somewhat analogous to the elaborate international trading partner system. Through the use of the trading partner networks, Northern Athabascans made declarations of war, sent messages of conspiracy between partners, arranged marriages, and in addition, traded goods and services with each other. Traditional marriage alliances were the vehicle by which women became the nexus of transactions between opposing kin groups in neighboring, usually Athabascan communities. Such marriages usually entailed a year of service on the part of the new husband. In this system, the net effect was that women stayed near their birth homes and under the visual protection of their matrikin, and men effectively became trade goods through the practice of the avunculate. In the Athabascan avunculate, boys aged six–ten were sent to live with matrikin for training by their classificatory maternal uncles. Often a boy would marry a daughter (child of an opposing clan mother) in the host matrikin family.

The dollar, by contrast, represents a completely different but interrelated set of symbols that are meaningful in the economic system of American users. For instance, banking is a U.S. institution frequently associated with the dollar as sign. Banking situates other cultural meaning webs, such as concepts of public honor, prestige, and personal integrity, into pieces of coded paper (some of which are dollar bills), which are still very alien to many Athabascan people. As mentioned in the previous chapter, cash as a sign began infiltrating Athabascan lives through the advent of the fur traders and gold miners of the 19th century and through large energy interests in the past five decades. So too has the addictive system insinuated itself throughout this same time frame. Despite occasional complaints about cash as a device that has degraded traditional cultures, Athabascans use and seek cash constantly and only rarely offer something as trade or barter instead of using cash. Envoys of mainstream society (teachers, missionaries, government agents, and researchers) have taught the Northern Athabascans many of the activities, politeness behaviors, and connections to other cultural complexes involving cash transactions. To the exact extent to which Athabascan individuals involve themselves in the many different possibilities of global cash transactions, these instructions have been useful. However, cash as sign connects to numerous other mainstream American signs that are not self-explanatory, such as using checks, banking accounts, money orders, and credit cards instead of currency. Use of the secondary symbols also implies other mainstream cultural webs, for example, that the customer has a source of cash income, and for those of mainstream culture this further suggests a continuing source of revenue, such as a job. Northern Athabascans have been successful during that past few decades in understanding and creating many new jobs in all of the villages, although most of such employment is of short duration or seasonal. The model of the profit motive, which Americans take for granted, is not encoded into Northern Athabascan lives simply because the dollar has entered. Profiteering is a secondary meaning web that is acquired through cultural media other than the presence of pieces of paper.

People in the Northern Athabascan villages can live with less cash than those in urban centers can, and they have no need to extend their meaning concepts of cash beyond their own perceived needs of it. Continuing implementation of sharing networks and supporting behavioral codes allow men and women to avoid total reliance on cash, so the requirements of maintaining a continued source of cash income are not the same as they are in urban centers. Moreover, Athabascan social discourse encourages partial employment rather than full-time jobs. Men, rather than women, are socially rewarded for maintaining hunting lifeways in the subsistence economy. Athabascan politeness codes encourage silence, and hunting skills require solitude. Both are habits that are rewarded in the intimacy of Athabascan homes. Also, some women and men are pressured by their families to abort their involvement in wage activities in order to be more involved in fishing and hunting. One of the consequences of all of these factors is that people often take jobs only for as long as they need the money and do not think of them as career opportunities, which is yet another complex of symbols in mainstream American culture that has not yet entered Athabascan meaning networks. There are some jobs that are filled repeatedly throughout the year by transitional workers. There are also certain individuals whose competency is so effective that they are encouraged to remain focused on the cash culture rather than on traditional village activities despite their personal wishes.

Northern Athabascan villagers often do not have much direct experience in banks and therefore do not have opportunities to learn all of the administrative procedures involved; sometimes they do not learn the underlying principles about preserving, accumulating, or otherwise revering cash that are intrinsic to the American system. Part of the mainstream apparatus of banking includes bank accounts, picture identification, knowledge of how to maintain a checking account, knowledge about which businesses if any might accept payment by check from a rural-based Athabascan person, and knowledge about the clothing, accent, verbal discourse, and body language required to engender trust in a non-Athabascan business in order to have checks be accepted. However, bankers are beginning to broaden their horizons to rural areas, and with trucks, boats, and houses now a part of Northern Athabascan society, Athabascans have begun to tap into the credit system of banks and the attendant apparatus.

It takes much more than understanding a mainstream language to adopt and become adept at the symbols of cash and credit, and Athabascan people who devote themselves to village life do not usually get sufficient exposure. One of the complexities of the present Athabascan economic system is that there are at least two codes of ethics and many aspects of social poetics involved. The ethical rules of reciprocity used in the village and those used by mainstream society differ and are to a certain extent mutually incompatible. In the villages an item given to a person within a sharing network implies vague debt (or generalized reciprocity in Sahlins's terminology) to the recipient on the part of the sharing network. When the recipient cannot give in return, then he or she incurs a generalized debt to the entire sharing network, not merely to the individual accepting the object. By this system of generalized reciprocity, a gift given usually brings a gift back from somewhere, and in trusting the system, a person's needs are usually met by continual impersonal generosity. For example, in January 1995, Janica, a white woman married to an Athabascan man, was very ill, and her husband was out of town. She had lived in Gwichyaa Zhee for many years, and most of the villagers knew her well. She had become blind and very weak with diabetes. Several people in the village stopped by her house with food or companionship until she recovered. One day a 79-year-old elder had someone drop her off at Janica's house with a pot of soup, whereupon Janica declared that this was completely backward. Janica as the younger should bring soup to the elder. Janica was well enough the next day to go to work and boast about the visit. It was an event that has the prestige value of royal patronage in other societies. Such an open-ended system of sharing and caring is common to many small communities, and those who are familiar with such customs also realize that there are many complex social meanings imbedded in each transaction. Even more important than the nuanced gestures linked with each exchange is the very fabric of sharing as an interpretive action. As in consensual decisions by which Athabascans seek to shift the center of decision making from one individual or group of individuals to another, so too do they shift and separate material goods from centers of accumulation to smaller, shared particles. Like decisions, which are thus left to continuous open interpretation by participants and spectators, food, money, and goods shared are also left to be used without restriction by those within the sharing network.

With the suppression of so many Northern Athabascan traditions, such as the system of religious beliefs, the sharing customs are no longer reinforced by a strong network of interconnected signs. Also, as mentioned previously, the trading links established by the former trading partner system have been obviated by international law. Likewise, the meanings of symbols involve a different realm of human relations and call into position new systems of moral behavior. An underlying principle of the cash economy is that the giver expects to receive in-kind cash, goods, or services directly from the recipient or the recipient's heirs. The cash culture replaced continual acts of open-handed generosity with transactions freed of human tension. Both systems contribute to bridging difficult areas in human relations, and each has limitations that are usually met with other cultural insignia. When two partially understood economic systems are actively in place, as in Athabascan land during this era, trouble arises when individuals remain undereducated not only about the existence of each but also about the philosophies underlying either or both. These subtleties are not taught in public schools. Moreover, they have no systematized instruction of any sort regarding traditional metaphysics, spirituality, or ethics.

Outsiders often make the assumption that Northern Athabascans have assimilated into mainstream society if they conduct any business involving cash. Indeed, many Athabascan people might believe such is true themselves. However, it takes full awareness of all of the apparatus that goes into using cash or sharing gifts to be competent in either economy. Athabascans did not have consistent methods of getting such knowledge in the 1990s. In one and a half centuries Northern Athabascans have not yet become fully part of the world's cash system, but they have been consumed by the addictive system that has undermined their traditional economies. The negative activities of the big energy coalitions and the intertwined forces of addictive economies work constantly against encouraging Athabascan efforts to achieve economic independence. Achieving independence will also entail more intense protection of their final resource, which is themselves.

Sources of Revenue

For the purposes of this study, I differentiate between revenue coming through Athabascan villages in name only and revenue entering the village economy as new cash input. I have made this distinction for two reasons. One is to give some indication of the actual cash used in the villages each year, and the other is to underscore the interconnectedness of Athabascan people to global economies through cash. Some revenue enters Athabascan communities as currency and remains until it is transferred into bank accounts. At that point it is removed from Athabascan hands. However, a great deal more of the revenue that is named in Athabascan formal agency budgets rarely enters the village store or other local establishments, as the funds are merely routed through agency bank accounts en route to other outlets. Northern Athabascans speak of themselves as isolated and separate from mainstream cultures and predicate their behaviors on that assumption. However, Northern Athabascans' connections to the outside world are both physical and economic. A single day spent near the Gwichyaa Zhee airstrip belies their independence:

> One bright afternoon in July 1995, I heard the engines of a C130 Hercules igniting and wanted to see it take off. I ran out the door of my cabin just as the craft began to taxi down the gravel airstrip of Gwichyaa Zhee. There was no wind, so the brown, volcanic dust that the aircraft disturbed churned in a wake behind it. I trotted to a point about one-quarter of a mile west of my

cabin in order to be directly below the plane as it ascended. I reached that point and waited for the huge craft to trundle slowly to the opposite end of the strip. It turned and moved toward me. Its speed was deceptive because of its clumsy shape and size. The trees lining the runway were shorter than the Hercules at their ragged 30-foot average height. The Hercules seemed to crawl, yet it was moving faster than any car could be driven in Gwichyaa Zhee. Dust curled over its backside and filled the runway with dirt that nearly hid the liftoff from my view. It was by then nearly even with the Frontier Flying service building and about one-quarter of a mile away from me. The pilot was turning the plane south almost before it reached the dot called me on the road below it.

The Hercules was one of the many such aircraft bringing cargo to Gwichyaa Zhee on that day. The sound any engine makes is heard for miles in northern Alaska. Most of my rural acquaintances are skilled in discerning not only aircraft from boat engines but also make and, by the day of the week and time of day, whose aircraft it is. All I could do was hear that it was big and close — hence, an aircraft. In this regard the skills of the outdoors combine with knowledge of the global community in harmony. In relative dissonance, however, the pilots and the aircraft remained at the airstrips, away from the community. Like so many artifacts of mainstream society, they remained isolated away from Athabascans but nonetheless brought multiple webs of meaning of their world to them. I estimate that only one-half of the revenue named in formal budgets for Athabascan people actually enters the local economy. According to my sources the amount of cash that flowed in and out of the village in 1994 was nearly $5 million. Table 1 lists some of the major sources of primary revenue.

There are a few large primary sources of cash that circulate through at least two other local hands before leaving the region. Among these are the welfare funds from state and federal agencies, which I estimate bring about $1 million per year to Gwichyaa Zhee. The two intermediary processes include those who cash the checks and then the local vendors. Checks can be cashed through the Alaska Commercial Company. Local vendors use the money at least one more time as payroll and to purchase local crafts or produce. Besides paychecks, other sources of incoming cash derive from tourism and sales from cottage industries. The city government of Gwichyaa Zhee also levies a 3 percent sales tax on all products sold in the community. It uses the revenue from the sales tax for local projects, such as paying youngsters to put street litter into garbage bags for later pickup by refuse employees. The tax thus forces some of the cash to circulate through the community following the same non-accumulation logic in which Athabascan sharing networks invest.

In Gwichyaa Zhee, which in terms of cash usage is more sophisticated and active than the other Athabascan villages in Alaska, cash is used in its material form as dollar bills, coins, and personal checks from reputably employed villagers. There are no bank offices, although one bank in Fairbanks employs a part-time person to sell bank accounts to people in the region (one of the transitional jobs that a number of people fill over the course of a year). Paycheck and welfare checks can be cashed at the larger of the two grocery stores. Some people have bank accounts, but most do not. Many people pay bills by first cashing a check (paycheck, welfare check, etc.) at the grocery store and then taking the cash to the post office to purchase money orders, envelopes, and stamps. Credit cards are not accepted at any of the local businesses. Personal checks are sometimes accepted and circulated as currency, as long as the check writer is known and reputed to have a reliable source of income. Table 3 provides an idea of the cost of living in Gwichyaa Zhee in 1994.

The practice of revenue in name only includes grants from state and federal sources, teachers' paychecks, and urban center lending institutions. Part of the funding that comes through construction projects en-

ters the local economy if Athabascan people are hired. Prior to the 1970s
and local hire regulations, employers usually hired laborers from out of
town. However, negative feedback from local residents all over the state
and ensuing legal action have inhibited this form of revenue hijacking.
The laborers employed to rebuild the Gwichyaa Zhee school in 1995, for
instance, were primarily Yukon River Athabascan men. A good deal of
the money involved in construction projects remains outside of Athabascan hands when it involves the purchase of building supplies and
construction equipment, which are available only from outside sources.
Moreover, reimbursement for transporting supplies, equipment, and
personnel remains outside of Athabascan territory by going directly into
the coffers of airline and barge companies, few of which are owned by
Athabascan business people. There are at least two Athabascan men
who have purchased aircraft and operate small charter flying services in
the region, one in Viihtaii and the other in Gwichyaa Zhee. At least nine
other commercial carriers operate in the region. As Table 2 illustrates,
they do a lot of business in Northern Athabascan land.

The funding for construction projects may not reach Athabascan
hands, but Athabascans benefit from their services, such as having
roads, flood control methods, airports, and public buildings. Occasionally the Northern Athabascans fund and implement their own projects
without using outside investment. The Gwich'in of Gwichyaa Zhee de-
signed and built the first water system in the 1950s with very little outside funding, but most subsequent public projects have been funded by
large grants from federal and state agencies. In the 1970s the men of
Vashraii K'oo supplemented the construction of their airport by bringing the heavy equipment required for the effort to the village themselves. Vashraii K'oo, which is situated in the Brooks Range, has no
roadways connecting it to any other community. To get equipment there
at less cost, Athabascan men from Vashraii K'oo drove D-9 Caterpillars
and other large vehicles across 200 miles of open tundra, rivers, and

mountains while state and federal officials observed their progress from helicopters overhead.

Some of the revenue for most such projects derives from the exploitation of the petroleum resources in Alaska. It is no coincidence that most villages in Alaska received funding to build airports during the 1970s shortly after oil was first taken from the north slope. The state government of Alaska used part of the oil revenue to build transportation devices to its remote areas. Such projects provided an outlet to distribute the funds to the public and brought remote Alaskan sites into the state economy. A decade later water system projects were built in the villages, again partially funded by state oil money revenues. Many people now take the services from such projects for granted. For instance, daily mail service, gasoline for motorized vehicles, and alcohol became part of the products sought and brought daily to Athabascan villages via these services with the ease of access provided by landing strips.

Another large source of noncirculating or outside revenue is from the U.S. military in the form of frequent cargo flights several times a month. A lot of large containers are seen coming into the village on military aircraft and are delivered to the so-called inactive U.S. Air Force base. The appearance of the large military cargo planes makes a startling contrast to the twin-engine aircraft usually importing private and commercial cargo to the village. While they may be intended for the federal Bureau of Land Management (BLM) facility located at the far end of the landing strip, the BLM usually receives all of its shipments and personnel at its own hangar. The military dominated Gwichyaa Zhee until 1986 by housing 1,200 or more soldiers in this remote village during the Cold War. In 1994 there were only five or six civilian employees stationed at the Air Force base, begging the question, Why do they need so many huge freight deliveries every month? The base was closed because when the Cold War ended northern Alaska was no longer considered a common entry point by enemy aircraft. Many people took me to see the now open base and conjectured with me about possible buried contaminants, and in 1993 and 1994 people demanded explanations from the Air Force about military contamination under the oddly shaped areas of sunken soil in four or five locations on the base. The Air Force has not responded to the questions about those areas but has stated that some of the areas cover storage facilities. One of the largest computers in Alaska is housed underground outside the entrance to the base adjacent to the huge satellite dishes that overlook Gwichyaa Zhee. It was used to analyze the satellite data.

The school district for the Yukon Flats Athabascan villages is one that receives large annual funding amounts, of which around one-third is payroll. An estimated 120 people are employed by the schools in these villages. Approximately one-half of those positions are teaching assignments, which means that they are held primarily by nonindigenous people. The other half is usually filled by Native residents. The Yukon Flats School District is reputed to pay the highest salaries and benefits of any employer in the area. Beginning teachers made an annual salary of $39,000 in 1994. Only a portion of the school district employees' payroll is used to pay for things in the village, as credit card companies, clothing outlets, telephone companies, and banks are owned and located elsewhere. The Yukon Flats School District is one of the largest employers in any Athabascan village, and it increases its popularity by making the schools the site of many public events. While only a fraction of the money involved in the school system enters the local economy, school officials try to offset public antagonism in other ways, such as offering school-sponsored trips for children into Fairbanks and other villages.

Cash as sign is complex in Gwichyaa Zhee. Mainstream representations and Athabascan residents encourage its increased usage. Residents are active in trying to find methods of slowing or preventing the practice of revenue in name only so that the village economies can benefit from it. Unless they do so, the implementation of schools and grant-funded projects simply represent sophisticated methods of resource extraction by designating Athabascan areas as a way station in shifting cash from one cash depot to another. Meanwhile, cash expenditures increase in both volume and complexity in rural Alaska.

The amount of money flowing through Northern Athabascan country without touching ground is impossible to trace, but the evidence of its passage is quite visible in such a small community, as mentioned previously. There are about ten residents in Gwichyaa Zhee (population approximately 730) per aircraft landings per week (roughly ten per day, seven days per week). See Table 4 for an indication of the volume in sheer weight coming into Gwichyaa Zhee. During the two years I was there, from 1993 to 1995, I shipped an average of 600 pounds per year to myself in groceries and other items. Table 4 notes that the combined total of commercial freight and mail that came into Gwichyaa Zhee by air in 1993 was 1,746,872 — or 2,392 pounds per person. A lot of the merchandize is ordinary mail, but groceries, clothing, fuel, building supplies, furniture, and alcohol are also shipped by air to the villages. The following sections detail some areas of expenditure in Northern Athabascan villages, particularly Gwichyaa Zhee, as do Tables 2–4.

Housing is by far the most expense-laden aspect of the local economy because it brings with it requirements for heating and lighting. People of Gwichyaa Zhee live in wooden structures, mostly single-family homes, although there are some multifamily houses. Most of the buildings are small one-story frame houses that are generally unfinished in one way or another. Local residents conceived of a way to bring running water into the village during the 1950s, and some houses and commercial buildings have both running water and indoor toilets. Not every house has both a sink with a tap to bring water to it from the public water system and a drain to remove waste to a septic tank. Most of the septic systems are incapable of processing a lot of water in one day, so householders are careful in the way they use water. Some households

Table 4. Freight Shipped into Gwichyaa Zhee from Fairbanks, 1994
(*In Pounds*)

Carrier	Commercial Cargo	Mail
#1	9,676	41,254
#2	69,631	58,761
#3	1,182	7,231
#4	3,326	34,477
#5	42,453	17,979
#6	12,436	18,881
#7	503	53,541
#8	—	40,558
#9	—	24,829
Quarter total	139,207	297,511
Estimated total pounds per year	556,828	1,190,044

Source: Data derived from information supplied by Frontier Airlines, March 1995.

have showers or bathtubs with running water, but many do not. There were four public showers and laundry facilities around the town, and eventually I discovered that I was not the only one who happened to schedule shopping trips into Fairbanks to visit relatives with bathtubs and washing machines. It was easier and less stressful on village resources to do it that way. In smaller villages, such as Tsee' and Vashraii K'oo, the public schools serve as the only hotels in town. The Yukon Flats School District charges rent to overnight visitors. Dinyee also offers the village health clinic for that purpose and collects lodging fees on behalf of the Tribal Council. Part of the fun of traveling to the villages is wondering where one might stay for the night, and part of the excitement of living in Gwichyaa Zhee was learning Athabascan codes of neighborly behavior.

Although I was told about some of the many bootleggers in Gwichyaa Zhee, I was never sure which of the homes in the village actually housed bootleggers:

> *"Don't stand in front of the window!" she told me. Her one and only window faced a rambling complex of structures that included a three-story, terraced log cabin. Beside it was a one-story building perched on five-foot stilts. Arctic heating system analysts thought that lifting buildings onto pilings kept more heat inside. I had just noticed a snow machine slide into position near the complex when she told me to back away from her window. "They're bootleggers," she whispered as if they could hear her. I moved back a foot or so.*

The complex next door was sprawling, and there were always many visitors to her neighbor's complex of houses during night and day. In view of her warning and my own observations, it seemed the better part of good sense to mind my own business regarding the details of bootlegging life in Gwichyaa Zhee.

When I left Gwichyaa Zhee on August 4, 1995, the city government was in the midst of an expensive flood prevention experiment. They elevated a few roads around the perimeter of the midtown and downtown areas by several feet. The road in front of the house I rented became a damp gravel barrier about four feet higher than it had been when I moved into the house in 1993. In 1994 my next-door neighbor raised her house seven or eight feet so that her home became higher than the road. My house was a tiny cabin that once had been about as tall as my neighbor's and higher than the road. In 1995 it looked like a discarded match-box forgotten among spruce trees, well below road height.

Some of the houses in Gwichyaa Zhee are owned fee simple, some are mortgaged through commercial lending institutions, and some are mortgaged through federally subsidized welfare programs. Many are rented. Table 3 includes a range of costs of renting homes in Gwichyaa Zhee in 1994. I paid $300 a month for a small one-bedroom house with partial plumbing, oil heat, and a propane stove. It was an average rental price. A few of the houses and other real estate are owned in a compli-cated process requiring the Tribal Council's approval to sell. Table 2 gives an indication of living conditions in each of the Alaskan Athabas-can villages.

Housing in Gwichyaa Zhee represents everything that colonial his-tory has done to rural Alaska, from imposing sedentary lives to making people live next door to bootleggers. Simply building permanent dwell-ings rather than making use of seasonal gear is the most prominent change (and despite the pious protests by some, I never heard of anyone in the 1990s living in a tent during the winter months as they did in pre-colonial times). A more subtle change is in the process of getting hous-ing financed. A few Gwichyaa Zhee residents have built or are building homes with their own money and muscle. There are many half-built cabins around the community that display the initial energy and re-sources of some individuals, and there are a few completed houses that are owned debt free. However, there are also many homes that are mort-gaged and several tracts of houses built with public funding. During the two and a half years that I lived in Gwichyaa Zhee two people died in two of the fires that destroyed three of these public tract houses because of faulty wiring. There is a stigma attached to those who live in public housing, which is voiced by the house tenants and neighbors alike. Phrases such as "Lousy HUD housing, what do you expect?" and "She lives in a HUD house," spoken with mixed contempt and apology, occur in conversations. Housing, like many facets of contemporary Athabascan life, is tinged with ambivalence about economic dependence, clever opportunism, and aspirations of personal potency.

There are grocery stores in each rural Alaskan village, and the nature of each store reflects in some way the character of the community. Inuvik, Northwest Territories, Canada, is one of the largest Northern Athabascan communities with approximately 3,000 people, of whom only a few hundred are Athabascan. Its store is like a department store with merchandise of all sorts. Despite the extreme distance from major urban centers, the costs in Inuvik are not high. The stores in Vuntut, Yukon, Canada, on the other hand, are among the most expensive in the region. Vuntut has 300 residents and is not on a roadway, and one of its stores provides only a few staple goods, such as flour and sugar, as well as some gift items for tourists. A couple of private individuals in Vuntut vend snack foods and cigarettes out of their homes. Some families in Dinyee, Alaska, have also made space in their homes to sell candy and soft drinks. The stores in Gwichyaa Zhee are the most well stocked in Athabascan country, and villagers from smaller communities go to Gwichyaa Zhee to do bulk shopping. However, many people from all villages (including Vuntut, in Canada, which is connected by river to Alaska) make monthly or bimonthly shopping trips into Fairbanks to buy food in bulk. Some people order food by mail, and others buy food occasionally at one of the two restaurants. Most people supplement their food intake with wildlife. The proportion of wild product usage depends on the presence of a successful hunter in the sharing network to which the people belong.

Food acquisition and usage make up another bundle of signs. Food signals nuances of pride, need, traditional sharing, self-image, waste, and welfare. Positive ideas are attached to what Athabascans call "Native foods," meaning game meat, game birds, salmon, and other fish.

Negative concepts are attached to packaged or purchased food. Although Native food is supposed to taste better, nearly every afternoon or evening flight into Gwichyaa Zhee from Fairbanks reeks with the pungent aromas of freshly baked pizza, a favorite treat for many of the villagers. While "Native food" has acquired a special meaning in an Athabascan nationalism, the food symbols of the larger world are popular in ordinary usage.

Since the early 1970s when airstrips were built in nearly every village in Alaska, rural Alaskans have begun to take part in the global cash economy. Whereas in traditional times they heated their homes with wood fires and transported objects by sled (sometimes dogsled), now their requirements for petroleum products are escalating. They use fuel to heat their homes and offices instead of wood. They use gasoline for motor vehicles (cars, trucks, four-wheelers, vehicles, boat motors, and airplanes) instead of dogsleds or their own feet. They use propane to heat cooking stoves and hot water heaters and electricity to light their homes instead of firelight. At least one-half of the Northern Athabascan houses still use wood for stoves. Getting the petroleum products to remote villages that are not on roadway networks is very expensive. In some cases the Alaska Native Claims Settlement Act (ANCSA) corporations or tribal councils have arranged to subsidize the cost of shipping and storing fuel. In Gwichyaa Zhee one commercial grocery store and another private business sell gasoline and propane. Another private business sells fuel oil and gasoline. These products cost more than double what they would in Fairbanks, which is the largest close city to rural Athabascan communities. The difference in price rests primarily in the cost of shipping. One tribally owned business sells electricity with a governmental subsidy. Private individuals occasionally sell cords of wood, and others will cut it into short segments and split the pieces into stove-sized lengths for a fee. Most families that need wood harvest and cut their own. To do so involves cooperating with the local tribal councils, which monitor not only who uses the wood but where it is used. They also try to prevent stripping the land in conformance with traditional knowledge of weather, flooding, and river current patterns. See Table 3 for examples of these costs in 1994.

> Earlier in the day I put some quarter-inch dents in a log while trying to split it. Dachan came to the door asking for work, and I told him the only thing to do was split wood. Because he had hurt his collarbone a week or so before, I thought he would not be able to do it. "I'm okay. It's not broke," he told me. So I handed him the ax and peered out a few minutes later. The ax hooked over his head and down in off-centered strokes. After less than a half hour he finished splitting a cord of wood, and I paid him $10.00.

One of the elders in the housing track down the road probably sent Dachan to me after seeing my ineffectual labors. Dachan was 15 at the time and seemed not at all aware of having extraordinary physical strength. For an Athabascan man or woman in the villages his strength was average, and so was the fact that he was using his body beyond its abilities. Dachan was there to make a little extra cash. A month later Itree paid him to clean the area around her doghouses of feces and trash.

Women, too, are expected to display physical strength. I discovered how much strength was expected one day when a woman delivered my new propane tank. The M&A truck backed into my driveway at the time promised. The driver pulled neatly up to the edge of my porch and stopped with one foot to spare. A young woman got out, lifted the 100-pound propane tank off the back of the pickup and carried it four steps up to my door. I thanked her and, after she left, rotated it in semicircles along the floor toward the furnace room, where I hooked it into the couplings that were waiting. The tank was so heavy that it left curved indentations in the linoleum. The men who had delivered the previous tanks always drove in, engine first, and then carried the tank 10 or 15 feet around the back end of the truck. Each of them had looked as if he was about to collapse under the weight. The woman who had just left my house worked at the smaller of the two grocery stores in Gwichyaa Zhee. She was 18, always wore makeup, and displayed the full length of hair that reached to her hips. That day she looked different because her hair had a fresh permanent. Except that her hair was longer than most, she looked and acted like other teenaged women in Gwichyaa Zhee. She was also as strong as any of them. After she moved out of town, there were rumors that she had dealt in cocaine, which would have been easy for her because of the free transportation to and from Fairbanks that she got as a benefit of working for the grocery store. That store has since been sold.

Like housing and food, fuel and energy resources are imbedded with marks of Athabascan self-awareness. Wood resources, which are local, are carefully protected by tribal usage regulations, and people bringing cords of wood into the village along the river routes are greeted with suspicion. All electricity is subsidized by the state government of Alaska, and some families can qualify for welfare funds for fuel oil. Thus, while heating methods have the primary meaning of keeping warm in a harsh environment, they are also laden with additional indications of economic dependence or independence, social capital, and environmental awareness.

Traditionally, Athabascan people made their clothing from the tanned skins of moose, caribou, and other fur-bearing animals. Their needs were simple, and most people owned little more than 20 articles of clothing during their lifetimes, including size changes from childhood to adult. Traditional clothing included parkas, boots, tunic, leggings, slippers, mittens, and hats. Now most people have at least one of these traditional items and own hundreds of garments made of contemporary materials and in modern styles (underwear, socks, shirts, T-shirts, jeans, baseball caps, shoes, seasonal jackets, dress clothes, bed clothes, etc.). In traditional times they fashioned containers made of skin and tree bark. Now they use packs, purses, and cloth carryalls for everything. One of the commercial stores in Gwichyaa Zhee supplies clothing, and people make irregular trips to Fairbanks to buy clothes from department stores and secondhand shops. Some people order clothing by mail. A few people make traditional goods for cash or trade.

In traditional times the average Athabascan house was a tent made of skin-covered wooden poles. They were temporary, built for easy moving from one seasonal camp to the next, and they were lit and heated by wood fires. Now houses are constructed primarily of wood in a variety of mainstream styles. They are now lit by electricity, and a few are plumbed for water. They require mainstream furniture: beds, chairs, tables, couches, and televisions. They have glass windows (with curtains) and framed doors and storage shelves. They require hardware in every nook and cranny. I pounded more nails into the walls of my rented cabin than were used to build it because the bags I hung on them became shelves, containers, and insulation. No one makes these objects in Gwichyaa Zhee or any of the Athabascan villages, and I had to mail myself used bookshelves as well as chairs from Fairbanks and Anchorage. One postal employee measured my folding card table twice to make sure it met size restrictions and then charged me the standard rate per pound, which came to $6.00.

Gwichyaa Zhee's economy was burgeoning during the time I lived there. Table 1 gives ample illustration of the modest wealth of the village in comparison to the small cost of living (shown in Table 3) in 1994. With expanding cash resources, more people owned and operated vehicles with motors than at any time in their history. There are now many snow machines, four-wheelers, trucks, cars, motorcycles, and special vehicles for construction and maintenance. All of such vehicles had to come into the region via barge (to Gwichyaa Zhee, Tsee', and Dinyee) or aircraft. I lived next door to the airport and witnessed many a Hercules,

DC-3, and other large aircraft land daily in Gwichyaa Zhee. Flat-bottomed riverboats with and without enclosures are the preferred mode of transportation during the summer. Several people made their own boats. Neeyahshii was very proud of the covered flat-bottomed riverboat that she and her husband built and used for summer excursions and hunting trips on the Ch'ôonjik River. Her husband insisted that she learn how to repair every aspect of the boat engine, just as he could, in case of emergency. When I left in 1995, she was already thinking of building a larger boat despite her husband's poor health. I asked her if she and her husband ever traveled along the Yukon, and she told me that they went upriver to Eagle once but that careful boaters will only travel along the rivers whose currents and channel patterns they know well.

Between 1993 and 1995 the number of cars and trucks in Gwichyaa Zhee doubled from around 100 to 200, and it seemed to me that almost no one who wanted employment lacked it for more than a few days of searching. Having the independence of a vehicle of any sort is a status symbol in rural Alaska. Few people walk even one or two blocks if they have a vehicle or someone to give them a ride. It was no surprise to me to see the increased number of vehicles every summer with the arrival of the barges.

Almost every household contains at least one telephone, a television, a stereo, books, magazines, and other communication devices. Some people have home computers. Smaller items can be purchased through the larger store, but everything else is purchased from cities in mainstream America where they are made. The City of Gwichyaa Zhee supplies cable television. It brings the wiring to the edge of one's house, and one has to figure out how to get it into the house. The same is true of the telephone service. The Athabascans of Gwichyaa Zhee were as computer literate in 1993–95 as any of my acquaintances in Cambridge were.

In summary, cash expenditures compete with sharing networks for the time and energy that Athabascan people invest in their economic experiences. Houses, which have heating and electrical expenses, require cash. The State of Alaska has encourage even the most traditional Alaska Natives to convert to cash usage by offering welfare income and energy subsidies to light and heat their houses. Autonomy is a valued Northern Athabascan concept, yet there are ambiguous symbols of cash and mainstream implications attached to nearly every means of achieving it. Subsistence hunters use guns rather than traditional bows or spears and thus require cash. Travel is never done by walking or snowshoeing except for fun in races or for short distances. Even dog-sledding has been replaced by snow machines except in races. In short, every facet of traditional Athabascan life is implicated in the cash economy, albeit without the meaning systems attached to cash as used in the mainstream or global economies.

The Council of Athabascan Tribal Governments

Until 1994 the Council of Athabascan Tribal Governments operated as a two-person office made up of Patricia Stanley, a white woman, and her Gwich'in secretary. In 1994 the organization grew from two to seven employees, and in 1995 it expanded to 35 employees working in four locations in two villages. Stanley has combined successful grant-writing skills with a personal vision about the potential of such a coalition. Over the years CATG has brought a good deal of revenue to each of the villages through grants for projects that have included traditional skin-sewing seminars, mentioned earlier, generator repair workshops, and resource management workshops. In 1994 it acquired an existing contract to provide health and counseling services to the region. Prior to CATG's administration of that contract, health services to the area were handled by Tanana Chiefs Conference. Tanana Chiefs Conference manages health and welfare programs in most of the interior Athabascan villages of Alaska. CATG's takeover of its contract in the Yukon Flats area represented one of the most significant Northern Athabascan efforts toward local rural control. Rural Athabascans have been actively seeking alternative routes to maintain their own affairs. For instance, in 1995 CATG offered a series of workshops instructing village counselors in Athabascan ways of dealing with mental health situations. It hired a Gwich'in instructor from Vuntut in Canada to conduct the last and most intense of the series. The object was at least twofold: first, to have Native counselors directing the response to local problems and, second, to explore the possibility of implementing Athabascan techniques in such situations.

CATG has also tried to back traditional skills in a variety of ways, including traditional land usage and language retention. One of its earliest such endeavors began in the late 1980s with a series of skin-sewing and beading workshops. Through grants obtained from various federal and state agencies CATG brought skilled skin and bead artists from all over Alaska and Canada to Gwichyaa Zhee for two-week sessions. The students have used their new beading and skin-sewing skills to make crafts to sell in gift shops throughout the interior of Alaska. One of the most interesting of these skills is called caribou tufting, which is a very old Canadian Athabascan technique nearly faded from usage during the 20th century. The artists dye small sections of caribou hide that has been carefully prepared to keep the hair intact. They then pull the hair through holes in a dilapidated piece of caribou or moose skin to achieve various floral or geometric designs. The results are very appealing to the tourist trade. CATG also introduced birch bark techniques through these workshops, as well as countless beadworking procedures and designs.

The villages in rural Alaska and Canada are so remote from the larger population centers that the only expedient transportation to and from them is via air. In order to have any economic or social connection to any other village or region anywhere in the world they must maintain electrical generators in order to provide airstrip landing lights and radio signals throughout the year. The generators, usually fueled by oil, are as reliable or unreliable as mechanical equipment can be. If they break down, someone has to fix them, and the cost of flying someone in to do so has been prohibitive both in terms of money and in terms of providing comfortable and hospitable lodging for the usually non-Native mechanics. The village councils often do not have enough money available for the former, and it takes culturally aware guests and hosts to facilitate housing an outsider for a night or two in an Athabascan household anywhere, city or village. CATG funded training for Athabascan generator operators from several of the villages in order to help them become more independent of outside help. The smaller villages (some as small as 35 people) have no more than one sufficiently trained operator. The result is that the village comes to depend heavily on the generator operator not only for that service but for others as well as that individual acquires training on other equipment or in other ways. Although this is not a perfect solution to a need for self-sufficiency, the villages gain some measure of distance from the foreign ways of mainstream society through the help of CATG.

Loss of traditional land and their resources has been one of the most distressing problems facing Northern Athabascans during the past 250 years. CATG involves itself in the issue in a number of ways, including resource management. With funds that somehow involve both federal and State of Alaska agencies, CATG has employees who assist in creating census data about some of the regional wildlife. It also aids in accumulating data about snowfall patterns, wildlife whereabouts, traditional land use areas, and other state-initiated projects. CATG employs several full-time and part-time resource specialists for these undertakings. In addition, CATG has sponsored several training workshops about resource management. The state and federal governments send their own employees to act as workshop instructors, and in some instances the University of Alaska has been approached to formulate the appropriate paperwork to enable workshop attendees to obtain university credit for the training at a nominal cost. Not very many people take advantage of the latter, and it is not clear that such credit hours can meet the requirements of any degree programs. Nonetheless, the attachment of such a negligible opportunity to a manufactured event embodies the nature of the tenuous and sporadic connections between Athabascans and mainstream U.S. society. The connections exist, but few people participate, and those Athabascan people who do are not particularly interested in understanding or maintaining them.

One resource management activity that has caught attention from the general Alaskan public, and to a limited extent the awareness of the people of Gwichyaa Zhee, is a proposal to introduce bison to the Yukon Flats area for adaptation to live in the wild. Some Athabascans object on the grounds that the bison might consume or destroy the plants on which moose and caribou feed. A species of bison used to roam in northeastern Alaska, but it is difficult to ascertain the ecological factors of that era. The bison may not have lived successfully with other large herbivores. CATG employees working with state officials contend that the bison would forage in areas that the moose do not use. The proposal is noteworthy in offering to restore something to the environment rather than extract it. There is little local interest in the project, which is typical of Athabascans. There is a general respect extended to those with special interests along with a mutual understanding that each person pursues his or her own dreams. The population is too small for any particular person to acquire a large following unless he or she happens to be charismatic or if the situation threatens the existence of others.

CATG seeks projects that develop both traditional and contemporary activities for Athabascans. In some cases it departs from established extractive strategies. One such extractive process occurs in language exer-

cises. During the past three decades Athabascan folklore has been recorded, transcribed in the Native language, and then translated for
publication into English. In a few instances documents written in English have been translated into all of the Northern Athabascan languages. As mentioned in the previous chapter, McDonald translated the
Bible into an eastern Canadian dialect of Gwich'in during the 19th century. Wycliffe translators have been translating parts of the Bible into
Western Gwich'in of Alaska. CATG sponsored the translation of a se-
cular document into Gwich'in in 1994. Two people of Vashraii K'oo
translated a portion of the proceedings of a scientific conference called
"People, Science, and Caribou" held in their village. The translation
challenged the translators in at least two ways: first to find comprehend-
ible ways to explain terms such as *cadmium, heavy metal,* or *nuclear waste.*
Second, they had to transfer concepts of Western science into Athabascan ways without demeaning either tradition. Although CATG printed
hundreds of copies of the document, only a few Athabascan people can
speak their own language. Even fewer read it. Nonetheless, the political
implications of that translation are not lost on Athabascan leaders, who
distributed free copies of it at the 1994 Gwich'in Gathering in Vuntut,
Canada. Translation services and literature written in a local idiom are
modes of social capital that, like the Takudh Bible mentioned in chapter
2, have become unsellable material capital to many Athabascans. The
Episcopal Church officials complain (or boast) that they cannot stock
copies of the "Indian" Bible or its companion hymnals because they are
stolen so quickly. In this context, discussion about revenue as U.S. currency falls a little short of a full understanding of how Athabascans actually perceive material wealth. Nonetheless, locating and counting
dollars provides a measure of how much potential wealth Athabascan
people have.

The revenue information presented in Table 1 is probably low in some
cases but high in others. The total of $17,969 represents approximately

$8.65 per hour in a wage-paying, 40-hour-a-week job. While there are several jobs in Gwichyaa Zhee that offer that kind of salary, there are many, such as the teaching positions, that offer substantially more. This table represents income that private households might be receiving on an annual basis, and, in my opinion, the income in Gwichyaa Zhee appeared to increase during the two years that I spent there. One indication that this is true is that CATG increased its salaried positions from two in 1993 to 35 in 1995. The major factor for that growth is that it acquired some of the federal grants operating the Gwichyaa Zhee Health Clinic, which already employed many individuals. In addition to that it increased its administrative staff from two to eight full-time employees, with several temporary and part-time employees. To my knowledge no other enterprise or agency in Gwichyaa Zhee has increased its payroll in any significant way.

In sum, subsistence and sharing activities play an important role in the ordinary conversations of Athabascan people. The conceptual frameworks that formulate the traditional religious principles of reciprocity among humans, nature, and the spirit world are present also in the sharing concepts of Northern Athabascans. As will be discussed in the next chapter, the same method of organizing religious thought and exchange into complex reciprocal networks also motivates the Northern Athabascan system of leadership and decision making. Before the advent of guns and motorized vehicles, any of the traditional activities just described would have required the full effort of an entire family. Now one or two individuals can accomplish most of the traditional work to satisfy their nutritional needs for themselves and part of their sharing networks in a few months without relying on their children or auxiliary help for much of the labor. A few families strive to maintain such standards, including Itree's brother, Vachaa, mentioned in chapter 1, who ran the family fish camp. Some say they do so for the sake of their children because they consider the activity to be better than the dangers of living in a city or growing up with alcoholism. Some families have tried what they call subsistence living for a while and failed for a variety of reasons. Concern for the health of their children encourages many parents to return to population centers where they can get medical help. In other cases, the individuals have not learned the skills needed for this kind of life, while others suffer from alcoholism or other addictive conditions. Some men maintain a subsistence lifestyle in preference to any other way of life (sometimes without input from the rest of their families) and often vocalize their objections to the cash economy. None of these people is in the majority, for at least in Gwichyaa Zhee cash is involved in most transactions.

The traditional leaders of a bygone Northern Athabascan era who led war parties against the Ch'eekwaii to the north and made trading alliances with the Tlingit to the south dealt with complexities in language barriers, histories of hatred, and transportation difficulties. The Athabascan leaders of today are learning new techniques in trade and warfare on a daily basis. Thanks to the colonial encounters, one major component of their new enemies is addiction. Contemporary Athabascan leaders must be knowledgeable about international politics, computer usage, and healing processes for themselves as well as their constituents. Athabascan women and women immigrants have made a transition from domestic circles to public service. Shroodiinyaa Ts'ivii, a lodge owner, is but one example of the many Native women entrepreneurs of Gwichyaa Zhee. Gwich'in author Velma Wallis has been introduced to the lucrative process of writing successful novels and in turn has introduced Gwichyaa Zhee to Athabascan-style philanthropy. She volunteers time and money to many local pursuits in an elaborate extension of traditional Athabascan codes of reciprocity. Patricia Stanley of CATG represents one of the most remarkable transitions of Athabascan standards of economic philosophy, which is moving from a male-dominated, ethnocentric model to one that allows and even cultivates her gender, multiple races, and national origins in their search for finding methods that emphasize indigenous solutions and Athabascan standards in order to counteract resource piracy by outsiders. Each of these women has introduced new meanings to the local Athabascan economy.

The Addictive System

Ann Wilson Schaef introduced a concept of society as addictive in 1987 with a book called *When Society Becomes an Addict*. Her theory is situated in psychological extensions of individual addictive behaviors that are translated into social paradigms. While Schaef's work is not akin to this study of the economic flow of funds through Athabascan land, her work led to my initial thought in this direction. The addictive system in Gwichyaa Zhee is manifold. One aspect affects individuals who become addicted to intoxicants and narcotics and act out addictive models of behavior. The other is the economic framework of this study, which centers on individuals, businesses, and agencies that benefit from and effectuate continued addictions. These fit a paradigm of enterprises at several levels of exploitation. First is the extraction of the physical, social, and financial independence of the addicted individuals. Second is the extraction of monies to outside vendors or agencies, including banks. Third is creating a resource base of needy people (the addicted, children of alcoholics, or codependents) and then using that resource for funding endeavors. Some of these funding projects are created to end the need itself. One, funded by the State of Alaska Division of Alcoholism and Drug Abuse, is ironically called Youth Survivors. The irony is that this education program for young Athabascans is funded by monies coming directly from taxes levied on the sale of alcohol. Bootleggers, liquor outlets in the urban centers and villages, freight carriers, and drug and alcohol counselors, among others, make a substantial amount of money by their involvement with addicts and addictive products. The entire multiplicity of positive and negative forms of exploitation constitutes the addictive system considered in this study.

Shoshoni reported to work at 5:00 P.M. one September afternoon in 1993. She was a waitress at one of the local restaurants in Gwichyaa Zhee. Instead of going to the kitchen, she went to the bathroom and vomited. Then she spoke to her employer, Shroodiinyaa, who sent her upstairs to lie down for a while. Shoshoni had just lost a lot of money gambling and suddenly realized how much she owed her bookie. She quit her waitressing job a couple of weeks after this event. A day or so after Shoshoni stopped work, Ts'ivii found footprints outside the lodge where none should be. It looked like someone with small feet about Shoshoni's size had broken into the main building. Shroodiinyaa and Ts'ivii declined to tell authorities or anyone else what was missing.

Until I lived in Gwichyaa Zhee I had never been aware of gambling as an addiction. Shroodiinyaa told me what had happened. According to her, Shoshoni went into a traumatic shock when she realized her gambling loss. Janica, who happened to be holding a workshop on gambling addiction that very week, said it is a shock akin to that which stuns the bereft when they awaken to the death of a loved one. Janica said that such illness is typical of the gambling syndrome. Shoshoni was also a cocaine addict. Physically she aged ten years in the two I knew her. In 1993 she was 30, but she looked a very unhealthy 50 by the time I left in 1995. I wondered if her two small boys would ever know her when they were 20. I never learned the identity of Shoshoni's bookie, although it would have been easy to get the information. The one bookie I did know did not hide this particular activity. While I was visiting her one day, someone came to the door and mumbled something inaudible. My hostess said cheerfully and loudly, ''Oh, you want to borrow a hundred?

Sure. Just sign this." They bent over a piece of paper, and my hostess lowered her voice so that I could not hear the rest of their conversation.

The addictive system includes the city-owned liquor store, 12–18 bootleggers, the bingo parlor, the Card Shack (a pull-tab outlet), private gambling clubs, and bookies. The City of Gwichyaa Zhee earned $122,000 in profits from the sales of liquor in 1995 (Fischer and Kelly 1996). No one knows how much the bootleggers or drug dealers actually make, as they conduct business in covert ways. Bingo and pull tabs are the only two legal gambling activities in Gwichyaa Zhee, and both are operated by the not-for-profit Elders Association, a group of approximately 30 people who use the proceeds for several public events. The Elders Association maintains a bank account, and in 1993–95 the only way to deposit cash into a bank account was to take it to the Alaska Commercial Co. store where the store would buy it by writing a check. The check could then be sent through the mail system. A night's bingo receipts averaged $10,000. Poker and other forms of gambling take place in private homes almost 24 hours a day. Prostitution does not have a formal capacity in Gwichyaa Zhee, but at least two groups of men invite women on a regular basis to their houses to give them liquor and other intoxicants for sex. Villagers called the busiest such establishment "Animal House."

Alcohol is the predominant form of addictive substance, but cocaine, marijuana, heroin, and a few synthetic drugs were also in use during the time I lived in rural Alaska. Adolescents use many chemicals that they conceive to be intoxicating, such as gasoline fumes, spray paint, and spray-on cooking oil. Many who are addicts of controlled substances pay for their habits through bootlegging. Cocaine users are reputed to be the most persistent bootleggers in Gwichyaa Zhee. Some of the bootleggers buy alcohol from the city liquor store and resell it to their customers. Some of them do so in a quasi-legal way by offering taxi services. According to some sources, the primary business of the taxi drivers is to go to the liquor store, buy liquor, and then go to their customers' dwellings. Some taxi drivers charge for the service according to how much liquor they buy rather than by the number of miles driven.

A few people work for money to buy liquor and for very little else. Avii, a man with severe alcoholism, worked for his sister one day at a time. She employed him because he was family, because she could coerce him into marginal honesty, and because in an emergency he was one of the few she could turn to for help. Because of his alcoholism Avii could only work a few days at a time before he succumbed to drinking in binges that lasted for days or even weeks, a drinking pattern typical in Gwichyaa Zhee. His cash goals were approximately $25.00, or the price of a bootlegged bottle of whiskey, a day. When he ran out of cash he begged for it from everyone. Because he rarely stopped drinking, he must have found ways to get alcohol between jobs that he and his family were reluctant to tell outsiders about. Avii was also a deadbeat dad by mainstream agency standards, which meant that his wages were garnished. He could work for no more than three and a half months with any given employer (or until the next quarterly tax reports had been filed and examined) before the employer was officially notified to garnish his wages. There were enough employers and odd jobs in Gwichyaa Zhee to give him protection in the form of isolation and misdirection so that he could continue to meet his personal goal of one-fifth of whiskey a day, $25.00.

The addictive system has an economic life of its own that consumes the energy of its victims and, through the healing machinery of various human services, provides steady income to many social workers, health professionals, and administrators. While a lot of money (some estimate between $5 and 10 million a year in Gwichyaa Zhee alone) circulates through the addictive system, the money does not constitute primary cash input to the village except in the form of payroll to those employed as counselors or health professionals. The most common negative addictive activities include bingo, pull tabs, poker, group sex, alcoholic binges, and bootlegging. By contrast, the most common positive activities in the addictive system are drug and alcohol counseling, workshops, seminars, church revivals, and public meetings. Most of these processes entail use of a wage-earning counselor and administrator. Often they require air transportation to and from either Fairbanks or Gwichyaa Zhee to one of the smaller villages. Occasionally they involve police force and court system expenses. Every workshop and revival brings new cash into the community through the inns, restaurants, and retail stores. These healing methods have proven somewhat effective in terms of their social goals. They have also proven an effective means by which state, federal, and commercial entities can profit from the addictive system. Much of the revenue involved in the positive aspect of addiction is revenue in name only as far as Northern Athabascans are concerned, but through the efforts of the tribal councils and the Council of Athabascan Tribal Governments, more of the grants generated for decreasing addictive behaviors are managed entirely by people in Gwich'in territory.

In June 1993 a Sashwap (inland Salish) couple from Alkali Lake Indian Reserve in British Columbia, Canada, was brought to Gwichyaa Zhee, Alaska, to give a workshop on alcoholism recovery. It was their second trip to the Northern Athabascan community of Gwichyaa Zhee. The first workshop they did in 1991 was picketed by local churches. The second workshop was not picketed, but people from the community complained to members of the Gwichyaa Zhee Tribal Council about the workshop. This workshop was one of three alcoholism treatment projects conducted in or near Gwichyaa Zhee that summer. The other two were retreats held in fish camps along the Yukon River. The only way to get to them was by boat. Camp participants were expected to stay in the camps for a week without alcohol or any mainstream distractions. The

Alkali Lake five-day workshop was held in the village, so participants were able to come and go as they pleased. All three of the treatment projects proposed to involve or introduce traditional healing techniques.

Complaints about the Alkali Lake workshop centered on the mystical techniques used by the Sashwap couple: they cleansed the facility by smudging with sage and tried to teach the participants to have visions (practices that are not remembered as traditions among Northern Athabascans). Some of the participants became nervous about these methods and left the workshop. They went to the Baptist minister, who was already aware of the couple's presence and had been active during the picketing of 1991. He called them New Agers who worshiped the devil. Unnerved participants also went to Shreevyaa (a pseudonym), a Tribal Council member, lay reader for the Episcopal Church, and director of the newly formed Youth Survivors program in Gwichyaa Zhee. Shreevyaa was one of the most outspoken women in Gwichyaa Zhee and normally advocated anything that is traditional as a solution for the future of Northern Athabascans. However, she was also a convinced Christian who had been training to become a deacon of the church and was in competition for this position with one of the men who organized the Alkali Lake workshop. The workshop was allowed to continue.

The two workshop leaders said they were sometimes criticized by Christian churches for their methods, and the Baptist Church in Gwichyaa Zhee was the worst of those critics. Their methods were focused on getting beyond their clients' anger, which they attributed to the control exerted by the churches and governmental agencies. They had instructed their 25 participants to take off their watches and to use "Indian time" during the workshop. They must have imposed some restrictions on Indian time, for their workshop occurred during the week of summer solstice. For Gwichyaa Zhee, which is north of the Arctic Circle, solstice is a two-month period of continuous day without darkness.

People can be just as active at 2:00 AM as they are at noon and often do not seem aware of the clock. The methods the workshop leaders developed for their village at Alkali Reserve were based on traditional Salish customs. They encouraged Athabascan participants to develop their own methods based on Athabascan traditions and maintained that they did not advocate using the Salish methods. This message was evidently misunderstood by some. A key irony in this event is that the state government ended up with the greatest burden of blame for having funded a cult-like event. This workshop reveals tangled webs of meaning and practice in its metaphysical, historical, and economic elements.

All three of the alcoholism treatment programs in force that summer were artifacts of Athabascan-initiated efforts to manipulate their own social and economic well-being. Part of the conflict over the Alkali Lake workshop lay in competition for clients and funding that kept all of the programs wary of each other. Fund-raisers from two separate organizations had proven successful in their endeavors. Gwazhał (mentioned in the previous chapters) and Shreevyaa were two such organizers, and this skirmish brought to the surface their history of mutual antagonism and opposing theories of healing. Despite the personal differences between leaders, many people benefited then and later from these imaginative attempts to bring about change.

In summary, the addictive system in Gwichyaa Zhee has two basic areas of activity. One involves physical addictions themselves, and the other, which is the subject of this study, embroils the entire Athabascan economy in yet another extractive process. Theorists such as Schaef have already postulated that addiction is a social phenomenon and not merely a personal dilemma. In this study I suggest that the addictions have fomented an economic system that is reproductive of itself and replicates a model of extraction instigated by Europeans centuries ago when they were first seeking riches from Asia. Gambling, introduced by the fur traders in the 19th century, continues to be both problematic and directly lucrative. In fact, the Elders Association is one of the most financially stable indigenous enterprises (albeit officially not for profit) in the community because of its profitable bingo and pull-tab business. Alcohol and other addictive substances are the most prominent and are very profitable. Most of those who benefit from addictive products such as alcohol are outsiders (urban center liquor outlets, freight carriers, drug cartels, counseling agencies), however, the only legal outlet for alcohol in Gwichyaa Zhee is the city-owned liquor store, which clears thousands of dollars in profit per month. Besides the liquor store, bootleggers, drug dealers, and taxicabs make sizeable incomes from liquor sales.

Healing programs have involved a good deal of revenue as well. However, some have brought cash revenue into the villages in the form of housing and per diem expenditures. These include the three treatment programs scheduled during the summer of 1993. For some Athabascan leaders per diem has become a form of income that ironically encourages them to seek out and remain in board member positions with entities that pay fixed amounts for travel, food, and lodging (scrutinized continually by their dissenters in the community). These entities include the Council of Athabascan Tribal Governments, the Yukon Flats School District, the Tribal Council of Gwichyaa Zhee, and the Gwichyaa Zhee ANCSA village corporation, among others. In the long run, Gwichyaa Zhee's economy is tightly interwoven with the addictive system and is not likely to become disentangled without system changes to the Athabascans' own emergent cash economy. Athabascan leaders not only are active participants in creating healing methods but, by and large, are in need of healing themselves. Very few of them have escaped the physical entrapments of alcohol or gambling. Some of them have approached solutions by openly using themselves as a measure of what needs to be changed. In this they follow one of the basic tenets of Alcoholics Anonymous. Most of the healing theories brought into Athabascan land are but a few years old and need time to demonstrate that they can be effective.

In the final analysis, the Northern Athabascans of Gwichyaa Zhee are prospering by some analytical frames and flagging by others. If one examines them from mainstream material insignia, they are burgeoning. If one uses health or sobriety as a sign, the prosperity of Northern Athabascans in the 1990s is questionable but not bleak. If one tries to measure intangible items such as the energy to try new ideas, then the prosperity of Athabascans is strong. When Athabascans speak of healing, they include not only their personal trials with addictions and illnesses but also the economic difficulties that have become part of their existence since the onset of colonialism in the 19th century.

4 Leadership: *Just One Mind*

The previous chapters have brought out the hegemonic forces of Northern Athabascan colonial history and multiple aspects of the local Athabascan economy. In chapter 3, I suggest that Athabascans have become the victims of yet another extractive process in the perpetuation of addictions through providers of addictive products and the therapeutic machinery that has been set into place because of addictions. Countering this exploitation are some Athabascan-initiated efforts to achieve economic independence, but they continued in a state of liminal economic instability throughout my research period. In addition, the Athabascans display frequent, but nearly unnoticed, moments of collective violence that I have classified as moments of a particular style of consensus. In light of their economic instability and propensity toward collective violence, I have suggested in chapter 1 that Northern Athabascans constitute one of many societies that use ethnic violence as a consensual form of politics. This chapter discusses Athabascan decision-making and leadership styles, as well as some of the traditional roots of these issues as contextualized in post–Cold War ethnic hostility, discrimination, and economic expansion.

The pressures of the past century and a half of negotiating boundaries between themselves and exploitive outsiders, their continuing economic fragility, and several traditional paradigms from Athabascan culture have led to a fusion of leadership styles and a multiplicity of decision-making processes. Athabascan leaders involve themselves in the economy and expound somewhat differing philosophies regarding

the most expedient or beneficial manners in which to strengthen Athabascan society. Despite performative differences, Athabascan leaders
share a common goal: local control over their economic and social lives.
Without local control leaders actually have nothing to lead because almost all power currently rests in the hands of mainstream U.S. or Canadian authorities. If the global trends observed by Maybury-Lewis (1997)
and others can be used as a predictive measure, then Northern Athabascans' small-scale collective violence exhibited through evictions marks
an emergent source of ethnic conflict in Alaska.

What authority do Athabascan leaders possess? They can garner support from their constituents in order to make business transactions,
solicit funding, and — with great restrictions — sell or lease tribal resources (land, mineral rights, forest products, and themselves as either
unsung Native Americans or people with social problems, depending
on the narrative suggested by the money holder). Social problems are
endemic in every Athabascan community and are a primary topic of
public and private narrative, including economic endeavors as discussed in chapter 3. As mentioned in previous chapters, Northern Athabascans include social problems related to economic hegemonies, such
as the requirement to use cash instead of other means of reciprocity, as
functions of social pathology. They are restricted from legislating crimi-
nal or civil laws, enforcing laws unless so authorized by the State of
Alaska, waging war, and issuing passports. As I mention in chapter 1,
they have found circuitous methods to rid themselves of unwanted people, and this they do frequently. In this chapter I ask, What do they want
to do? There is no collective that can be said to represent all Northern
Athabascans. Rather, each village or group works toward its own ends.
For instance, the Venetie Tribal Government (IRA) asserts that its lands
are U.S. federal Indian Country and is engaged in a legal battle with the
State of Alaska, which challenges its right to levy taxes and legislate civil

law. Gwichyaa Zhee and leaders of other Alaska Native Claims Settlement Act (ANCSA) villages can express but a disconnected interest, however, as leaders of ANCSA villages must work within regulations imposed on corporations by the State of Alaska, and doing so leads them away from an established federal staging ground for negotiating sovereignty (which the Venetie Tribal Government [IRA] employs) and confines them to the smaller construct of state government. As Herzfeld remarks about bureaucracy and the state, those that are dominated by a system must "rehearse the logic of the state itself" with every transaction (1992:109). In this regard, the Venetie Tribal Government (IRA) rehearses a federal logic, while the ANCSA village tribal governments act out an anomalous tertiary position at once situated between federal and state authority and yet subordinated to the state government.

Women have played significant roles in constructing and critiquing Athabascan society through public discussions, writings, and modes of instructing their children. During the time I was in Gwichyaa Zhee I saw them taking a strong position instituting revisionary moral values, especially about rape. A recent double trial of a former Gwich'in chief brings to light some of these issues:

Iłt'at (a pseudonym) was accused of rape by Isleta Cross (a pseudonym), who came into Gwich'in country some years ago. She went to the Venetie Tribal Government (IRA) to offer her services as a fund-raiser and grant writer, and it accepted her offer willingly. She said she was an undocumented Native American. She was gone from the region before I began fieldwork. Iłt'at was one of the chiefs of the tribal government while she was there. He had a reputation as a sexually indiscriminate man. Descriptions of Cross were equally unkind. Nonetheless, Cross filed charges of rape against Iłt'at in 1993 with the State of Alaska as well as with the Venetie Tribal Government (IRA). Iltł'at was arrested and released on bail. During that period he returned to Viihtaii, where the tribal government brought him before a closed tribal court to ascertain his guilt or innocence by Gwich'in law. Three Athabascan women from Vashraii K'oo traveled to Viihtaii to testify against Iltł'at, and after lengthy deliberation, the tribal court found Iltł'at guilty. He was banished from the village. A few months later, in spring 1994, Iltł'at was found guilty by a jury of Athabascan residents in a State of Alaska court in Gwichyaa Zhee. Iltł'at was sentenced to eight years in a jail in Fairbanks, Alaska.

This case was the strongest and most public example of censoring of certain Athabascan intergender behaviors that I encountered, but I also witnessed many similar events of a smaller dimension. Most such acts of censoring were made by women who verbally chastised men for making sexual advances toward themselves or other women. Several women, both Athabascan and non-Athabascan, told me about their confrontations with men or warned me to be wary of their proclivities. Many of these women spoke out about cases of child and adolescent sexual molestation.

There are many Northern Athabascan women who take positions of leadership as entrepreneurs, administrators, project leaders, and state or federal politicians, although not very many have become village chiefs. Likewise, most of the warrior chiefs lauded in Athabascan oral traditions are men. In this respect, Athabascan history and leadership can be perceived as dominated by a masculine world, although there are a significant number of exceptions. However, ordinary conversations among Athabascan women and their writings address life and leadership in a different light, one that depicts men as undependable in economic and domestic spheres and sometimes morally objectionable in private life. Belle Herbert (1988) remarks on the selfishness of men several times in her autobiography, as is mentioned in chapter 2. This is a typical statement from her bilingual text:

> Dinjii vanh daį' too hee dinjii hadal.
> Duuyee tr'injaa ts'a' tr'iginjii.
> Tr'iinin geetak hee aghwaa googaaa
> kwat ts'a' oondaa niginjik.

> [The men left in the morning while it was still dark.
> They never helped the women.
> Even if they were packing babies,
> the women would set up the tent.] [Herbert 1988:18]

These issues of intergender disparity and conflict are addressed in more detail in the following chapter, but they have significance here with respect to conflictual symbols of personal perfection and leadership in Athabascan communities. One is a cultural ideal of individualism that directs each person to act with as much emotional, physical, and economic independence from others as possible. The other is a cultural ideal of conformity through consensus that suggests that every Athabascan somehow knows "the" Athabascan way of thought, word, and act. By this ideal, those who do not know these ways are not truly Athabascan. Later in this chapter I describe some of the ideals of consensus that are expressed by Athabascan leaders. The key thought here is that ideal Athabascan codes of behavior, if any exist, are supposed to be tacitly understood and enacted. In effect, all repeated behavior becomes acceptable because of this ideal of social silence, whether or not all Northern Athabascans agree with it or can live with it. In the double court case described previously, it took public outcry by Athabascan women to alert each other that they object to rape. Northern Athabascans practice of consensus is thus twofold: one is si-

lent consent based on repetitive action, and the other calls for public debate, commentary, and, in this case, a review of role models and other
leaders.

One of the tasks of this chapter is to explore some of the underlying
paradigms or theories that configure an essentially indeterminate Athabascan leadership complex. Some of the underlying theories stem from
traditional culture (religious traditions, issues of consensus, and concepts of strength), while others have emerged from the administrative
requirements imposed on Northern Athabascans from outside governmental agencies in the form of complex paperwork to reify the bureaucratic discourse of the government at the local level. Each of these concepts is interlinked with knowledge of the numinous and is further
woven into the fabric of two other ideals in Athabascan behavior: their
notion of consensus and Northern Athabascans' sign of private and
public strength. These Athabascan traditions work in an unwieldy partnership with the mainstream requirements of hierarchical administrative control. There is no overarching model for Athabascan leadership,
leaving individuals struggling with the ambiguities of their complex
roles. With multiple governmental policing and funding interests alive
in Gwichyaa Zhee, the Western administrative models predominate in
every situation, although in recent years they find resistance and intolerance in many Athabascan behaviors. The governmental sources are the
Gwichyaa Zhee tribal council, the incorporated city government, the Yukon Flats School District, the state government, and several depart-
ments of the U.S. federal government. Besides these, there are two occasionally competitive not-for-profit agencies that engage in aspects of
Athabascan villages. These are the Tanana Chiefs Conference and the
Council of Athabascan Tribal Governments. Each of these entities has
control over many elements of ordinary Athabascan lives.

Northern Athabascan decisions and leadership paradigms are drawn
from their traditions of religion, consensus, and strength, as stated pre-

viously; but, in point of fact, their decision-making processes are constrained by and in tension with the underlying patterns of behavior of American government and business. For instance, with respect to religion, Northern Athabascans' geographic position at the confluence of three major river ways, including the transecting Yukon River system, in precolonial North American trading networks encouraged them to incorporate the largely compatible cosmological ideals from Siberia and other Native Americans. In other research (1990:301–306) I have argued that there is a correlation among a Canadian Athabascan mythological figure, "He Who Sees Before and Behind," the middle clan group of Northern Athabascans, and Siberian trading influence. Northern Athabascans were also part of the trading networks of the Tlingit of the Northwest Coast culture area, whose bipartite kinship system was adopted by Athabascans closer to them but only superficially by Northern Athabascans, who are farther from the Northwest Coast culture area. Evidence of the extent of precolonial trading networks is found in oral traditions that incorporate culture heroes such as Ch'iteehakwaii, who resembles heroic figures in Athabascan legends of other regions; origin stories about the formation of the earth, which resemble the Mohawk creation story; and elements of the moon and star motifs, which organize coastal Iñupiat religious beliefs; as well as short stories that have nearly identical counterparts in Siberia.

One effect of trade contact was the emergence of a highly defensive paradigm of traders-cum-warriors who invested in imported and traditional forms of *shan* (black magic), *nagwahtsi'* (other magic), and *vat'aii* (mental strength) for their mutual protection. Most Northern Athabascans distinguish linguistically several kinds of practitioners of metaphysical skills. For instance, Gwich'in Athabascans employ the terms *dazhan, gininlyaa, neeyahshii,* and *ginkhii,* among others. In so doing, they adopted some of the defensive measures and worthwhile identity markers of their trading partners in order to enhance communication while simultaneously attempting to maintain safety from potential enemies. Northern Athabascans have done the same in their relations with environmentalist organizations by incorporating elements of environmentalist jargon into their discourse. Among the defensive measures they maintain are shunning and banishment.

Like Slobodin, I heard many stories about the strong medicine of men/warriors of the past who used shamanic power to rescue their people or effect other mystifying endeavors. Slobodin writes, "For tactical reasons, and also because warfare and homicide involved many magico-religious precautions, warfare was hedged about with very many restrictions" (1981:522). One of the untested assumptions about traditional Northern Athabascan warfare is that women were not active participants in the violence. I suggest that because physical strength (vat'aii, as discussed later in this chapter) is demanded of both Athabascan women and men this is probably untrue. There are Athabascan legends and myths about women who were present and active in one capacity or another during battle. The story presented in chapter 2 by Itree's grandmother is typical of this genre.

Nowadays Athabascans are obstructed by far more than the religious differences they have with Euro-Americans. This section describes pertinent elements of Northern Athabascan religious traditions that have motivated the behaviors of Athabascan warriors, traders, and decision making for centuries, as their oral traditions indicate. Athabascan concepts of mental development and strength incorporate and inform the idea of consensus, one word for which is yinjih. Bound into Northern Athabascans' sign of strength are notions of physical, emotional, mental, spiritual, and group strength. Athabascan theories of the numinous, albeit blurred and patched together, underlie all of their leadership activities.

Athabascan religious experience of the 20th century is an indeterminate complex of beliefs and behaviors embracing several associated reciprocal cultural webs that were woven together into a comprehensive precolonial religion. Dominating their religious thought is a concept of supreme power that controls and benefits all creatures which is referred to by two interchangeable terms: *k'eegwaadhat* and *vit'eegwaahchy'aa*. *K'eegwaadhat* indicates "heat" as well as "that which gives orders." *Vit'eegwaahchy'aa* means "that on which we depend." Both refer to something powerful and ubiquitous that has no identified physical construction, and the sign itself makes up the object, which is ineffable, and its numerous representations (including dreams, human and other spirits, and mystical or inexplicable events), and many Gwich'in equate this sign with Jesus or God. Gwich'in religious beliefs incorporate a system of power and its usage that may or may not be conceived as originating in vit'eegwaahchy'aa or k'eegwaadhat. Traditional Northern Athabascan leadership required proven success in communication with the sacred for hunting, war, trading, and healing. Much of this activity was related to dreams that contain prophetic data. For instance, a Gwich'in traditional trilogy of narratives features powerful leaders, including Ko'ehdan, Vasagihdzak, and Ch'iteehakwaii (Fast 1990; Mishler 1995; Slobodin 1981). Just as the models established in these oral traditions do, Athabascan people often treat each other and other creatures without mercy or compassion. Life in the inclement subarctic environment and what it takes to make a living there systematize Athabascan religious and social theory.

A tangential symbol for all people committed to a mystical calling is the system of behavior that is self-effacing to a certain extent (*gwintsii veegoo'aii*). Individuals are expected to behave as if their public missions are self-evident and perceived for their present or future public value (Marilyn Savage, personal communication, 1992). Also, communication between human beings and sacred entities forms a key component in Athabascan discussion of the numinous. All religious activity is centered on perceived receipt of communications from the sacred via signs in nature, dreams, or messages delivered by human spiritual intermediaries. As it is with other Native American peoples, hunting ethics are interwoven with the customs pertaining to reciprocal relationships with nature and spirits. Hunters must be respectful of the wildlife as their contribution toward a reciprocal renewal of wildlife, environmental order, and human life. Hunters (both women and men) anticipate dreams or other signals from the numinous and acknowledge their debts toward the animal world and spirit world in terms of knowledge, respect, and mutual protection. In this age of environmentalism, subsistence hunting behavior has received more attention than most other Athabascan behavioral clusters because of its reliance on nature. Another aspect of the numinous is psychic ability, which encompasses a full range of mental activities described in the traditional Athabascan language. Consensus is one of these mental activities: *yinjih ch'ihłak* (of one mind) is a theory that people can act in perfect awareness of other people's thoughts with or without speaking and with or without occupying the same space. Although yinjih ch'ihłak has telepathic overtones, Northern Athabascan people I met use the spoken word to communicate.

Northern Athabascans have many ways to express their experience of the sacred, such as song, dance, and other forms of body language, in their multiple languages and English. Sarah James of Vashraii K'oo talked about it in public speeches and performances. She has recorded one of the several traditional Gwich'in drum songs in a compact disc collection ("Caribou Skin Hut Dance," on *Arctic Refuge*, a gathering of tribes by Soundings of the Planet, 1996), which I heard in public gatherings as well as in private homes in Gwichyaa Zhee, Vashraii K'oo, Viihtaii, Fairbanks, and Anchorage. Although there is no way to empirically ascertain how Northern Athabascans experience the numinous, it can easily be said that they forefront prayer in every decision-making event, whether personal or public. As a Canadian Gwich'in man from Vuntut put it:

> Every time we have a meeting for Native people, as we demonstrated today with a prayer, a few words of prayers for that strength that we ask for. This morning it was done in Gwich'in. If it was translated, that prayer would say that these people would work together in the next few days towards the common good of the land, the animals, the air and water, and the fish and that the peoples would work together in the future. [Grafton Njootli, Vuntut, Yukon Territory, "People, Science, and Caribou" Conference, Vashraii K'oo, November 6, 1993]

Other Vashraii K'oo people spoke to me about mystical events or sacred experiences. For instance, one of the chiefs talked to me about a gravesite that he and Gilbert had come across by chance several years ago. He described the odd way that Gilbert was attracted toward the spot and their mutual but unusual compulsion to dig into the soil. From the look of the rotting fabric of the deceased's cloth shirt, his traditional Athabascan paraphernalia, and other objects in the burial place, they estimated that he had lived over 100 years ago. They reburied the human remains but divided between them some of the glass beads that were near the body. My host took his tiny collection of those beads out of a hiding place in his house to show me and made sure that I did not touch them. He told me the grave and the beads were sacred. Northern Athabascans tell stories about a mythical woman who wore dentalium shells. She was the wife of Ko'ehdan, who named her Ch'atthan Vee (Dentalium Shell Woman) after he rescued her from the Ch'eekwaii who kidnapped her (Julia Peter, personal communication, November 19, 1989). The same mythical woman is called Latpatsandia (Prize Woman) by Canadian Gwich'in (Fast 1990). The trope of white shells has multiple potentials in referent. First, it refers to trade with the people of the Northwest Coast region. Second, it resonates with Koyukon legends of the three-clan system that once dominated the Yukon River valley, mentioned in chapter 2. Third, it calls to mind the White Shell Woman in the Apache and Navajo (Southern Athabascan language speakers) creation stories. Another man showed me the three eagle feathers that he had found on different expeditions into the woods around Vashraii K'oo. He described the experience of each journey and his discovery of each feather. Such events are always imbued with importance and separation from ordinary life, even though the stories about finding them are fairly uneventful. I would suggest that in each of these instances the Northern Athabascans I was with were trying to communicate their numinal experiences as something they do with anyone at any time, rather than going out of their way to do so for me, an anthropologist. I heard many like experiences while I lived in Gwichyaa Zhee. The verbalized and public aspects of traditional Athabascan religious beliefs have been dominated, sequestered, and largely obliterated, but these commonplace conversational themes in Northern Athabascan land indicate that there are habits of thought and communication that maintain some elements of their ancient codes of metaphysical belief.

Northern Athabascan religious specialists have traditionally included Athabascan women as well as men, although there are some issues of gender segregation. For instance, men were not expected to be midwives, although contemporary women accept men (Athabascan or non-Athabascan) as medical practitioners during pregnancy and childbirth. In the 1980s, Indian health officials decreed that all births under the care of their health service must occur in one of the regional urban centers. This effectively stopped the privilege of choosing between or using both Western medical facilities and traditionally trained midwives. By contrast, women were not expected to become warrior shamans. However, if they had other shamanic gifts (such as dreaming or healing), they were called on to exploit them. With the advent of Christianity, these endeavors were sequestered. There are as many women as men involved in the Christian posts as there are men in Athabascan villages. Many Athabascan men and women have become lay readers, and in Gwichyaa Zhee both men and women have indicated interest in learning to be deacons of the Episcopal Church. Several men and one woman have become ordained ministers. In sum, both Athabascan men and Athabascan women are expected to develop awareness of the numinous and make use of it in social contexts.

Shifting Sands in Athabascan Consensus

A Gwich'in elder once told me, "We do everything by consensus. We just know what everyone wants. We know the best thing to do without talking about it." The elder was expressing one of the most common ideals voiced in Athabascan territory. It is an ideal that has many modes of display in Athabascan communities. Consensus is another habit of thought fitting into a larger framework of Athabascan semiotics. It is one of the most important aspects of Athabascan decision making. Northern Athabascan consensus displays in everyday experiences, crises, public elections, and their efforts to heal from the complex of ideas subsumed under the general Athabascan narratives about their social problems, such as addiction and poverty. Athabascan consensus incorporates a few methods for legitimized sanctions to violations of Athabascan norms, such as the tribal court discussed in the rape trial. The court represents a conjoining of smaller, more private efforts to effect public change. Other methods of reprimand include shunning and banishment. Consensus as Northern Athabascans use it for informal joint actions (such as banishment or communal acceptance and constraining the presence of some strangers, such as myself) is often enacted as a shifting point of accountability that locates meaning in transaction rather than in social actors. By "shifting accountability" I am referring to the use of informal communication (primarily gossip circles and established codes of reference), which can convey habitual webs of meaning along established patterns of social networks. For instance, when Andrew Dakota offended a Gwich'in mother (in the incident described in chapter 1 in which the mother of one of his pupils caused him to be evicted), she used the informal network of her family to effect a series of shunning and violent events to frighten Dakota and force the school district to fire him. She did not use any of the formal processes, such as speaking with the principal, the tribal chiefs or council, or the school board officials. The method she chose was a customary pattern of public behavior requiring little discussion and relatively little public awareness of the situation. Often these evictions are attended by complaints about white people (vaanoodlit) and outsiders (oonduk Gwich'in). Athabascan habits of projecting animosity toward outsiders have led to a routinization of cooperative expulsion that they effect with little communication with each other. This form of collective action contrasts with another form of consensus that Northern Athabascans use in building coalitions and devising new projects. Such consensus building tends to be situational, serving an ameliorating, problem-solving goal, whereas patterned consensus used by Northern Athabascans in evictions has the effect of fomenting ethnic exclusivity.

A semiotic review of performance is useful in discussing aspects of leadership to shed light on the process of communication that occurs during an eviction. I have referred to it as shifting accountability whereby the decisions made for any eviction process are continually relocated from one person to another and never remain the responsibility of any given individual for more than a few moments of time. In the Dakota eviction (chapter 1), for example, a Gwich'in mother told key members of her family and other people about her distress. I heard about it indirectly through one of the gossip circles. One or more of her kinsmen covertly threatened Dakota with gunshots. The identity of the attacker was never officially revealed, although I suppose that if I had pursued the issue, I could have found out through informal gossip channels that are open even to other outsiders. The only action taken by a public official was that of the principal, who suggested that Dakota remain away from the village for an extended period and then removed him from unsupervised classroom teaching afterward. She eventually passed responsibility on to the school board, which failed to extend Dakota's contract another year.

Evictions of people who perform certain categories of unacceptable behavior have become routine, and the method of executing them involves a shifting of accountability. Such consensus allows Northern Athabascans to make potentially contentious decisions with a minimum of discussion as long as they follow established patterns of behavior. By invoking the term *consensus* they suggest that their culture (a trope adopted from anthropology that they have found a useful means of insulting outsiders) privileges them with an ineffable power to know what they, and their neighbors, are thinking — hence, avoiding the need to discuss the issues. Athabascans' use of consensus allows an illusion that they have succeeded in doing what they "all" wanted done.

The custom related to shunning and evicting behaviors also invokes an impression of social solidarity that might not otherwise exist. I describe two complex evictions in chapter 1 and a third at the beginning of this chapter. Each eviction was effected through an act of consensus, although in fact there were no public meetings about either of the first two events. There was simply a common idea that the people had to go, and no one defied the overwhelming pressures brought to bear in each situation. As Athabascan people use consensus, it involves communication of opinion through precedent, gossip, public meetings, and

Jakobson-like shifters to steer action. A consensual shifter is sublimely useful in pointing toward the transitional actions in an event rather than freeze-framing any given moment for closer analysis. This form of collective action does not occur in dealing with new ideas, such as what I thought of as a growing movement against sexual violence among Athabascan women. In that case, consensus takes place in the form of public meetings, trials, and elections. When it comes to making communal decisions for new forms of collective action, Northern Athabascans hold meetings and voice their opinions as often as possible in public areas.

One useful characterization of what might pass for traditional consensus came from Clarence Alexander of Gwichyaa Zhee, who described the way he was taught by his grandmother. In this description Alexander not only defines one of the key parameters of Athabascan consensus (learning without asking questions) but also signals one of the determinant issues about Athabascan culture that give rise to ambiguities between two cultural ideals: that of individualism and that of conformity. In describing his grandmother's pedagogical style, Alexander stated, "She would make me sit without speaking until I understood what she wanted me to know. She wouldn't tell me anything. I had to understand it myself." Implicit in Alexander's description of the Athabascan ideal of consensus is an underlying hypothesis of mutual comprehension of the ground rules that motivate any given situation. Inherent in Alexander's statement is that the ideal Gwich'in must exert individual mental agency in order to conform to Gwich'in t'eeteraa'in (their way of life). Athabascan individualism in this sense is a far cry from idea of "being true selves independent of any cultural or social influence" (1985:150), which Bellah et al. suggest of the U.S. ideal of individualism. Alexander's statement also exhibits another central difference between American and Athabascan cultures. Learning in this silent mode is antithetical to the agonistic displays of U.S. learning styles. Athabascan individualism, on the contrary, seeks to find ways to integrate with cultural or social influences. Athabascan consensus does not signify mental telepathy, although there were many who suggested the possibility. In practice, they talk about every issue in gossip circles, at public meetings, and on the radio. The radio station in Gwichyaa Zhee, which began operations in 1993, was funded on the strength of arguments like these:

> Our people in Jałk'iitsik, they're not too familiar with caribou herd, but if they want our support, we are willing to support these people. Like Vashraii K'oo people, we are 100 percent with you on this caribou management, and we mainly live on moose diet in our area. . . . I just want to say to these [Vashraii K'oo] people that we're supporting them as much as possible and tell my people when I get back home how important this meeting is about our caribou wildlife. . . . I was thinking that all this information should be provided to this radio station to these outlying villages. See what we're doing right here in meeting, what we talk about. This information should be out to these villages, besides who's representing their own village. He might not provide all the information to his people when he gets home. It should be in the air in the radio station. [Than Yinjihaadhak, Jałk'iitsik, "People, Science, and Caribou" Conference, Vashraii K'oo, November 8, 1993]

Athabascans also rely on customary common sense, patterns of action that emerge from repeated, accepted (or ignored) past activities or expressions. These customary patterns of thought are the lessons that Alexander had to learn at an early age, and he had to learn them without asking if he had guessed right or wrong. Alexander is but one of many Athabascan men and women who spoke to me about consensus. While many actions do not require much discussion, the people of Gwichyaa Zhee make frequent use of public meetings, simultaneously complaining that there are not enough meetings and stating that there are too many. At such public meetings some are quick to voice angry complaints about actions with which they disagree. Consensus, then, is a combination of using customary patterns of decision-making behavior with each new event and accepting criticism after the fact if or when there is a joint action of complaint against it. With respect to the two evictions described earlier and some of the others that occurred during the time that I was in Gwichyaa Zhee, there was no public outcry against the actions leading to banishment, for the habit of eviction has become a paradigm of collective behavior in Gwichyaa Zhee. The trials of Iltł'at, however, do not fall into the patterns of performed collective violence already instituted in Gwich'in. Rather, they reflect a significant change in public attitudes and processes with respect to intergender behaviors that have become habitual among Athabascan men and women, a manifestation of routinized violence against women by Athabascan men. The trials of Iltł'at display a consensual action on the part of a faction of Gwich'in people (primarily women) who forced another kind of public censure by urging a tribal court hearing, a rare occurrence in late-20th-century rural Alaska. The otherwise shifting sands of Athabascan consensual authority were stopped in this event for intense public review throughout Alaska's rural communities. Even so, the tribal court had to share responsibility in reprimanding the accused rapist, as the State of Alaska court system was already involved. The double trials of Iltł'at bring to light at least two forms of consensus: one that is the habitual deflection of accountability in familiar situations (permitting other similar intergender behaviors by other men or Iltł'at himself) and another that seeks potential systemic review or broad-based public consciousness of a revision in Athabascan values. Other such social reformations in demographic loyalties occur with each new marriage, business venture, and outside endeavor. Significant changes in family alliances show up in village elections, trials by jury, and community-wide traumas. Homicide, accidental death, house fires, and suicide are examples of such upsets that occurred while I lived in Gwichyaa Zhee. While changes in Athabascan social behaviors are being cultivated to heal their social problems, forms of consensus continue as primary modes of decision-making or other public behaviors.

Consensus displays in nonverbal public ways as well. In 1993 my sister and I went to the Northern Athabascans' General Assembly meeting in Inuvik, Northwest Territories, Canada. There were no other strangers present, and Esther and I were introduced to the group at the beginning of the meeting. When lunchtime came someone brought in food, and there was a brief announcement that they would take a break. Without another word all of the elders moved into the serving line. No one else got up even when the elders were nearly finished, and Esther and I assumed that the food was only for them. We were discussing where we should go ourselves when one of the traditional chiefs invited us to join him in line. As soon we got there all of the rest of the people silently got into line behind us.

There were, of course, a number of factors operating there besides consensus — respect for elders and visitors, Athabascan politeness, and deference to one of the inherent contradictions in Athabascan culture: the absolute right of individuals to make their own decisions (rather than always to behave consensually), and, as one Gwich'in woman suggested, Canadian respect for order. It was in essence a striking example of consensus operating wordlessly, spontaneously, and so smoothly that it seemed as if the people there were acting with one mind. It involved coordinating at least four different kinds of action by different factions in the room. As was their due, the 20–30 elders present moved as a group without regard to anyone else present. The remaining 50–70 people, including a handful of children, refrained from doing anything until one of their members extended the invitation. Then, on the proper cue from my sister and me, the outsiders, they moved in unison just as they had waited in unison. As Durkheim might explain it, they were transported as a group beyond who they are as individuals to a cohesive body with one purpose, however inconsequential it might have been to those present.

There is a juncture between consensus (acting with one mind) and ideas about culture (a body of shared knowledge, ideas, or rules). In this case the people of Inuvik share a body of knowledge that dictates when to wait and when to move into line. Consensus presents an opportunity to implement rules and other cultural ideas. In Inuvik it presented an opportunity to display courtesy to visitors without having to force any one person to take responsibility as host in a shifting performance of accountability. After the meeting moderator announced lunch, his involvement in officiating ended, and responsibility for creating order fell to the routine practiced by the local elders of getting into line first. Once they were there, however, there were no established habits for all social actors to implement, and the Northern Athabascan people present simply waited in communal silence until the responsibility was assumed momentarily by one of the tribal leaders present. My sister and I removed responsibility from him by getting up, and that action transferred responsibility of collective action to the rest (who took it without delay). In this situation consensus became a vehicle by which they reminded themselves and their guests of the value they place on elders. Consensus can also conceal discordant ideas. In other words, they used the practice of waiting for the elders as a conventional symbol of who they are as Athabascans, but the action of waiting may have generated individual feelings of animosity or impatience that either they did not display or we did not see because of the overriding principle of courtesy in this situation. In other circumstances, Northern Athabascans' ideal of performance based on absolute individualism and independence might be exercised.

One Gwich'in term that encompasses the idea of consensus along with mutual mental awareness is *yinjih*, a derivative of *-inji'*, which denotes mental action. In spite of experiences seeming to testify to the contrary, many people told me that Northern Athabascans live in harmony with each other. Having an ideal of harmony (however much it is fulfilled or not fulfilled) encourages Northern Athabascans to leave open a way to incorporate consensus into political and social objectives. The actual enactment of harmony is a far more subtle issue. Athabascans are prepared for opportunities to achieve mental harmony but arrange their lives toward acting in spatial or emotional independence of each other. *Harmony* in their usage is not synonymous with *nonviolence*. Rather, it is an ideal toward some sort of independence. Seen in this perspective, violent evictions occurring with a minimum of public agitation (i.e., a state of harmony) are part of an established method of peacekeeping. As the episode of the Langfield family eviction suggests, Northern Athabascans exist with violence and allow things to happen as they happen until something or someone fails to conform with Gwich'in ideals or what they are then perceiving as ideal behavior. As the rape trials indicate, they are processing new modes of thought about intergender behavior that take precedent to a certain extent from American women's efforts to reshape mores about sexual violence. While I was in rural Alaska, one of the methods Northern Athabascan women had already instilled into patterned behavior was shunning men and teaching their daughters to shun adult men. Shunning in this sense conforms to ideals of Northern Athabascan independence and isolation. Shunning is a Northern Athabascan value that serves as a stepping-stone toward personal survival. Although shunning can interfere with consensus, it also serves consensual efforts that forward cultural survival. I discuss shunning behaviors in greater detail in the following chapter.

It takes a fairly broad focus to understand acts of shunning as contributing to Athabascan unity, especially when people selectively shun each other as well as outsiders, unless it is taken in the context of ethnic

identity issues and ethnic violence. It has long been noted that Gwich'in
Athabascans have a consistent sense of themselves as a separate people
rather than as simply human (Slobodin 1981:527). The same cannot be
said of other Alaskan Athabascans. For instance, most Koyukons who
were younger than 60 at the time of this study identified themselves first
as Athabascan and then as Koyukon, if they knew the term. Most
Gwich'in of the same age group or older identify themselves first as
Gwich'in and then as Alaska Natives. Part of this stems from the fact
that the word Gwich'in is one of the few self-selected indigenous tribal
names in Alaska. It is an act of consensus that they were able to collabo-
rate sufficiently at some point in their history to first see themselves as a
group and then to so name themselves. They achieved consensus in that
regard despite considerable political upheaval and conflict with another
highly valued cultural ideal, which is to view themselves primarily as individualists. Gwich'in people can and do use consensus on a daily basis
without much effort and yet insist that every child learn to be as independent as possible. How they resolve these inherently opposing ideals
is quite simple. Most of them watch in silence, waiting for negative reactions against their behaviors. In some Gwich'in communities it is customary to voice criticism with loud voices in public places, and therefore
some people tend to make continual "mistakes" in the eyes of their
compatriots. This is the lot of many Gwich'in chiefs, who are elected,
voted out, and reelected time after time. Some of their mistakes are forgotten, while others are not.

Consensus-building techniques were implemented at some of the
more successful meetings in rural Alaska. By "successful" I mean that
the voting participants closed themselves around the events within the
meeting spectrum instead of diverging to discussions on other matters.
By the sheer numbers of decisions made and administered by the end of
the two years I observed it, one organization in particular, the Council
of Athabascan Tribal Governments (CATG), displayed effective use of

consensus. CATG has united several village entities in joint initiatives during the past decade through constant use of public forum and election-format consensus.

Sometimes Northern Athabascans have crossed the U.S.–Canadian border to help make informed consensual decisions. One of the chiefs from Tetlit Zheh in Canada used all of the communication mechanisms available to him in order to make a decision about permitting the building of a petroleum pipeline through his region:

> The panel was chiefs so I told them, "Okay, let's get the twin otter on this. Get our four communities together. Let's take a load over to Fairbanks and see this Alaska pipeline." No problem. We done that. We took a good look at it. We talked to the Natives over there: down to Minto landing, the Native peoples there, what damage it did to them. What they did to their moose and caribou. So we had information. We went home, and we gave all that information to our four communities. When we met, they all came. Everybody said no to the pipeline. Until today there's no pipeline there yet. [Johnny Charlie Sr., Tetlit Zheh, "People, Science, and Caribou" Conference, Vashraii K'oo, November 6, 1993]

Mr. Charlie's method of gaining information to make long-range plans is something most Athabascan leaders try to do. Some of them have made decisions that they have since regretted. For example, the Venetie Tribal Government (IRA) agreed 20 years ago to exploration for oil on the Venetie Reserve. Now that the tribal government is fighting oil development in the Arctic National Wildlife Refuge, the exploration, which found nothing to interest big energy concerns, is a point of embarrassment in its relationship with environmentalist groups.

In summary, consensus as Northern Athabascans use it is a complex practice used in many public circumstances of collective violence (including shunning and evictions) as well as acts of hospitality. Athabascan consensual behavior has been impacted by U.S. election practices, which base public action on nonunanimity, but otherwise American influence on Athabascan social life and nonpolitical use of consensus remains ambiguous. A primary effect of consensus in patterned situations is that it covers indeterminacies by shifting accountability as an event unfolds. The indexical process of Athabascan consensus pointing to transitional areas of action is similar to the logic used in Athabascan traditional sharing networks (as discussed in chapter 3). Like sharing and consensus, eviction follows a pattern of logic that avoids situating accountability for public action in any given individual while simultaneously spotlighting the unwanted person until he or she is gone. In a like manner, sharing the meat of a slain moose has the effect of marking the virtue and skill of a hunter while simultaneously dissipating the carcass into the social sphere of the hunter. The semiotic of a continuously shifting zone of accountability to avoid accumulating either wealth or blame works for most situations in Athabascan society. Athabascan decision making, like sharing, displays itself as action oriented, de-emphasizing individual agency in culturally prescribed formulas in favor of underscoring the shared relationships and responsibilities that connect all actors in any given setting.

Women play several roles in Athabascan consensual activity. Although none of the roles is distinctly their own in format, gendered social spheres have resulted in separate gossip circles and, thus, have resulted in some differences in the roles women play. Women as victims of violence have initiated public meetings, demanded tribal court hearings, and implemented modes of training their children (discussed in the next chapter) to accentuate certain types of shunning behaviors. Yet, in contradistinction to the conformity required in collective or consensual behavior, Athabascan individuals are applauded for their personal acts of strength, physical, mental, or public, as will be discussed.

Paradigms of Personal and Societal Strength

Three Gwich'in terms encapsulate central concepts of Athabascan strength: *vat'aii* (personal mental or physical strength), *dat'aii* (strength through the demonstration of public accomplishments), and *yinjih* (acting with one mind). The union of individual to public strength in the root word *t'aii* is an indication of the logical integration of the (by Euro-American standards) disparate notion of the individual versus society. By Athabascan ideals, both as they perform them in contemporary settings and as they are originally expressed in their indigenous language, individuals and their social environment are bound together in strength. Strength, as Northern Athabascans use it in descriptions of themselves or others, refers to a combination of mental stamina, focus, and physical execution. The social extension of this concept, dat'aii, also brings in similar issues of perseverance, group sustenance of a single idea, and material or physical evidence of its accomplishment. These values are implied in Northern Athabascans' adage "We suffer, we endure, but we continue on" [Khaiinji' ch'iidhat gaa nihk'it ahaa] (Peter 1979:48). Northern Athabascan concepts of power underlie many Athabascan expressions in conversation and literature. A root word of the first two concepts, *t'aii*, is expressed by the late Belle Herbert (as noted earlier), who was born in the mid-1800s. Herbert uses the word *t'aii* to denote strength from a sacred source that characterized her medicine skills: "Zhyaa gwats'at ree K'eegwaadhat t'aii zhik shaa daatth'aa" [But from then on (an incident that publicly revealed her to be a medicine woman) the strength of the Lord was in me] (1988:77). The word *k'eegwaadhat* may be from the Takudh Gwich'in dialect of eastern Canada. It bears a similarity to the modern Alaskan Gwich'in word for heat, *gwadhah*. The similarity of the words evokes images of a possible traditional belief in the sun as creator, which is common to many Native American tribes.

T'aii is also a root word that acts as a stem or morpheme for the many ways in which the thought can be expressed. T'aii embodies skills and moral values that people inherit from their ancestors, including the skills to think: "There's a feeling, and you know in your heart by dreams and thinking that this is what it means" (Savage, personal communication, October 1992). T'aii means "the wisdom of your ancestors" (G. James, personal communication, January 1995), "their strength and the strength from ancestors before them that is carried through" (Savage, personal communication, October 1992). Northern Athabascans' concept of t'aii is closely tied to mental effort in the form of *nint'aii*. *Viyinji' nint'aii* means "his or her strong mind, a mind with great powers of concentration." *Viyinji' nint'aii* also suggests the ability to use the mind to organize and internalize extremely complex ideas, such as the concept of the sacred. T'aii also represents a source of energy or force that connects all living and nonliving things to each other. A Gwich'in metaphor that draws on this idea states that every human heart contains a bit of caribou heart, and likewise every caribou heart has a bit of human heart (Slobodin 1981:526).

The late Wally Peter of Gwichyaa Zhee told me in 1994 about a traditional exercise used to develop viyinji' nint'aii. In the old days young men learned to be warriors by running all day without stopping and without taking any refreshment. When they began the ordeal in the morning they were given water from a squirrel skull. They were to spit the water back into the squirrel skull at the end of the day and were considered successful if the water filled the skull. The idea behind this exercise as well as vat'aii and viyinji' nint'aii is that the individual puts all thought of physical discomfort and limitations behind him- or herself in order to focus on an objective. In traditional Gwich'in oratorical practices a speaker or storyteller would use the phrase "viyinji' nint'aii" at the beginning of a statement or utterance and afterward would use a variation of the word for strength, such as *dat'aii ha'*, to emphasize the mental strength of the person being described (Savage, personal communication, 1992). Mental abilities (viyinji' nint'aii) are also linguistically linked with the concept of completion or finishing a goal, yiinjii. Likewise, aspects of strength, vat'aii and dat'aii, are linguistically linked to concepts of the sacred.

Vat'aii represents individual power in thought or action, while dat'aii emerges as the power of accomplishment that an individual accumulates over time through the use of vat'aii. Gwich'in who understand the term associate dat'aii with social action. An individual is thought to have achieved dat'aii when she or he does something for the group in a socially constructed manner. For instance, the dat'aii of the nine year old, Ninjii, who killed his first moose (described in chapter 3) was recognized in a disguised potlatch for his achievement of a preliminary phase of adulthood. The potlatch (which normally would have included the final sharing of the moose meat, except that the hunt occurred months before the potlatch) was also an act of dat'aii on the part of family members, who were thus publicly acknowledged for raising a good or productive hunter. However, the potlatch and praise of Ninjii sent blurred messages that left him in great doubt about the import of his accomplishment, one of the many indeterminacies of contemporary Athabascan life. I have also given an example of a young man who chopped wood for me in an exercise of vat'aii (personal strength). John Fredson, founder of the Venetie Reserve that led to the formation of the Venetie Tribal Government (IRA), was recognized for countless acts of dat'aii on behalf of his tribe. He brought about protection of the land, schools, postal service, and other services. Ultimately he expressed supreme dat'aii in sacrificing his health and life to use his education (he was the only Gwich'in with a university bachelor's degree for many years) for the common good of the people. His life has been commemorated in numerous ways, through biography, the name of a school, and a well-publicized reburial ceremonial.

In the everyday world of Northern Athabascans, vat'aii means work:

chopping wood, hauling water, lifting heavy objects, repairing mechanical devices that an expert would normally be called in to do in a city. In a village of 730 there are not enough people to do all that is required, so almost everyone does many things that a city person never does. They take their physical strength for granted. That which constitutes vat'aii becomes a matter of everyday fact, which continues forward from traditional narrative. The values implied in *vat'aii*, *dat'aii*, and *consensus* are encoded in traditional tales such as that about Ko'ehdan ("Without Fire") and contemporary works such as Wallis's 1993 novel, *Two Old Women*. The elements of vat'aii in the Ko'ehdan tale are manifold: a man walks in midwinter for several days without food or adequate clothing trying to find help and succeeds. The hero, Ko'ehdan, uses survival skills, intelligence, physical strength, and endurance (all Gwich'in ideas that are linked to mentality, strength, and the numinous) to reach his destination. The Ko'ehdan narrative is also a story intended to teach young Gwich'in about dat'aii. The hero proves dat'aii to his followers by first successfully passing the tests of strength and endurance that they devise for him (he has to survive a shower of arrows shot at him by his proposed band of warriors), then by success in hunting for many people, and finally by leading his men to the village of the people who kidnapped his wife and massacred the rest of his family. There he proves ultimate dat'aii by killing the leaders of the raid against him.

The tale of Ko'ehdan is a favorite Gwich'in story. Many Gwich'in legends and myths are about survivors in modern times. The late Steven Peter was one such man who demonstrated dat'aii for Vashraii K'oo during a time of starvation:

> One summer dawn in 1994 I walked through St. Stephen's parking lot in Gwichyaa Zhee. At that hour almost no one else is awake, not even the mosquitoes. I felt the comfort of privacy and had been entertaining myself with fragmentary thoughts about nothing in particular. Bemused and content, I

was inattentive. A shadow to the right jerked me alive. In that moment of fright and defocused eyesight I thought it was a bear and stopped dead still. Instead, it was Steven Peter, who was then 87, a habitual early morning walker. In relief I laughed and told him what I had thought. He smiled without surprise and continued on his way.

When he was younger, Steven Peter (1907–97) used to walk the more than 100 miles from Vashraii K'oo in the southeastern foothills of the Brooks Range to Gwichyaa Zhee on a routine basis. There are no roads between the two communities except for a traditional winter trail. Almost no one makes that trip on foot nowadays because they have snow machines for winter travel and because air travel between the two villages is relatively inexpensive ($80.00 one way in 1994). In a low-flying aircraft one can see enough of the terrain below to understand some of the dangers. The area close to Gwichyaa Zhee is called the Yukon Flats because it is flat. From the ground there are no naturally tall reference points to mark distance or obvious direction. Northern Athabascan men and women whom I know do not go anywhere unless they are themselves absolutely familiar with every aspect of the trails or rivers or are with someone whom they trust to have that knowledge (*yitinjyaah-chy'aa*, "she or he trusts or depends on him or her"). Those who know the river are adept at recognizing variations in the water: rocks, changes in the channels, obstacles that were not there before. Likewise, muskeg is very deceptive in its surface appearance. People can drown in something that looks like solid land. Winter travel can be a little easier because the trails are usually frozen and more easily marked, so one need only worry about the wolves. In the summer the wolves are a minor problem compared with the hordes of insects that consume anything with blood in it.

An elder, Myra Francis, told Gwichyaa Zhee schoolchildren about the time her uncle, Steven Peter, made an emergency trip from Vashraii K'oo to Gwichyaa Zhee in midwinter. She later learned that he arrived with blood-soaked feet that had been lacerated by the pressure of the webbing of his snowshoes. He had walked night and day to get there as soon as possible. Gwichyaa Zhee people donated food and medical supplies to be flown back to the starving people in Vashraii K'oo. Mrs. Francis ended her story with an injunction that she and other elders were trying to teach the youngsters survival skills so that they might avoid "getting stuck" as her Vashraii K'oo relations did. The following story was told by Myra Francis in Gwichyaa Zhee, and transcribed and translated by Mary Fields, in 1994:

Tr'iinin naii gooraatan oo'ok trał tee
Children all they teach them out brush among

nee-goorahaazhik ts'a' gwaraak'ik, geegwiichy'aa
they take them and they build fire things

t'igwii'in. Zhah haa chan zheh gwarahtsii
we do. Snow with also house we build

chan geegooraatan ji' gwik'iikwak gaageheendaii eenjit,
also we teach them if by that they will know that way

goodhaii nagaanaii ji'. Gwagaa chan duuyee
get stuck they happen if. Even though also never

gwik'it t'ogwagwa'in. Izhik gaagiindaii ji' goovoinyaa
that way to them. There they know if I want

gaa reh deegoohałiyaa enjit.
even though what should I do for them.

Every tale has at least two sides, and although this story is one of clearly demarcated heroism or dat'aii, the narration about this event as told by the man's wife is one that couches the valor of her husband's excursion in context with the number of times that he left her in isolation with their small children for weeks on end while he visited friends and relatives in Gwichyaa Zhee or elsewhere (Peter 1992). Athabascan children grow up knowing the strengths and weaknesses of their parents and the perils in which the occasional unpredictability of their behaviors leave them.

In summary, the foregoing has been a discussion of traditional Gwich'in concepts of sacred power or strength as derived from a root word, t'aii. The morpheme t'aii can be modified linguistically to reflect many subtle variations of power, including number, case, and applications. Vat'aii, for instance, refers to personal strength that seeks to concentrate on a core element of one's inner self. I have further described uses of vat'aii as seen in the ancient Gwich'in narrative of Ko'ehdan.

Athabascan men and women discuss and teach three ideals that can serve as a basis for judging the moral appropriateness of leaders and decisions but are countered by many opposing indications of indeterminacy. These ideals appear to be the blurred remains of Athabascan religious traditions that continue as symbols of mental, physical, and public strength that are evidenced in linguistic patterns, such as the root word t'aii. While the language is obsolescent, the patterns governing the behavior endure via other conduits of social behavior, such as surviving harsh weather. In this regard, women are expected to have the same kind of skill and knowledge about surviving in the harsh environment as men; however, Athabascan women have traditionally been portrayed as victims of violence from men. Public and personal strength are common denominators for all of the paradigms of Athabascan leadership or, for that matter, everyday life in Athabascan territory. An Athabascan leader is expected to demonstrate not only the strength of body (vat'aii) that has come to be expected but also that his or her public actions can be challenged if they do not conform both to common expectations of public merit and to what the leader has indicated is his or her vision for the people (dat'aii).

The Indeterminacies of Athabascan Leadership

Contemporary Northern Athabascan leadership is fraught with tension between the disunited traditional paradigms of the past and the problems of present-day economic processes, which are outside of the expectations of traditional Athabascan culture. The knowledge base that served to cohere Athabascan paradigms and narrative flow has been depleted, sidestepped, or eradicated. Today's Athabascan leaders follow models that are indeterminate in shape and scope. One of them is the warrior model for which shamanic powers were once expected. Another is the trader paradigm, a leadership position that emerges from the trading partner networks and which has been described previously in chapters 2 and 3. The trader system serves leaders in being aggressive when seeking economic ventures. The third paradigm, gwintsii veegoo'aii, invokes images of a visionary leader who responds to callings from sources beyond the immediate needs of him- or herself or the village. The last paradigm is the administrative model that is an outgrowth of colonialism. Athabascan leadership is rarely assumed to be the province of any single individual or any given agency, for there are many conflictual mainstream agencies making demands on leaders. Rather, individuals who know how to navigate the administrative tides of mainstream regulations do what they can as situations arise. American authorities and outside agencies are viewed with mixed habitual resentment and equally habitual hope for rescue.

The term *gwintsii veegoo'aii* is one of several that are translated into concepts of leadership in English. Most of the Northern Athabascan terms so translated incorporate a concept of rank. Another term, *kohk-waii*, is the word most often translated as "chief." A third term is *vigwid-dhin*, meaning "he or she is important, intelligent, or valuable." Its plural form, *kogwiddhin naii* could be used to refer to an entire tribal council. A fourth term is *gwoo'aa kit*, meaning "leader." Finally, *gwak'aahtii* means "guardian," and *t'ah'in* means "warrior." Each of these terms draws on traditional patterns of thought regarding all the factors in providing food, shelter, and protection to small groups of people in an extremely harsh climate with potentially hostile neighbors.

Northern Athabascan paradigms of leadership invest trust and dependency in transient displays of numinal power that come to and through individuals but are not necessarily fixed personal attributes of any single human being. Every leader must reaffirm his or her numinous abilities by demonstrations of personal strength (vat'aii) and public strength (dat'aii) and by meeting all reciprocal social obligations. In precolonial times the reciprocal obligations included relations with nature (moose, caribou, or sheep), human beings (the sharing network), and the spirit world, which gave leaders luck in finding wildlife. Today, with the contemporary influences of Christianity and secularism, the spiritual aspects of leadership have been undermined.

These Athabascan terms, like the language itself, are obsolescent; however, they are useful in understanding that traditional leadership responsibilities were encoded into several different areas of expertise. Itree and others suggested that there was a traditional hierarchy that ranked these notions of leadership with respect to each other. Theories about traditional ranks also shimmer in discussions about the matrilineal kinship system that once prevailed. While a system of logic that expects to categorize people hierarchically infiltrates ordinary Athabascan conversation, so, too, do counterbalancing behaviors leveling all people to independent individualists. Another tension exists between the symbols of warrior behavior and the system of behaviors nested in gwintsii veegoo'aii. The warrior model displays three key behaviors. The most dominant are public actions of strength (dat'aii), whereby leaders notify their constituents when they have achieved a significant success. However, the moral code implied in gwintsii veegoo'aii (described later) requires a certain amount of restraint in this area. Restraint, thus, is the second behavior used in warrior-style leadership. Restraint is shown as an economy of words spoken with force (talking loudly or actually shouting), rather than refraining from speaking at all. The third behavior of the warrior paradigm is taking responsibility for monitoring the activities of strangers. This is an age-old custom featured in many traditional tales, such as the Ko'ehdan legend mentioned earlier. When the starving Ko'ehdan arrived at a new village, the residents waited until their chief approved before they fed the collapsed man. Because I was an outsider, I witnessed this behavior several times. For instance, a month after Steve Ginnis took office in 1993 I witnessed him shouting at another graduate student in anthropology who was doing a study on hunting techniques. He wanted to know why she had not presented him with a proposal about her work. I stood there for a moment, waiting for my turn to be confronted, but something took his attention away from us. Both of us had submitted materials to the Tribal Council Office before we arrived at the village, trying our best to follow unclear guidelines of research ethics. I went to his office a few weeks later to give him some of my findings. He read everything carefully and had a few minor suggestions that I found useful for this final writing.

The attributes of the warrior paradigm must have been incorporated into a larger scope of Gwich'in Athabascan leadership, which includes the visionary model of gwintsii veegoo'aii, but gwintsii veegoo'aii has been reduced to habits of action that appear alternatively as humble, modest, spiritual, and ineffectual. The term *gwintsii veegoo'aii* refers to an uncommon person who is associated with both social moral good and qualities of the numinous. *Gwintsii* means "largess, bigness, much."

Veegoo'aii implies rank or state, either spiritual or material. Together the concepts refer to a person who bears great responsibilities. Gwintsii veegoo'aii is a paradigm of encoded moral behaviors that define leadership as being something beyond the individual. Like the Northern Athabascans' ideal of consensus, which depersonalizes events by the use of shifters to point toward transitional elements rather than any given individual or part of the sequence, so, too, does the paradigm of gwintsii veegoo'aii de-emphasize the individual and individual agency in the same way. By contrast, the warrior model emphasizes the personal attributes of the individual, as do the meanings invested in vat'aii (personal strength). These contradictory ideals of Athabascan leadership result in conflictual statements about the integrity of any given individual who makes decisions on behalf of Athabascan communities.

Athabascans locate power within the processes of their own minds but cherish an ideal that the best solutions reside in the force of collective thought. The ideal of consensus reminds each of them — or if consensus does not seem to be effective in any given moment, they will remind each other — that they should act as one and not as stellar heroes. Leaders are usually careful to couch their conversation in Athabascan-style humility, which mixes forceful behavior with expectations that others will recognize their importance without explanation. Many people speak of Northern Athabascan chiefs prior to the mid-1960s (in other words, prior to statehood and the ensuing changes in governmental policies toward Alaska Natives). According to such memories, earlier chiefs were held in awe, their autocratic decisions obeyed without hesitation. People can identify by name and action a number of such men. When it becomes necessary to take some control over a situation, most find ways to take responsibility without taking overt control over other people's actions. The decentralized official actions surrounding the Langfield family eviction exemplify the Athabascan deployment of power in this sense. For instance, the police chief did not shoot the dogs but did take responsibility for the action. The tribal chief offered free transportation out of Gwichyaa Zhee but did not order the family to leave. The city manager found ways to reimburse them for the loss of the dogs, and he, too, avoided telling them to leave town. No one declared him- or herself to be in charge, but the family's departure was nonetheless expeditious and inevitable. Individual contests for control in Athabascan territory occur incessantly, as they do elsewhere, but in some circumstances, when public expressions of power transpire, no single Athabascan ever seems to be at the helm.

Northern Athabascans have many examples of leadership behavior in history. Chief Peter, born in 1882 in the T'eedriinjik River area near Vashraii K'oo, is described in tribal minutes as a good chief characterized as both a good medicine man and a man devoted to the concept of sharing his harvest with those of his sharing network. In other words, he displayed evidence of being both powerful in the warrior style and responsible in the gwintsii veegoo'aii style. The language of the following statement about Chief Peter also displays the linguistic restraint used to describe chiefs: "He was chief on the title of moose, caribou and sheep and muzzleloading gun. He got those and served the people. He was not the only one [who] had a muzzleloader, but he always killed some animals. He was a good luck man for meat and always split it with the people. He always made service for the people" (Campisi 1991:27).

Self-aggrandizement is criticized by Athabascan people. For example, Velma Wallis, the author of *Two Old Women*, then in her early thirties, worked hard to prove her modesty after her book was published and immediately sold out. In order to appease the people of Gwichyaa Zhee she talked to many of the elders both before and after publication in order to inform them of her book, as well as to seek validation of the version she presented. She gave two public readings, donated $1,000 to the university library in Gwichyaa Zhee, volunteered many hours of her time at the public radio station, and vowed repeatedly that she was still unchanged, still the Velma that they had always known. Interest in censoring her abated a month or two after the second reading and after all of her gestures of modesty had been observed. Only the elders can escape overt criticism. That which an elder might say or do is rendered difficult for a younger person to critique. For instance, a highly respected Gwich'in elder from Vuntut in a speech to an international Athabascan audience referred to the sense of loss that she considered has been experienced by Northern Athabascans: "People have been talking about the land and the caribou since I was young. And yet it is like we are lost, lost somewhere. That's how it seems to me" (Niintsyaa Gwich'in, 1989). It is worth noting that she, the acknowledged elder, did not attempt to pinpoint a cause or a beginning point to this condition. Sarah James, mentioned earlier, a younger, more politically active Gwich'in woman, took that step. At the same Gwich'in gathering, Sarah James of Vashraii K'oo said, "A lot of times I think about Indian people, what they had to go through, through that 'Great Change' that was forced on them. I remember some part of it in a story." This is a phrase that James has used in other public speeches. James, lacking the authority of being an elder, first invoked the name of her grandmother, Sarah Tritt, and told the audience about the kind of education she got from her parents and her grandmother. Even with that she, in a style similar to the Vuntut elder's, qualified her phrase "the Great Change" by saying it came from a story. All of this reflects the ideals and trials imbedded within consensus and gwintsii veegoo'aii. Northern Athabascans maintain a culture holding that no one individual has authority over another. In order to make any meaningful statement to the outside world James devised ways to indicate that others had permitted her to speak as she does. If she failed to do so, or if she were to say something that does not satisfy any one of her people, she would face the tribulations that Velma Wallis did and later overcame. To be Gwich'in means walking a tightrope supported by assumptions of traditional knowledge, the glosses and traps of consensus, and the conflictual codes of humility attributed to gwintsii vee-goo'aii.

Traditional tales speak of the chiefs, such as Chief Peter, as making frequent use of medicine power. Although many people spoke to me about medicine power and described it to a certain extent, I never saw it in use. What I did see were several instances of charismatic authority that sometimes seemed as if they were magical. For instance, one of the chiefs in Vashraii K'oo came four days late to a conference in his village. There were already nearly a dozen other Native leaders in the conference room who had established their presence during the previous few days. Gideon James arrived shortly after lunch had been served. As soon as he arrived, two or three of the Northern Athabascan leaders present escorted him around the room to meet some of the invited guests. Although James is a short man, he seemed to sweep around the room with such innate authority that he seemed tall, with royal robes swirling around him. None of the other conference participants, including the state senator, who is a very charismatic Koyukon Athabascan woman, attracted that much stopping power. Part of it had to do with the reason for his absence, which he described in a brief speech in which he outlined the parameters of a long court battle in which the Venetie Tribal Government (IRA) has been embroiled for many years. Warrior chiefs may have used medicine power at one time to enforce their words, but James seemed to use the charismatic charm that he was born with or had cultivated to captivate the, by this time, exhausted audience. Everyone held quiet for this brief talk even after he shifted to more personal and mundane matters.

U.S. Indian history also shapes Northern Athabascan leaders. James's audience appeal may have been enhanced by the force of the history that led to the formation of the Venetie Tribal Government (IRA) and its option out of ANCSA. By contrast, both Alexander and Ginnis of Gwichyaa Zhee are chiefs in ANCSA villages with traditional Indian Reorganization Act councils, meaning that they must weigh all decisions with respect to the legal issues that constrain them under the Alaska Native Claims Settlement Act of 1971, which are often in opposition to the options available to domestic dependent nations under federal law. Their counterpart in that respect is Gideon James of Vashraii K'oo, who has led the Venetie Tribal Government (IRA) through a series of legal battles to gain Indian Country status with the federal government in an attempt to further federal recognition of their sovereign status. In essence ANCSA places the State of Alaska in an ambiguous role vis-à-vis the nation-to-nation status between Alaska Natives and the U.S. federal government, which leads the state government to contest any authority that the tribal governments have in situations in which the state's authority is threatened, such as in levying taxes. The Venetie Tribal Government (IRA) leaders shaped their discourse around the litigious framework of U.S. federal Indian law and seek political alliances to emphasize their sovereign status because they opted out of ANCSA in 1973. In this regard they have invested in a reciprocal relationship with environmentalists who are interested in preserving the Arctic National Wildlife Refuge from development. As Maybury-Lewis puts it, indigenous peoples are "regularly accused of 'standing in the way of development'" (1997:31, 145), an accusation that the Venetie Tribal Government (IRA) addresses by joining forces with international entities that deliberately stand in the way of development. ANCSA-dominated chiefs, Alexander and Ginnis, on the other hand, work with theories of economic investment and corporate statutes.

In the weeks before the 1993 village election, just when I was starting fieldwork and the experience of writing assiduous field notes still governed my life, Ginnis was just as busy as I was in moving quietly around the village, talking to people about his bid for election. We stood out because we were both walkers at a time when most people used motorized vehicles. We spoke to each other guardedly when we crossed paths, me, the anthropologist, him, the future chief. Ginnis spoke to me about his hopes for the potential of a Compact agreement with the Bureau of Indian Affairs whereby the funding designated for Gwichyaa Zhee by the federal government would be granted directly to the tribal council, rather than going through Tanana Chiefs Conference. Ginnis spoke his language with apparent ease, as he did English. His alcoholism is public knowledge, yet I never saw him drunk. He made sure he attended every significant event in Gwichyaa Zhee that might have an impact on the future, and he was always challenging those who might do something to harm his community. At statewide conventions he was one of the half dozen people who routinely stood up at the microphones with suggestions to reword almost any key proposition, suggestions that were phrased in the highest of "Robert's Rules of Order" formality. Ginnis was dubbed the "Potlatch Chief" in contrast to his predecessor, who was considered a warrior-style chief. Whenever Ginnis attended statewide or national Native meetings he presented himself as a traditional chief by wearing his handmade, fringed, beaded jacket.

Ginnis's predecessor and election opponent Alexander favored working toward total economic independence through local initiatives rather than maintaining dependence on federal funding. Alexander was voted out of office in 1993 in a runoff election in which 111 people voted. Ginnis got 58 votes, Alexander got 29, and my landlord, Earl Cadzow, got 19. Ginnis made door-to-door campaign stops, and Alexander and Cadzow did not. Alexander cofounded the Council of Athabascan Tribal Governments and had been working for it for the past decade. The by-laws of CATG require that only the elected chiefs of each village have any voting authority in its actions, so Ginnis, perforce, replaced Alexander at CATG as well as in the tribal government of Gwichyaa Zhee. As it happened, Ginnis was chief of Gwichyaa Zhee when CATG achieved one of the largest coups overturning economic hegemony between Northern Athabascans and outside enterprises in 1995 through the acquisition of the village clinic.

One of the primary impacts of mainstream hegemony regarding Northern Athabascans, as in most Native American communities, is the need for leaders who administer rather than control power. The history of Northern Athabascans has entailed multiple forms of negotiated relationships starting with the fur traders of Canada and culminating with the present situation of global friction among extractive models, moral reform (environmentalists and spiritual revivalism), and poverty. The economic and social complexities of these forces in Northern Athabascan society display an asynchronous or warped reaction to the larger movements of international tensions. For example, the removal of over 1,000 troops from Gwichyaa Zhee in the mid-1980s collapsed an artificially swollen population from over 2,000 people to less than one-half that size. Despite the sudden change, there was no appreciable change in the local economy: I did not find vacant houses or apartment complexes, and there were no empty offices or stores. No one spoke of job loss or material deprivations. The Cold War had ended, and the economic reaction in Gwichyaa Zhee was simply a loss of 1,000 bodies from the village.

The larger society and its economic pressures have required mediators, people who can communicate with both insiders and outsiders. There is no standard model for success in this area. Children who speak English without an appreciable accent are brought into exchanges in order to help parents check into hotels, order food, purchase objects in stores, or translate, even though all parties may speak English. The best mediators are adults (Athabascan or non-Athabascan) who are literate, articulate, versed in office technology, and understand how to manipulate indifference, ignorance, and fear of Native people in bureaucratic agencies. Patricia Stanley of CATG is one of the most successful such mediators. Stanley (a white woman) has combined two invasive, mutually transparent cultural signs. One of them is that of the administrative secretary, which incorporates submissive body language, verbal charm, technical proficiency, and a constant awareness of having an inferior status in a bureaucratic system. The other is that of the gwintsii veegoo'aii paradigm, which calls for overt mannerisms of humility combined with determination to run a system without formal or public approval to do so. In many respects the American secretary enacts the behaviors encoded in Northern Athabascans' gwintsii veegoo'aii model. One of Stanley's objectives is to maintain constant communication between herself and all of the chiefs with whom she works. This is an ideal favored by many of the Northern Athabascans chiefs whom I interviewed or heard from in other circumstances.

Contemporary Athabascan leaders try to be competent in their usage of traditional signs, paying particular attention to the moral imperatives of Athabascan traditions. Athabascan leaders of the late 20th century are pulled in three directions. First, they are asked to be mediators who can communicate effectively with both their own constituents and outsiders. Second, they seek economic development solutions to create greater independence from welfare. Third, most participate in or encourage healing efforts for both humans and the environment. Many leaders express awareness of the disparity between Athabascan ethics and mainstream practices.

In summary, the successful contemporary Athabascan leaders make use of each of the paradigms available to them: they enjoin blurred acts of cohesion that some of them call consensus; they act out gwintsii veegoo'aii strategies; they enact fragments of traditional codes of warrior behavior, such as harangues testifying to the purity of their individual visions and actions; and they reproduce elements of mainstream models of bureaucracy. They also make use of the educational materials available to them, particularly when it comes to their environment. Many of them worry about the health hazards that have been dumped or left behind in their region, a dilemma in many other parts of the world. Others worry about the hunting resources that they continue to rely on for a certain percentage of their annual diets. Some feel compromised by their incomplete understanding of how others use this information. This dilemma surfaced several times at the "People, Science, and Caribou" Conference held in Vashraii K'oo in 1993, sponsored by CATG.

Women, such as Patricia Stanley, often serve in leadership positions in Athabascan territory. While I lived in Gwichyaa Zhee, they elected a woman mayor, and one woman ran for the office of chief but lost. Four of the several former women chiefs and city managers of Gwichyaa Zhee are still active in less exalted but nonetheless public positions. Women, more often then men, are employed in full-time administrative jobs, perhaps because they tend to have better mainstream educations than their male counterparts do. A better education usually means greater fluency in English and more technical proficiency in office equipment. In terms of promoting ethnic divisiveness, Athabascan women tend to be as vocal in expressing anger about and toward outsiders as are men.

To be an Athabascan leader requires great sacrifices in time and pride. Nonetheless, successful Athabascan leadership takes strength from each of the paradigms and theories named previously. Some of the models issue from the remnants of Athabascan religious traditions no longer taught with conscientious effort, leading to extremely varied uses of politeness codes, mystic experiences, and moral criticisms. Added to this is a widespread incompetence in bureaucratic skills, such as being able to read or write English well enough to administer a grant or apply for another. Behaviors such as depression or alcoholism simply add to the confusion. There are not very many Athabascans who can avoid the latter and implement the former. Those who do so are prized. The net effect is that Athabascan leaders come and go, but individual projects succeed through dint of communal action and need.

5 Women: *She Who Is Ravished*

In the previous chapters I have introduced Athabascan history in northern Alaska, as well as their local economy in the late 20th century and processes of Athabascan leadership. This chapter portrays the mental environment of Athabascan women as mothers, the behavior of daughters in the absence of their mothers, roles of Athabascan women in social cohesion and disruption, and Athabascan women as activists. This chapter thus brings together many of the topics discussed in previous chapters but reframes the inquiry through the practices of individual women's responses to raising children in Gwich'in when faced with the ever present dangers of contemporary life: alcoholism, drug addiction, rape, child abuse, and poverty. In other words, their lives follow patterns familiar to women throughout Native America.

While I was in Gwich'in, I spoke with many women about themselves. One of those women is Shreevyaa (a pseudonym) of Gwichyaa Zhee, a woman who represents all of these factors in one way or another, even though she is not a mother herself. She was one of the eight or nine individuals in Gwich'in territory who designated themselves as my watchdogs — people who kept track of my general activities and my progress in research. Shreevyaa was one of the most aggressive in this respect. She would come to my cabin or stop me in the street whenever she saw me to challenge me with direct, often personal, questions.

"Where have you been?" (Her voice was strident as it usually was.) I cringed inwardly and made some inane comment in reply. I had a few pages of my writing for her to review and had brought copies to "Native Village," as they

called the Tribal Council Office. "Talk to me," she commanded, pointing to her office. She spent the next hour or more talking to me, informing me of her theories about local education and politics.

Shreevyaa had held many Gwich'in leadership positions, including president of the Gwichyaa Zhee Alaska Native Claims Settlement Act (ANCSA) village corporation, Tribal Council member, member of the Yukon Flats School Board, and executive administrator for the Youth Survivors organization. She was one of the most powerful leaders in Gwichyaa Zhee. She terrified me by her direct, openly critical oversight of me as an anthropologist. In her forties in 1993, she exhibited a driving force for what she wanted to see changed in Athabascan society. She also tried to reinstate some of the traditional Athabascan cultural patterns, such as environmental survival techniques, community awareness and participation in every new project, and use of consensus. The rapport she had with Athabascan youths was clearly affectionate and trusting. She liked children, and I often saw her with one or more sons or daughters of other people. In the details of her approach and in terms of what she had accomplished in her various positions of leadership, she had as many supporters as she had detractors. She was not popular enough with other Athabascan women to be considered a role model, yet her very lack of popularity was a paramount aspect of an Athabascan leadership style that both creates Athabascan solidarity and isolates Athabascans. Despite these polarities in demeanor, Athabascan women like Shreevyaa of Gwichyaa Zhee are actively striving, with tenable success, to make social change.

Northern Athabascan women, both of the past and in the present, play significant roles in their history, economies, decision making and leadership, and, perhaps more than anything else, shaping methods of social control. In oral histories, Athabascan women factor into oral traditions as strong, solitary women who are capable of surviving on their own in harsh conditions. Women's stories (past or present) are part of the living traditions of Athabascan women and serve as models by which they form self-images. Contemporary Gwich'in novelist Velma Wallis has written two novels based on traditional stories about women, testifying to the present viability of their moral codes in Athabascan life. I discuss the first of these novels in greater depth later in this chapter. She wrote both of them through frequent consultation with elders in Athabascan communities. Athabascan women are also active in writing their own histories in the form of autobiographies.

In chapter 3, I describe the influences of Athabascan women on the local economy. In this respect, women are involved in both informal and formal economic sectors. Their informal economic activities include such legal projects as skin sewing and other handicrafts, as well as outright illegal activities, such as bootlegging, or sanctioned, but disapproved of, things, such as bookmaking. As discussed in chapter 3, the traditional sharing networks form a social core of cohesion by enforcing more or less continual dispersal of material goods throughout the community. Athabascan women are situated in positions of control in such networks. For instance, the most meaning-filled part of a moose carcass is its head, and hunters bring that part to the most important woman in the individual sharing networks as a symbol of respect to that woman.

In chapter 3, I describe in some detail the integrative force of alcoholism, gambling, and drug usage that binds Athabascans to a global addictive economy, a bondage from which they are trying to escape in word, if not yet in deed. One indication of the success of their efforts is that individual sobriety efforts have become instituted as social capital, starting with the rise of a statewide sobriety movement in the 1980s. Besides the traditional work of their domestic circles, women and men alike have inaugurated incipient systemic changes to counteract the negative effects of addictions. One of the first public events I attended at

Gwichyaa Zhee was a youth-oriented conference on drugs and alcohol, initiated by Shreevyaa.

In chapter 4, I discuss the role of the nearly silent consensual evictions, which often include collective violence. These events range in overall effect from spreading rumors to open gunfire. Because evictions are a central trope of social solidarity in Gwich'in territory as well as other parts of Alaska, in this chapter I discuss women's involvement in the exclusionary and inclusionary processes that initiate the evictions. One of the conclusions I draw from this analysis is that like the processes of sharing networks and the processes of consensus, caring for children is expected to be a shared responsibility in extended families and communities of social intimates. This form of child care and training, ironically, exacerbates one of the cultural contradictions among Athabascans, which is that they become socially and emotionally independent of others while at the same time weaving intricate fabrics of social interdependence within their society. In the following pages I discuss several family situations that illustrate that the Athabascan approach toward social healing violates their ethos of individualism while at the same time creating new barricades in social isolationism.

In addition, these activities border on nationalism without yet incorporating the institutions of a nationalist movement. In my numerous discussions and interviews with Gwich'in women I realized that the Gwich'in processes of social solidarity and expressions of nationalism are gendered. Women's methods differ markedly from more conventionalized (in mainstream perspectives) political efforts of Athabascan men. Athabascan male political leaders generally pursue the political courses already in place in the United States for American Indians, while the Athabascan women leaders of Alaska generally teach the behaviors that signal an Athabascan model of cultural survival beginning with birth and continuing through old age, behaviors that denounce otherness, if not yet expounding on Athabascan identity as an operable sign. Like most such models, the lived expression of them is dependent on the life experiences and physical parameters hampering or enhancing the mental ideals of the individual. These mental codes frame the goals of Athabascan social integrity as independent, emotionally aloof, and yet dependent on family and a community for approval. The tension between these poles of dependency is rendered all the more difficult because of cultural expectations of stoicism.

Native North American Women's Studies

What do Native American women want to know about themselves and each other? There is a burgeoning body of autobiographies, biographies, and theoretical analyses about Native American women throughout the continent. Scholars in Native American women's studies, for instance, often position their work either in debate with mainstream anthropologists or as paradigms of their own cultural milieu, and they thereby often create images of cultural continuity that are unrealistically seamless. Native American scholars such as Gretchen M. Battaille (1991) and Rayna Green (1983) have provided annotated bibliographies of work by and about Native American women. Green (1983:4–8) describes the historical changes in attitudes or issues surrounding Native American women during the 20th century, beginning with the 1930s focus on individuals, the 1940s interest in psychoanalysis, and the 1950s studies in family structure and maternal behavior. Feminist approaches to Native American issues began in the 1960s and continued through the 1970s (Green 1983:7–8). Battaille and Sands (1984) have compiled autobiographies of Native American women, commenting on the marginalized status of such work in literary canons. Unmindful of the marginality, some Native American writers have encouraged indigenist literatures, terming such publications a genre in bilingual writing (Brant 1994:x–xi). Weaver balances such euphoria by stating that "such a de-

velopment [writing in indigenous languages] is, at best, temporally remote and, at worst, highly unlikely" (1997:174n61). A glance at the publishers of some of the books by Native American women is testimony
enough to Weaver's caution. *Half-Breed*, the autobiography of Maria
Campbell (1973), published by a number of small presses, including
the Saturday Review Press of New York, exemplifies publishers' simulta-
neous doubt about the value of Native American women's stories in tension with the ongoing demand from readers for them. Campbell reveals
a life tormented by self-doubt, alcohol, and living on the fringes in Canada. She also describes how as a half-breed she was a pariah in both
white and Indian communities. Everything she wrote mirrors similar
events or conditions about which Northern Athabascan women discuss,
criticize, and agonize.

A vivid example of indigenous women exploring their own realities is
Daughters of Abya Yala: Native American Women Regaining Control, published
in 1992 by Book Publishing Company of Summertown, Tennessee. This
small text, compiled and written by Wara Alderete, Gina Pacaldo, Xihuanel Huerta, and Lucilene Whitesell, includes works by indigenous
women of South America, Mesoamerica, and North America. In this text
Native American women address the starkness of sexual abuse and
other forms of violence that have raked through indigenous lives. The
book was created as part of a collaboration within the International
Council of Indigenous Women that met in Samiland, Norway, in 1990.
Although not proposing a theoretical or analytical structure, *Daughters of
Abya Yala* gives evidentiary force to the central thesis of my study, which
is that Athabascan women are actively struggling to find new models of
behavior to counteract the ravages of alcoholism and other addictions.

Native American anthropologists have begun to work in the area of
indigenous women's issues. For instance, anthropologist Beatrice Medicine, who is herself Sioux, has written a few works about the multiple
hegemonies encountered by Native American women (1978, 1983). In a

chapter in *The Hidden Half: Studies of Plains Indian Women*, she counters a stereotype of Indian women as docile beasts of burden with her research on Plains Indian warrior women, women who took their place in their traditional societies in roles that were culturally accepted and accorded them power and prestige (1983:267–268). Medicine's work comes to us from the lonely position of being a Native pioneer in a field dominated by white academia in which she is marginalized even by other women anthropologists. Nancy Parezo, editor of *Hidden Scholars: Women Anthropologists and the Native American Southwest* (1993), for instance, does not mention Medicine or any other Native American anthropologists who work in the Southwest, such as Clara Sue Kidwell (Chippewa-Choctaw). The Native Americans who are included are simply referred to as linguistic collaborators whose efforts in language should be encouraged.

Medicine collaborated as editor with Patricia Albers on *The Hidden Half* (Albers and Medicine 1983). Albers's contribution to that book is "Sioux Women in Transition: A Study of Their Changing Status in a Domestic and Capitalist Sector of Production" (1983). As the title suggests, Albers has taken a Marxist approach to the study of Native American women in which she correlates a rise in Lakota women's community authority and influence with an increase in their economic productivity (1983:217). Albers points out one of the dilemmas of Lakota men, which relates to the problems of some Alaska Native men in the 20th century, which is that Lakota men's social influence is not highly valued "because it was ultimately granted or denied through the federal government in compliance with wider corporate interests" (1983:219). Alaska Native men have not been so highly dominated by the federal government, although many Athabascan men will testify to their anger at the many, and increasing, governmental constraints that are placed on Native men's activities in Alaska.

Caroline James (1996) describes the roles of women and men of the Nez Perce. James points out that Nez Perce women have been forced to

become more independent because of an increase in single-parent (usually the mother) households, which cause the women to act more force-
fully not only in the home but in the community (1996:216). James
found that Nez Perce men are considered to be undermined by the lack
of jobs available to them (something that is also true in Athabascan
communities, where women tend to hold more jobs than men do).
James cites one woman as follows: "I think many of the men are not
able to find a job. It's not because they are not capable of finding a job,
[but] because of the society in the way it was . . . trying to take over the
land . . . and make the European culture the dominant force. They
would deliberately undermine the men" (1996:217–218). The Nez Perce
women also discussed the relationship between mainstream domination and alcoholism. Both Albers and James have illustrated by style and
content a point about studying women in any Native community:
women often identify and discuss their economic and political efforts in
connection with the ways that their men are undermined by mainstream
enterprises and governmental agencies, as well as alcoholism.

Some non-Native authors, for example, Marion E. Gridley (1974)
and Jane Katz (1995), have produced collections of Native American
women's autobiographies. Gridley's collection includes stories of some
of the more notable Native women in history, such as Pocahontas, Sa-
cajawea, the Tallchief sisters, and one woman from Alaska — Elaine
Abraham Ramos, a Tlingit from Yakutat (1974:162–168). Katz includes
a story by and about Sarah James of Vashraii K'oo (1995:221–229). Still
other scholars, like Cherokee writer Jace Weaver, have edited works
written by Native American peoples. Weaver (1996), in a text addressing
Native American concerns for the environment, taken from a 1995
North American Native Workshop on Environmental Justice, includes a
short article by Norma Kassi (1996) of Vuntut, Canada. Kassi is a well-
known Gwich'in political activist in the Canadian Yukon. Some Native
American women leaders have also had their stories written with the

help of professional writers. Wilma Mankiller's 1993 autobiography was written by Mankiller and Michael Wallis. Mankiller was elected chief of the Cherokee in 1985. In the book they include the noteworthy federal legislation and policies that have affected the Cherokee and other tribes during Mankiller's lifetime, such as the 1953 "termination policy" that affected over 100 tribes in the United States.

For those researchers who engage in the polemics of anthropological debate, the issues are situated in two much larger and contested arenas: one of rhetoric on changes in culture and the other of the stylistics of writing stories of women who are seen as materializations of idealized Native communities. Nancy Shoemaker (1995) breaks her anthology of Native American women studies into two slightly different areas: (1) the status of women versus men and (2) the effects of colonialism on Native American communities and women. Shoemaker points out one of the most common European observations about Native Americans during the early colonial period, that "the freedom allowed women and children" was antithetical to the strict patriarchal control that was expected in the families of the colonists (1995:7). Comments such as this are reminders that cultural lenses can work for and against the anthropologist. While the comment is about freedom, we cannot know what parameters for freedom were in effect at the moment or why it would seem so unusual to the colonists. In any event, Athabascan women of this century might seem equally, if not more, free to the same observers. In general, Shoemaker posits, the effects of colonialism influenced material culture.

Archaeologists have also proposed new insights about Native American women. Cheryl Claassen and Rosemary A. Joyce (1997) have brought together a number of essays about prehistoric women in Mesoamerica and North America. In general, Joyce and Claassen suggest that the authors in this anthology "contribute to a destabilizing effect of the burgeoning literature on the archaeology of gender and of women"

(1997:8). Using archaeological records, they have postulated about women as hunters and warriors, as well as women's menstrual huts. Using symbolic constructions in weavings and gendered goods (pottery) these authors have suggested theories about early women's social prestige and sexual orientation. Brumbach and Jarvenpa (1997) have written about Chipewyan Athabascan women as hunters, thus challenging many theories that men are the hunters and women are the gatherers and keepers of the home. They include interviews with contemporary Athabascan women from a small Chipewyan community, as well as historical reviews of census records beginning in 1838. They conclude that women hunt closer to home than men do and concentrate on smaller animals, "although the two patterns overlap considerably" (1997:29). These patterns conform to stories about Athabascan women's and men's hunting patterns prior to the 20th century. Nowadays, the Athabascan women who hunt usually do so in partnership with men.

Native American women writers have addressed women's issues in an effort to find, as Inés Talamantez puts it, "a new schemata, one that forces us from the constraints of a Western patriarchal paradigm of control, one that takes us beyond victim status and blame" (1995:389). In her essay "Seeing Red: American Indian Women Speaking about their Religious and Political Perspectives" (1995), Talamantez presents a break from other academic traditions by analyzing the lives of five women (including herself) through a combination of their own voices and her experiences of them. The words of each of the women, including those of Talamantez, are drawn from widely different ideological, religious, and political viewpoints, which are united first by the consistency of Talamantez's theme of models of social change through religious beliefs and second by her emphasis on religion and the way that religious beliefs ground the lifeways of each woman. Talamantez suggests that the ritual patterning of religious traditions can be seen in many Native American efforts to sustain indigenous people of today.

Religion, or their traditions regarding the numinous, is a dominant theme among Athabascan people, despite the many forms it presently takes. Because of colonial missionization, Athabascan religious traditions have been fragmented, resulting in ambiguous attitudes and applications. Nonetheless, religious models of one sort or another impelled the solution patterns taught to a child of one alcoholic mother (discussed later in this chapter) whose family was invested in both Christian and traditional religious theories. Whatever the source, whether it be social models and solutions of other Athabascans, the advice of Native elders, or the proselytizing of missionaries, many Athabascan seek some form of spiritual relief to lessen their stresses.

Some do not seek religious counseling but, rather, follow patterned behavior that resonates with Athabascan traditional customs. Like the Isánáklésh Gotal (female initiation ceremony) of the Apache described by Talamantez (1995:410–417), the Athabascan tradition of puberty seclusion was intended for women in their adolescence to define the moment when a woman achieves adult status. Some Athabascan families continue to encourage and sometimes achieve traditional puberty isolation for their daughters, but there is no record of a related ceremony of the magnitude celebrated by the Apache. I suggest that because of the harsh environment, waiting 10 or 15 years for a child to mature is and was too long for security reasons and that Athabascans have learned to mark maturity beginning with toddlers. The case studies I have included in this chapter are suggestive of such a pattern of early training in survival.

Mainstream feminist studies have been useful in framing and reframing some of the key areas of analysis regarding issues in gender negotiations. Marilyn Waring (1988) points out the invisibility of the work that women do in many areas of social and familial life. Waring's text resonates with the complexity of processes that devalue women's contributions in Athabascan communities when viewed through criteria for standard U.S. business practices. In 1971 Sherry B. Ortner proposed a stratigraphic plan for studying women's social positions as inferior to those of men throughout the world (see 1996). She has since rescinded some of this early theory, particularly the first flat assertion of universal female subordination, a statement that many Athabascan women might dispute. Nonetheless, I found her initial broad sketch of potential gender hegemony useful as a starting point to study elements of Athabascan women's society that problematize their lives. Ortner's three levels of analysis are (1) women are symbolically subordinated to second-class status in all societies, (2) symbols of womanhood vary from culture to culture, and (3) there are many dichotomies between cultural ideals about women and women's actual experiences (1996:22). Using these propositions to contemplate women's lives for late-20th-century Athabascans both reveals greater complexities at every level and helps organize some of the data about Athabascan patterns of social pathology and healing, recognizing that these terms are overburdened with theories that come from a number of disciplines within mainstream society. The Athabascans use some of the terminology involved in discussions about healing, but they have not yet compiled their own compendium of theories about what constitutes healing or pathology.

With respect to the first "universal fact," as Ortner puts it, of women's global symbolic second-rate status, there is indirect evidence that Athabascan women were considered to be subordinate to men in traditional times in terms of decision making regarding group movements through their seasonal rounds. In this respect, the oral traditions represent a conflictual view of whether women were considered to be full members of community councils. In the contemporary era, there are no behavioral suggestions that Athabascan women consider themselves anything other than individuals, variegated in their responses, such as being affectionate, contemptuous, impatient, proud of men or themselves, supplicating when in need of help, or romantically patronizing toward Athabascan men in the 20th century. Nonetheless, there were a few Athabascan women who were rumored to be dominated and physically abused by the significant men in their households, but physical abuse cannot be taken as a statement of a generalized second-class status, and the instances of such abuse in Gwichyaa Zhee are not broad based enough to be considered indicative of a social trend.

I was aware of one battered woman whom I call Yaajat (a pseudonym) who was known to be abused frequently. A small woman (no more than 90 pounds), Yaajat was the mother of four children at the age of 23. I thought when I first arrived in Gwichyaa Zhee that Yaajat's otherwise chiseled features were marred with a birth defect. The large area of purpled skin around her left temple and eye area was there for several weeks, and I was surprised to notice it was gone about three months later. I was told that her boyfriend beat her and that she often had bloodied clothes and black eyes. A few weeks before I left Gwichyaa Zhee in 1995 I saw Yaajat riding a bicycle with an infant on her back and herding her three other children on bicycles around her. As was usual for her, she kept her eyes averted from me. Unlike most Athabascan mothers, she did not shout instructions at her children as they proceeded down the road.

Yaajat was one of the dozen women about whom I heard rumors of physical abuse by their spouses or significant male companions. By contrast, I also heard one case of a man who was chased around the outside of his house by his angry, knife-wielding wife, and there were many situations in which the abuse was mutual and mostly verbal. When people (usually women) told me about such beatings, they spoke with a lack of emphasis, as if it were a predictable, albeit perturbing, aspect of life. Lack of tonal or volume emphasis typifies some Athabascan speech acts, and some Athabascans prefer to use that style for all of their speaking habits. Others incorporate shouting and wide tonal ranges frequently. Thus, speech patterns did not provide a consistent clue toward Athabascan attitudes about physical abuse.

Athabascan women are frequently just as physically strong as an average urban man and seem to have no model of behavior that expects men to offer to serve as their burden carriers. It was the absence of this mainstream urban system of creating and providing porters through specific politeness codes that I recognized a significant difference in the range of performative models of Athabascans. Neither Athabascan men nor Athabascan women expect to carry anyone else's burdens unless that person has the social authority to ask them to do so. Athabascan matrons, for instance, ask or order others (usually children and adolescents) to carry objects for them.

Others who oversaw my progress during my fieldwork included the two successive first chiefs of Gwichyaa Zhee, Clarence Alexander and Steve Ginnis; the executive administrator for the Gwichyaa Zhee Tribal Council, Barry Wallis, and his sister, Linda Wallis Wells; the 1993 mayor of Gwichyaa Zhee, Donald Peter; Itree (or Marilyn Savage), who was a City Council member, a Tribal Council member, and member of the ANCSA corporation Board of Directors; one of the chiefs of the Venetie Tribal Government (IRA), Gideon James; and his sister, Sarah James, spokesperson for the Athabascan Steering Committee. There were many others in Vashraii K'oo and Gwichyaa Zhee who followed my progress as I bored them with numerous copies of my initial drafts of this study. All of this placed me at the lower end in a position where I was occasionally asked to perform small tasks by near strangers (both men and women) and pointedly not helped (until I was there about ten months) when it was obvious I needed assistance.

Ortner's other two suggestions for systematic study of women's lives have proven more fruitful for inquiry of both traditional and contemporary patterns of gender negotiations. Ortner's second point (signs of womanhood) reveals many aspects of what Athabascan women expect of themselves. Physical strength is a dominant theme, as is emotional distancing from spouses and children. The latter is more or less counterbalanced by expectations of asserting social control through motherhood and age. Social independence is taught through rituals and is the way many Athabascan families organize the lives of their children. The routines not only save lives but teach toddlers proactive measures of independence from their mothers (see the later section regarding daughters raised in the absence of their mothers). Finally, Athabascan physical ideals are influenced by Western stereotypes in terms other than beauty — but, rather, in conventions of body measurement. The following example illustrates a multifarious difference in Athabascan attitudes toward body in contrast to those of the American mainstream:

> One morning near Christmas 1994 I waited for a flight out of Gwichyaa Zhee. It happened that I was the first passenger to arrive. A seasoned bush plane traveler by this time, I marched in, took a seat, and waited until the clerk noticed me. At his request for my weight I called across the room "140" without a qualm. Another woman came in and at the appropriate moment told the clerk that she, too, weighed 140 pounds. I looked up. Thin. Her snow pants hung loosely around her waist. She probably added all of her clothes and her handbag into the total. A few minutes later another woman came in who also said that she weighed 140 pounds — a very substantial 140 pounds. I buried my head in my book.

Lying about weight can be an act of vanity, but 140 pounds hardly fits within mainstream standards of feminine beauty. In this case, the weight is a compromise among vanity, safety, and political caution. For more than a century the Athabascans have been controlled by doctors, missionaries, police, and public administrators who have taken land, their children, and themselves away from their homes for reasons as arbitrary as weight gain or loss. The political ramifications of weight are not great, but they do exist for Athabascans. For instance, Athabascan women during the 1990s have been required to give birth in Fairbanks or Anchorage rather than in their own villages, as was common until two decades ago. Based on concerns expressed about complications during birth, all women receiving health care through the Indian Health Service are now housed in Fairbanks for the last eight weeks of pregnancy, often without the benefit of extended family member support. Spouses or other family members can be housed with them during this period at the family's expense. Women with medical conditions (such as obesity or underweight) may be removed for a longer period of time. This regulation coincides with a national increase in medical malpractice suits resulting in high insurance rates. Thus, while the dangers of giving out weight information are not significant, Athabascan people are generally cautious about providing any personal information to public officials.

Nor is weight of cultural significance. Athabascan men seem to admire obese women with as much enthusiasm as they do slender women. Thus, while Athabascan women use makeup and wear the latest in clothing designs that also meet with their lifestyles, they are not concerned about what size clothing they wear. They chose jeans over skirts and invest more money into stylish outerwear than on blouses or sheer scarves. Not only is laundry a problem, but there are also no dry cleaners in the villages, so woolens and silks are saved for use in the urban centers, which people visit often. Slenderness is not a factor in beauty, but having to announce out loud one's weight in mixed-gender or culturally diverse company admits a point of vulnerability in front of people who can use the information in many forms of discrimination. Signals of weight are thus signals of potential political intrusion to which both Athabascan men and women are attuned. The standard weight given by Athabascan men is 200 pounds, a figure that is equally unbelievable. Because political dimensions are a part of Athabascan physical indicators, factors of body size are just as important to Athabascan women as they are for urban American women — but not for reasons of measuring beauty. Weight is merely one of many tropes that are overtly similar to those of mainstream women but for which the cultural meanings assigned to them differ markedly.

In one form or another, most of those writing about Native American women's issues emphasize the social pathologies of private lives or public situations. In the final analysis, a schema for understanding Athabascan women's issues has to be taken framed with a clear awareness of the political and social conditions that might affect their mental environment. During the 1990s addictions and the addictive economy became issues that impact Athabascan women everyday and therefore also must be taken into account when trying to understand Athabascan behaviors. The areas that I have found most theoretically productive are acts of mothering, behaviors of daughters, and acts of social reproof. Most of these areas of Athabascan life display either a continuity with an Athabascan past or a combination of that continuity in conflict with addictive behaviors of the many present-day political dilemmas that face Native Americans.

Acts of Mothering

Many Athabascan women become mothers during their adolescence. Marriage by U.S. laws is by turns encouraged, ignored, and resisted. Christian Athabascans and missionaries encourage marriage, while traditionalists or other social rebels discourage it. Until 1995 there were financial advantages to being an unmarried mother without discernible support from the father(s) of the children. The U.S. federal program called Aid to Families with Dependent Children (AFDC) provided food, medical care, and an income that was sufficient for most families' needs in Athabascan villages. Although federal legislation passed in 1995 has severely impacted AFDC benefits, there are other forms of public assistance that have continued. One of these is the state-administered program for foster children, which pays families who take in children who have been abandoned or removed from their birth homes. Often relatives of such children take in both the children and the monthly stipend attending them. If there are two or more children, the revenue for their care is enough to cover the food and housing expenses for an entire family in rural communities as long as the family can supplement its nutritional needs through hunting, fishing, or sharing networks. Athabascans who use welfare revenue are not criticized in direct terms; however, those who manage without public assistance make sure that everyone knows it in numerous ways. Those who do not have regular employment might sell their personal possessions between paychecks and make sure that potential buyers know how the money will be used and why it is needed. Because the number of full-time jobs in Athabascan villages is finite, this strategy is looked on as a practical solution. Others do odd jobs or sell handicrafts and publicize their resourcefulness in daily conversation, which often leads to new sales (especially to itinerant anthropologists or other researchers). Thus, deciding whether or not to marry is a complex economic issue that Athabascan men and women taken under serious consideration. Divorce is another matter that is nuanced with difficulties in Athabascan society. Because divorce requires entering into the Alaska legal system and its attendant forms and procedures, divorce is rare. Separation, sanctioned or not, is far more common.

Mothering in an addictive system is equally complex, in terms of both how it happens in the cultural context of the community and how mothering is perceived in the legal framework of the Alaskan court system. Most Athabascan children are raised by their mothers in single-parent relationships, while the rest are parented by a combination of family members (including one or more of their biological parents) and outsiders. Some children are raised by grandmothers if the mothers are active in addictive cycles. Others are removed by state agencies and become pawns in the legal tensions between tribal governments and state or federal authorities. A few children are raised in tightly structured environments by parents who are concerned about addictions and the abuses surrounding them. A few children are raised by male parents (not necessarily biological fathers) as their primary caregivers, and even fewer are raised by single-parent fathers (or the male equivalent). My comments generally refer to single mothers and their methods of raising children in communal settings. As sexual abuse of subadult women is a known problem in Athabascan communities, I also concentrate on how daughters are trained to deal with intergender situations. Some of these complex situations are unpacked and analyzed for their social and political implications in the following pages.

The situation I will describe portrays an average event in the parenting life of a woman, around 35, who is married. She and her husband are from two of the smaller families in Gwichyaa Zhee. The Laraa (husband's) family (a pseudonym) is tightly knit and described by other Athabascans as "half-breed." There are several Laraa households in Gwichyaa Zhee. The Tl'ee (wife's) family (a pseudonym) is also described as a "half-breed" family and is closely connected to the family of my mentor through a first cousin on her mother's side, Itree. The husband and wife lived for months at a time in the outlying areas around Gwichyaa Zhee, where the husband hunted and trapped for food and extra money. Vagwaahtai' Laraa (a pseudonym), the wife, occasionally worked for money or volunteered at the Gwaandak radio station as a disk jockey and also worked at the Council of Athabascan Tribal Governments in bookkeeping.

Vagwaahtai' picked her children up each day when school was over and was strict with them in certain details. The following is an example of her method of enforcing simple rules of behavior:

> Vagwaahtai' Laraa arranged her toddlers on the snow machine. "Put your foot up!" she shouted at the middle child, whose boot had been on the snow, rather than on the runner, where it could snag on something and cause the child to fall out. She checked them again and then stood on the runners between the second and third child. Slowly, she pulled the snow machine into the street, standing up.

Everything about this scene is distinctively Athabascan, from the use of snow machines as a customary winter vehicle in the 1990s to shouting at the children when speaking at a lower volume would be audible. I have already discussed the custom of speech volume that was normal in Gwichyaa Zhee. In addition to making sure that the children were safely tucked onto the machine, Vagwaahtai' also had each child fully clothed in polyester fiber-filled snowsuits and thermal boots, with hats and gloves. Her method of standing on the runners was not safe, but it was safe enough in the low-traffic, nonwindy conditions of Gwichyaa Zhee. It was also a matter of stature to be seen standing on the runners while driving, as she displayed the agonistic bravado characteristic of some Athabascan women. She could have put the children into a sled attached to the rear of the snow machine, as others did. If the family had had enough money to own and garage a truck, she would probably have picked them up that way, as trucks had a high prestige value in Gwichyaa Zhee in the 1990s. Vagwaahtai' Laraa performed her mothering acts in conformance with Athabascan standards, part of which entails calling attention to her methods through strategically loud speech, displays of bravado, and making sure that her children were visibly protected. Her public performance, which replicates that of many women, reinforces a

certain standard of toughness among Athabascan parents, a reverbera-
tion from oral traditions.

   This was a common sight at end of the elementary school day, with
mothers like Vagwaahtai' collecting children at the classroom door.
Most preadolescents who lived farther than a block or two from the
school were escorted home by relatives, usually a mother or aunt. Exceptions were rare. One woman, also married, went with her husband in
their truck to pick up their daughter after school. I saw the family often
and noticed that the daughter had two general modes of behavior: she
was very reserved when not with her mother and extremely uninhibited
when she was with her. I call her Gwintsal, a pseudonym. One day I happened to be passing the rear entrance to the school at 3:00 PM, just as
school was over. Gwintsal was sitting at the top of the steps, waiting for
her parents. She looked at me but other than maintaining steady eye
contact with me, made no other signal of greeting. I was a little surprised, for we knew each other rather well, but I also recognized this as
the kind of training Athabascan girls get from their mothers, as I will
discuss in the next section. Just as I was debating whether I should greet
her myself, I saw her parents coming around the corner, and I waited
until they arrived to say hello. The following typifies Gwintsal's behavior in company of her mother:

> Gwintsal barked at me as she scrambled on all fours across the classroom ta-
> ble. I was arranging speakers on two of the tables for an audio course that
> was scheduled for later in the evening. As I filled one table, she moved to the
> next. Finally we were finished, and I went into the lobby where her mother,
> Neeyahshii (a pseudonym) was working. Gwintsal hopped off the table and
> crawled on the floor after me. I sank into my favorite easy chair for some idle
> chatter with Neeyahshii before they went home, leaving me to oversee the
> evening audio-conference classes. Gwintsal crawled under her mother's desk
> and eyed me. As her mother and I talked I forgot she was there until I felt

warm fingers untying my shoes. As soon as she unraveled the knots, she re-laced and tied them back into place. Neeyahshii offered a mild, "Leave her shoes alone, Babe," while I shifted my left foot forward so that Gwintsal could reach it more easily. Gwintsal's shoe-tying stage was over by the time I left Gwichyaa Zhee. By that time she was already seven. Shoestrings and barking happened when she was five.

I have included this cozy incident to illustrate the sharp contrast between this behavior and that of girls who are in the absence of their mothers as described in the following section. Outside the school Gwintsal displayed the reserved behavior that her mother encouraged and which I noticed in many other children. Because I also baby-sat and volunteered in the schools a few times while I was in Gwichyaa Zhee, I know that Athabascan children have different behaviors for different occasions, and I suggest that each of these situations creates informational environments that contour family behaviors.

Neeyahshii told me of experiences with her older daughter that worried her with respect to the safety of both her older and her younger daughters. Neeyahshii lived near the infamous ''Animal House,'' which was the private dwelling of an Athabascan man whose friends used it as a central place for constant drinking. They invited women of all ages to drink with them and waited until they were inebriated before raping them. One morning Neeyahsii had hung some clothing out to dry. The clothing included both her own and her five-year-old daughter's underwear. Later in the day the underwear was missing. Neeyahshii and several other women told me about this kind of incident to warn about my own neighbors, as well as to present alternatives that worked for them. It is this sort of communal parenting and coaching of parents that reinforces the kind of performative action that I witnessed so often among Athabascan mothers. In her case her presentation of self was bifurcated to include her public negotiations regarding her position in the Atha-

bascan sobriety movement that began around 1987, as it did in the rest
of Alaska. The other part of her activities located her within the general
spectrum of Athabascan knowledge of mothering. In each case, the performances were public and gave the appearance of opening the woman
to public censure or praise. While these behaviors pull alcoholism and
child care forward as common topics of conversation, it should be noted
that the selection of such proscriptive subjects was limited while I was
in the region: they spoke of alcohol rather than cocaine or heroin use
and of protective child care techniques rather than child abuse or sexual
assault. According to their public testimony and private conversations
with me, even these few areas of social pathology were new within the
past two decades, coinciding with the importation of state-funded mental health care counselors.

Some women have been able or are determined to incorporate elements of traditional livelihood into their parenting process. In chapter
1, I mention the couple that used Itree's family fish camp in the summers as a twofold mechanism: one to prepare dried fish for winter use
or trade with others, and the other to give their children a chance to
learn traditional values and work habits. In July 1993 they invited me to
spend a weekend with them at their camp. It was an opportunity for me,
a city-bred Native, to learn or at least contemplate some of the survival
skills that my mother had learned and in part had taught her children.
While I was there I watched how one very efficient woman mothered
several children at once:

> "So, sue me," Hułyakk'atno' said without interest to a child who was ar-
> guing that she had promised him a treat and moved the family steadily to-
> ward the fish-cutting table. "Son, could you fill my water cup and bring it
> here?" she asked of her youngest. Hułyakk'atno' is a Koyukon woman mar-
> ried to a Gwich'in man (Vachaa). Vachaa brought a bucket filled with seven
> or eight silver salmon. Hułyakk'atno' directed both her husband and her

nephew back to the river with the tub for rinse water. She cut armholes in a
big, dark green garbage bag and put it over her head. It covered her torso.
She handed one to me. She surveyed the crowd of children and me that sur-
rounded her and assigned everyone a task. I got to cut fish backs (an undesir-
able fish part but a task sufficiently elevated to differentiate me from the chil-
dren). Hułyakk'atno', Vachaa (her husband), and his brother had the major
jobs of cutting and filleting. The children each had fish-gutting and cleaning
jobs. Within 45 minutes all of the fish were neatly strewn across poles in the
smokehouse, with fish eggs and smaller parts spread over netting in the hot,
bright sun. There was a bucket of tails and other dog food that was taken to
a holding area for the half dozen dogs that were tied in the woods on the west
side of camp.

Fish camp revolved around Hułyakk'atno', then mother of seven. She
supervised the family production of dried fish and reshaped the Athabascan fish camp to suit her sense of aesthetics. She and Vachaa had
landscaped about four acres of the camp by cutting down a number of
black spruce and cottonwood trees, pushing the camp farther back into
the woods. After the fish cutting was complete, she went back to the
kitchen tent area and began the second and largest meal of the day, con-
sisting of an open-fire baked salmon and a rice casserole. With putter-
ing and seeing to each child, the meal was ready in about four hours. It
was the last meal of the day. Besides me, there were two other guests:
German men who were canoeing down the Yukon River from
Whitehorse in Canada to Gwichyaa Zhee in Alaska. They had asked to
pitch their tent in the encampment, which already held five or six other
tents and various lean-to structures. They helped Vachaa and his
nephew, Chihshoo, with some of the heavy work around the camp. Vachaa asked the three of them to bring some logs from the river below up
to the camp. I watched as the two German men, who looked very ath-
letic, struggled up the steep embankment with one of the logs. Chih-

shoo waited until they reached the top and walked up easily, carrying a second log on one shoulder by himself. No one said anything about the disparity in body strength, although Vachaa did not ask for the third log that was waiting below.

The finished smoked salmon became food for winter, gifts for relatives, and items for trade or sale, all activities supervised by Hułyak-k'atno'. Hułyakk'atno's primary income derived from the sale of beaded objects. In this area she developed a strong reputation among shopkeepers in Fairbanks. Her tufted caribou skin objects and beaded bags and earrings are distinctive, and she manufactured hundreds throughout the year. She pulled out her beads and the jewelry she had been making, and I bought a pin. One of the German men commissioned something to be sent to him in Europe. The money she made on beading allowed Vachaa to work part-time or seasonal jobs rather than having to get a full-time job, although he found full-time work in the years following this study. Whenever there was a fair or craft show, he made sure that her products were on display. Vachaa and his wife were acting out one of the revivalist models of family unity that has been tried by Athabascan families with partial success since the early 1960s, when one of the Athabascan leaders removed several households of his extended family to a remote area along the Ch'óonjik River for a few years. Medical problems, educational requirements, and persistent alcoholism caused them to move back to Gwichyaa Zhee. A smaller segment of the same family tried it again in 1993 but moved back to Gwichyaa Zhee in 1995 for the same reasons. With the encouragement of so many Athabascans, families such as those described here are constantly reminded of the aspirations of their coevals and kindred to establish some sort of idyllic Athabascan lifeway based on hunting and fishing.

Athabascan Daughters in the Absence of Their Mothers

Athabascan women are involved in forms of routinized or routinizing social behavior akin to those of Athabascan sharing networks and evictions to the extent that the logic underpinning these activities draws its force by leveling authority derived from material goods or political power. These actions are the emergent responses taught by parents to their daughters and sons in reaction to addictive behaviors, which include physical abuse of women and children. In terms of social problems, Athabascan women are far more diligent in sustaining or reviving social relationships than men are, although both Athabascan men and women of the late 20th century have been active in initiating solutions to social problems.

An event occurred during my first week of fieldwork in 1993 that came to serve as a paradigm of routinized problem solving that I observed throughout Athabascan territory:

Ch'idinghìt [a pseudonym] walked up to the telephone in Shroodiinyaa's [a pseudonym] kitchen and dialed. Moments later I heard her penetrating voice announce, "I'm at the Lodge. Come get me." She hung up and went to the dining room. Ten minutes later she was gone.

Ch'idinghìt was five years old when she placed this call to one of the cabs in Gwichyaa Zhee. It was January 1993, one of the coldest winters on record in Alaska. She had walked to the lodge from her mother's house, about one-quarter of a mile to the north. Her mother, Nihtak (a pseudonym), was drunk again. Ch'idinghìt had followed instructions set up by her great aunt. Even at five, Ch'idinghìt knew that it would be days before she saw her mother again. Her mother's drinking binges sometimes went on for weeks. When she drank, Nihtak drank to oblivion. Sometimes Nihtak's family did not know where to find her. Ch'idinghìt was fortunate in having a big extended family on her mother's side that protected her whenever Nihtak was drinking. Her great aunt, Veek'aii (a pseudonym), had joined the Baptist Church at the invitation of one of Nihtak's younger sisters and, with the support of the preacher and the rest of the Kwaiitryah (a pseudonym) family, including Nihtak, taught Ch'idinghìt how to cope when she woke up to a house with no heat or food. Ch'idinghìt went to the private Baptist school for her first two years of education. After a while the Kwaiitryah family withdrew her from the church school and entered her into public school. Some of Ch'idinghìt's relatives belonged to the Episcopal Church, and others were struggling to maintain or rediscover their Athabascan religious traditions. The family was well known in Gwichyaa Zhee for reading and talking about religion, often engaging in passionate debates over ideological issues. The decision to remove her from the Baptist school was partly ideological and partly financial, as the church school levied tuition costs.

Every once in a while Nihtak would say that she wanted to get sober; however, the state-funded treatment procedures are very strict. In order to enter the first level of treatment, she had to be sober for five consecutive days. Whenever Nihtak was sober for that long, she did not seek treatment, although she was encouraged to do so by her family. She continued a cycle of binging between periods of sobriety. When she was sober, she was employed, so she was employed off and on during the time I was in Gwichyaa Zhee. Ch'idinghìt's father was serving time in a Fairbanks jail; Nihtak tried to arrange occasional visits between him and his daughter. I was told he was an Eskimo carver. His contributions to Ch'idinghìt's overall support system were thus tentatively factored into the family agenda but not in matters of training. Ch'idinghìt was one of many Athabascan girls who were taught to find solutions to their physical predicaments. The Kwaiitryah story epitomizes solutions that Athabascan women find to counteract social problems represented by addictions, which include psychological, physical, and emotional abuse of women and children. This case study exemplifies how an Athabascan family has jointly targeted issues (days spent drinking) that in other communities might have been limited to moral criticism of the addiction of the drinker without proactive efforts by the family on behalf of the addict's victims. Children in less supportive family settings became wards of the State of Alaska. The members of the Kwaiitryah family whom I knew avoided that kind of censure of their kinswoman and instead focused primary, pragmatic attention on the multiple trained responses they had developed to help the daughter, Ch'idinghìt. These issue-specific performative structures elicited immediate response in various, but coordinated, ways to Ch'idinghìt's needs and occasionally to those of Nihtak herself.

Like the routinized consensus of evictions described in the previous chapter, this is a model of planned routines that requires communal effort to reinterpret symbols that are otherwise centered on the addicted person (in this case, Nihtak, the mother) to symbols that are instead centered on potential victims of an addictive system. The Kwaiitryah family, including the addictive mother, created a performative structure for the daughter to guide her actions when clearly defined signals occurred. Thus, while five-year-old children in other families in Gwichyaa Zhee or elsewhere might simply await the return of an alcoholic parent in a freezing house without having been taught what to do, the Kwaiitryah family has carefully trained Ch'idinghìt first to recognize signals and then to follow a step-by-step procedure to preserve herself. In addition to help from their own kin, the Kwaiitryah also included non-Athabascan help as part of the child's help structure by going to a local church. In another solution-intending structure, they sought help from the local network of mental health care agencies on behalf of the alcoholic mother. It was not coincidental in this respect that Veek'aii (the mother's aunt) worked for one such agency. The structure to help the addict was less effective than that for the daughter, but, nonetheless, the idea of forming family-based support structures is demonstrated in the effectiveness of the child's actions on that day and others like it.

The following situation with a three-year-old Athabascan girl illustrates how early childhood training in emotional independence begins for some Athabascan families. This event occurred during the fourth biennial Gwich'in Gathering, which was held in Vuntut, Yukon Territories, Canada, in July 1994. At the last minute 18-year-old Lidii (a pseudonym) asked if her three-year-old daughter Tr'iinin (a pseudonym) could go back with her grandmother Ch'izhee (a pseudonym) in a four-passenger aircraft, which would also hold me, the pilot, and one other passenger. Lidii brought Tr'iinin to the airstrip, and as soon as the elder was able to distract her granddaughter, Tr'iinin's mother ran to the corner of the nearest building where two young men were waiting. The child's grandmother and the other passenger were both obese, and I had the only lap with space available, so Tr'iinin was consigned to me. Tr'iinin saw her mother's fleeing form and began to whine and squirm. Her grandmother caught my eye, and together we began to babble in false animation about the blue sky, trees across the runway, and the exciting airplane that we were about to enter. After a few minutes Tr'iinin relaxed. When we finally boarded the aircraft, Tr'iinin dozed off even before the plane started its taxi and slept soundly during the entire two-hour flight. She exhibited neither interest in me as an individual nor nervousness about sleeping on an unfamiliar lap.

Tr'iinin's mother, Lidii, was used to an active social life among her age-mates, and there were teenagers from six of the Athabascan villages present at the gathering, as well as teens from Fairbanks and Whitehorse (two small urban centers). Normally Tr'iinin would have been left with one of her aunts in Gwichyaa Zhee during this kind of event, but neither of them had come to the gathering. These two women were at the airport with a four-wheeler to pick up the three year old, while someone else came to pick up their mother. The two women regarded me in silence and drove away. As they pulled away from me Tr'iinin caught sight of me and nodded. Everything about her behavior suggested habits learned, if not precisely taught, to cope in the absence of her mother. Although not all Athabascan children are taught emotional independence in this manner, many are, and I suggest that their independence is a culturally taught solution to specific situations. The overnight absences of mothers are among the most common situations in addictive families.

These behaviors are more clearly defined in older girls. Another situation involved a six year old making a trip without her mother. After making initial preparations to leave the Athabascan region in July 1995, I was returning to Gwichyaa Zhee from Fairbanks. There were three other passengers already waiting at the flight service company office. One was a little girl whose family I knew:

> Ch'ahdit [a pseudonym] was six, just out of kindergarten. Her aunt smiled in relief to see that a woman would be on the flight. Her mother, Vagwaahtai' [a pseudonym], who was waiting in Gwichyaa Zhee, had called the Fairbanks office several times to find out where her daughter was.

I had never met Ch'ahdit's aunt, although we knew of each other. The other passenger was Ch'adantł'oo (a pseudonym), a man who was universally trusted in Gwichyaa Zhee. Ch'adantł'oo was one of my mentors. He was the executive administrator for the Tribal Council and, in his own words, the "primary benefactor" to the university because he had initiated and sponsored so many educational programs through the local branch of the University of Alaska in Gwichyaa Zhee. Ch'adantł'oo would have been the little girl's chaperon on the aircraft, a position that was automatically transferred to me without a word of query or acceptance. I did not quite realize the transference had happened until the boarding announcement was made and the aunt kissed her niece goodbye and then pushed her toward me, not Ch'adantł'oo.

There are many ambiguities about this incident. The reason she elected to push her niece toward me was not simply because I am a woman. Not Gwich'in by birth and not known personally to the aunt, I was an outsider-cum-insider (introduced then by Ch'adantł'oo as a two-year resident of Gwichyaa Zhee and a Native woman), and her action simultaneously revealed to me my final status in Gwich'in territory, as well as the tenuous interaction between imagined roles based on ascriptive characteristics and awareness (expressed by silence, hesitations, and body motions made by all of us) of the multiplicities of danger or innuendoes of danger present to the child during the next hour. By this time in my tenancy there I had become aware that normally Athabascan women would entrust a small child, especially girls, to another Athabascan woman rather than to an Athabascan man unless the man was the father. There were half a dozen men in the two Athabascan communities I knew best who were often called on to baby-sit. One was Gideon James, chief of Vashraii K'oo, a man whom I often found taking care of children from the village either because he was asked to baby-sit or through traditional tribal adoption. He told me that when he was a youth, he was sent to live with his grandfather for a few years in an Athabascan tradition of education. Likewise, he took in nephews or other kin to train in the same way. Another was my landlord, Earl Cadzow, who was voted Father of the Year by the statewide Alaska Federation of Natives in 1994. These men had achieved a status elevating them above gender stereotypes in Athabascan. Ch'adantł'oo was another such man.

In view of the obvious concern for the girl, I wondered about the mixed messages offered in her clothing. She wore a bright red dress with hearts decorating the pockets and shoes. Almost everyone in Atha-

bascan territory wears jeans except for the women who belong to the
Baptist Church. They are required to wear skirts at all times. Likewise,
the teachers, who are expected to be role models, tend to pattern their
apparel after that of urban American teachers. Sometimes little girls
wore dresses, but it was not a convention shared by many. Ch'ahdit's
dress was, therefore, a marked but indeterminate symbol of femininity
that did not match the symbols in common usage by Athabascans. The
multiple meanings imbedded in heart symbols and party dresses that
are extolled, systematized, and criticized by mainstream U.S. audiences
through commercials, advertisements, greeting cards, movies, television, newspapers, books, and magazines are not as much a part of the
rural Athabascan meaning system as they are in urban centers. Most
Athabascans have and watch cable television (but do not have many opportunities to explore or understand all that they see), buy and send
some greeting cards (but this is not a widespread convention), and read
books, magazines, and newspapers that are available to them (although
there are no bookstores, and only the small university library is available
to them). I wondered if the hearts evoked images of the indeterminacies
of idyllic romance compounded with theories of female debasement to
Athabascans as they do in mainstream America. Can they signal the
range of failed communication between genders about implied emotion
and assumed obligations generated by perceived romance to Athabascan women, as occurs elsewhere?

My coffee-table conversations with Athabascan women were often
about these topics. I had listened to many terse stories of fights between
couples, tingling speculations from women about their latest lovers, la-
conic sarcasm about the behavior of a boyfriend or husband (her own
or someone else's), and warm reminiscing about the early days of long-
standing relationships. All of these Athabascan stories seemed like (by
content) and yet unlike (by style) stories that women of urban communities tell. The economic and social obligations generated through the

relationships enacted in Athabascan society are vastly different from those of their urban sisters, giving these stories an Athabascan twist that differs in marked ways from the urban counterparts I have heard and told myself, primarily in terms of personal safety.

> *When the announcement was made, I walked with the Valentine-bright Ch'ahdit to the aircraft. She was quiet while I buckled her seatbelt and attentive when the pilot explained the procedures. As the plane lifted, her reserve fell away. She squealed when there was minor turbulence, and she looked at me for a cue. I smiled back, and my calmness seemed to give her license to become ebullient. She bounced in her seat and played hand signal games with me. I kept an eye on her seatbelt, relieved that she managed to remain enclosed for the entire 45-minute flight to Gwichyaa Zhee.*

The difference in Ch'ahdit's behavior toward me on the ground and then in the air is noteworthy. I had observed Ch'ahdit in company of her mother and aunts since she was three. Until she turned five she stood out from the rest of the toddlers in Gwichyaa Zhee because she ran when others walked or sat. It had been commonplace to watch her mother or one of her aunts lift an absentminded hand to grab and hold her for a moment in order to slow her pace as she raced around public areas. She came from one of the tight-knit conservative families in Athabascan society. The Laraa family was large, represented by several households. Ch'ahdit's parents were among the several who were trying to live a traditional subsistence lifestyle. This entailed living in Gwichyaa Zhee from late spring through early fall and in a winter home where the father hunted and trapped. They tried a combination of solutions to meet the public school requirements to educate their children. One of the boys was given a home schooling program by his father's sister, instead of attending the regular fourth grade class with his age-mates in 1993. He was enrolled in the Gwichyaa Zhee public school during the two following years. Ch'ahdit was enrolled in kindergarten for part of the spring semester in 1995 but had been taught at home during the bulk of the year before. I observed her kindergarten class one day and was surprised to see her as a solemn, still person, focusing intently on the project assigned to her, just as most of her classmates did. The joyful energy she had displayed as a three year old had become contained. She was in that latter mode of reserve at the airport, and I was to see her don that reserved persona again before the end of the trip:

> About 30 minutes into the flight I pointed out the enlarging strip of the Yukon River. When we saw the four Gwichyaa Zhee antenna towers, Ch'ahdit settled back into serenity. When we landed, I unbuckled her seatbelt, and she closed herself away from me. She moved carefully to the aircraft door and made no reply to the male ticket agent who joked with her at the entrance to the aircraft. He ignored me completely as I followed the girl out of the plane. She walked toward her mother as slowly as would any middle-aged woman and hopped on the back of a four-wheeler. I caught one last glimpse of her as she relaxed her body against her mother's back.

This deliberate assumption of specific mannerisms, I posit, is as carefully taught as were the procedures that guided Ch'idinghìt to Shroodiinyaa's lodge to call a cab.

In a community where social workers have reported that nearly every woman has been sexually abused and children are victims of abuse of many kinds, it was not unusual to see a six year old already able to focus her consciousness inward. It was not uncommon that a six year old would know when to arm herself and when it was safe to relax. For Athabascan women, vat'aii (strength) first involves developing a hard rind of mental plating from the moment they are able to understand their mother's rules about public behavior. Little boys learn to do so as well. Those more conversant with traditional beliefs understand this as a primary form of personal development in ritualized independence, some of which stems from Athabascan traditional culture.

The foregoing have been discussions about Athabascan daughters who have been taught in the absence of mothers by their families. In previous chapters I have suggested that sharing networks and eviction processes both exhibit an aspect of Athabascan logic that works to disperse material goods and social power throughout a framed community. The same logic is also apparent in teaching children how to cope with addictive behaviors. The family or community at large shares in training its infants, if not the youth. Thus, the leveling logic that grounds Athabascan social interaction also provides parents in the (temporary or permanent) absence of the biological or legally appointed guardian. This group behavior works in harmony with individual parenting techniques when functional adults are around. Some less fortunate Athabascan children either do not get this kind of training as toddlers or else become emotionally or physically separated from parental support by the time they reach age 10 or 11. In the present global addictive economy adolescents are a primary target for incorporation into the sale of addictive products. In nearly every Western society adolescents are victimized by entrepreneurs in the addictive system, and the Athabascan traditional culture does not provide a comprehensive model of continuing the training begun in early childhood. This can be seen as a carryover from traditional modes of conceiving of adulthood, when adulthood in the traditional Athabascan society was ritually marked with menstruation or a boy's first kill.

Putting It Together, Tearing It Apart

This chapter has so far presented Athabascan women as mothers and daughters. Women's roles in these capacities are implicit in mapping and shaping moral attitudes about addictions and sexual abuse, as well as in areas of political control. Women inform the lives of the children they parent and serve as role models to their daughters. By protecting their children and their relationships with men, they also delimit the intergender relations they permit and demarcate the relationships that they will tolerate with others, particularly outsiders. Those targeted for eviction are often so marked by women whose boundaries have been breached. With respect to political pressures, both Athabascan men and women have suffered the calumnies of social abuse through colonization. I suggest that there are demonstrable gender differences, resulting in specific effects on women and therefore reactions by women to the political hegemony of the various entities representing outside government. With respect to medical practices, for instance, women have submitted to the social indifference regarding their bodies expressed in the administrative requirements about where they should give birth. Western medical administrative procedures configure other areas of Athabascan women's lives. Gynecological problems are treated in cycles depending not on the illnesses (unless there is a predefined emergency of this nature) but on the schedule of the Indian Health Service doctors who tour the Alaskan hub villages (regional centers) throughout the year. When the gynecologist arrives in Gwichyaa Zhee, the women are notified and, if they need help, must come in at that time. This chapter deals with the protocols that women use to determine who will be shunned and who will be included in their social circles.

Shunning and Inclusion

The events surrounding the eviction of the Langfield family described in chapter 1 as well as the abandonment of the two elderly women described in Wallis's 1993 novel (discussed later) encompass a resilient Athabascan tradition of closure against each other as well as outsiders — shunning. Such closures are not permanent or impenetrable, but it takes a good deal of effort on the part of the shunned to overcome the barriers. Athabascan culture provides counterweights to this negative aspect. The shunning barrier is not permanent, nor does it consistently favor those who have been shielded by it in the past. The chief who was found guilty of rape (mentioned in the previous chapter) exemplifies someone who was once honored and then was discredited by a large (but not uniform) force in Athabascan society. Generally, however, once people become accepted into an Athabascan community, they fall under a particular kind of security. The following incident occurred in 1994.

Janica (a pseudonym) is blind. On October 3, 1994, I escorted her to the podium where she was to say a few words to the people assembled for a bilingual conference at Gwichyaa Zhee. It was not a long walk — about 100 feet from the rear of the multipurpose room. Eyes glared at me. I thought that if she stumbled even once someone would come to her and snatch her from my careless hands. A woman from Jałk'iitsik watched me with studied contempt as I confused Janica by failing to warn her about an electrical cord in our pathway. We managed the rest of the trip with a few joking remarks. When she was finished we made the return journey. The eyes that followed were slightly less hostile. Janica is a white woman who married into the community over 30 years ago. All of the glaring eyes that day were Athabascan, from Gwichyaa Zhee and other communities. She belonged to them, while I was still an outsider. I had lived in Gwichyaa Zhee nearly two years by then. Janica was surprised at my comment because she did not realize how much a part of the community she had become. Her history with Athabascans was one of occasional shunning. At one time she fought accusations of having used witchcraft. Because of these accusations she was barred from teaching at the public school, though not from community life in Gwichyaa Zhee. Janica's story is one that displays the give and take of Athabascan shunning activities, which can include evictions.

Women and Evictions

I thought I had become a victim of such a process myself in 1993 when I was feeding Itree's brother's dogs in her absence.

"Go back to Rampart, bitch! I shot the dog!" a woman's voice shouted at me over the telephone.

It was August 7, 1993, and I had just reported the loss of one of Itree's dogs to the city police officer who was patrolling the area. While I was standing beside his vehicle, he made an announcement about the dog over the radio. I had just finished feeding the dogs when Itree's telephone rang, and I picked up the receiver to hear these words. I mentioned the incident to Itree and her family. During the course of the next few days her brother made inquiries and discovered that K'aii had shot the dog. When K'aii had heard the announcement over her police scanner, she had called me at Itree's house. K'aii had a reputation for drinking heavily. She was one of the most colorful Athabascan women because of these overt displays of verbal hostility. She often rode around the village on a motor scooter and occasionally stopped to shout at or chat with me, depending on her mood or sobriety. Everyone who knew her told me that she was actually very kindhearted, and whenever we saw her alone, she presented an air of diffidence. On the other hand, whenever there were other people around, she donned the gruff demeanor by which I first identified her. K'aii's dual self-representations caricature the "disemia" (what Herzfeld terms dual modes of behavior — each suited for specific cultural events) that I found common in Athabascan women. In private they behave with verbal reserve and in public they assume voices and mannerisms of defiance or belligerence. I am tempted to say that Athabascan men did this as well, if not to the same extent, but in fact I did not spend as much time with men as I did with women, and therefore my data are skewed toward the feminine.

While no eviction ensued from this event, I knew of a number of women who had been evicted — some with legal force, others with Athabascan collective violence. Athabascan women dealt with these issues with as much violence as Athabascan men did. One of K'aii's sisters attacked the local police chief (a woman) with a knife and was arrested, convicted, and served a few months in jail during 1994. In addition to her jail sentence, she was officially barred from reentering Gwichyaa Zhee by the state court system. K'aii's family supported her sister's efforts to be allowed back into the village after her sentence was over, indicating the political force of the family. It was K'aii's family that had the schoolteacher evicted in the incident concerning Andrew Dakota (a pseudonym), which I mention in chapter 1. A few months after Dakota left, yet another high school teacher was shot at by teenaged boys on several different occasions. One day she had had enough and caught an afternoon plane out of the village without stopping to pack her bags. All of these events and the several others I found out about had one thing in common: violence. It is not clear that all of the evicted individuals were so treated because of social trespasses, although in each of the most public cases, the violations were brought to light. The violations are not always clear to those evicted. For instance, I am not sure what, if anything, I might have done to injure or insult K'aii. When I asked, she laughed at me. It could have been the alcohol, or it could have been because I am an anthropologist — hence, a historical enemy in any Native community. In any event, nothing more was done or said in this regard except to give me a significant awareness of the Athabascan process of eviction as motivationally and procedurally complex, violent, and frequent.

Rites of Mourning, Rights of Grieving

One of the most sensitive areas in Athabascan community behavior is intergender relations. If the rumor mills are to be relied on for evidence, then almost everyone in Gwichyaa Zhee engaged in promiscuous and chaotic affairs simply because they were either male or female. While some people were visibly engaged in sexual affairs with other than their sanctioned partners, it seemed to me that most were not and, moreover, that in villages as small as Gwichyaa Zhee or Vashraii K'oo, nothing is secret. During my second month in Gwichyaa Zhee I accidentally left a bag of groceries at the post office just before 5:00 PM on Friday. The post office was closed when I realized the problem, and I knew there was nothing in the bag to link it to me and considered it lost. I bought other groceries later and forgot about the bag until I got a phone call on Monday morning to notify me that the bag was behind the counter — I could just ask anyone for it. In view of that quality of intimate public awareness of each other, little can be kept secret. The foregrounding of sexual indiscretions in casual conversation points to the importance placed on mutual trust in intergender relations.

The following case of a funeral from which one woman was barred provides a heuristic event that describes the collective measures that Athabascan women take regarding sexual transgression:

> A couple of women came into Shroodiinyaa's restaurant and asked me who I was. It was January 1993, and I had just begun fieldwork. I told them the basic facts: name, anthropology graduate student, trying to do fieldwork. They stared at me without expression and then asked for some sodas. I was the only one present in Shroodiinyaa's restaurant at the moment, as Shroodiinyaa had run an errand. I sold them the cans, and a few minutes after they left, Shroodiinyaa walked in. "What did they ask you?" she demanded. I told her, and after a moment she said, "They were trying to find out about the funeral. I'm glad I wasn't here."

Between enigmatic half-phrased references to the life histories of at least a dozen strangers, Shroodiinyaa told me a about a secret funeral for a local non-Native pilot. The more I asked, the more confusing and annoyed Shroodiinyaa became, so I shut up and remained baffled about the funeral for the next few weeks. Eventually I pieced the story together. In September 1992, a non-Native flight service operator crashed in one of his own aircraft, leaving behind a widow and a mistress, both Athabascan women of Gwichyaa Zhee. The widow and the pilot had separated a year or so earlier. She had moved to Fairbanks with their children during the separation, and she returned a few months after his death to resume her career as an elementary school teacher in Gwichyaa Zhee. The widow was a Ch'ilik, my pseudonym for one of the largest families in Gwichyaa Zhee, while the man's mistress was of the Ch'ookwats, a pseudonym for a smaller family with origins in Vuntut, Canada. The Ch'ookwats, although from another region, were nonetheless numerous enough in Gwichyaa Zhee to engender significant tension within the village. There were many affinal ties and distant consanguine connections between Shroodiinyaa's family and each of these two families. Shortly after returning to Gwichyaa Zhee, the widow donated one of her husband's aircraft to the Baptist Church, as the minister was a pilot. The funeral was held somewhere else in Alaska, and the mistress was never informed of its time or place. Of note in this situation is that the castigation of the mistress was not aimed at her or the pilot while they were engaged in their affair but, rather, at her efforts to participate in public mourning for him, a means by which her state of affect regarding the dead man could have been — but was not — equated to that of a sanctioned widow and, thus, might have entitled her to receive the approval and comfort of a putative Athabascan public.

Gendered Courtesy, Gendered Defense

More common examples of intergender behaviors follow patterns set in custom and oral tradition. The following event illustrates aspects of ordinary gendered courtesy in Athabascan. One morning I was walking past the white graveyard to the post office as a middle-aged couple walked toward me. It was unusual to see a man and a woman walking together, and this was doubly so because they walked side by side. The woman beamed at me, and I smiled back. The man stared straight ahead. About ten feet away he nodded slightly and said hello. The woman's face registered shock, and I know that mine mirrored it. He kept his eyes locked firmly on nothing directly in front of him. The woman also looked straight ahead. I walked past without further ado.

I rarely saw men and women walking together in Gwichyaa Zhee, although I often saw couples riding on four-wheelers and in cars or trucks together. It was more common to see two people stop to speak to each other briefly and then move apart. Occasionally I would see a couple walking in a straggling line, one ahead of the other. In this case the man had violated Athabascan gender codes by addressing an unfamiliar woman (me). The woman relayed her reaction to me even though we did not know each other and did not speak of it either then or later. Her initial happiness and later distress were obvious and helped me formulate my response, which was (I hoped) polite avoidance.

Prior to the 20th century, most Athabascan marriages were arranged, leaving flirtation to have negligible to negative value. Another effect is the minimization of a need for verbal communication between genders. This continues to a minor extent through separate gossip or social circles, although I encountered many male/female combinations engaged in companionable conversation with each other and was never aware of gender-coded language except with respect to menstruation and childbearing. Discussions about menstrual difficulties generally occur in women-only groups and take the form of complaints, requests for or offers of practical or therapeutic help, or solicitation of comparative biological information. In these discussions I found Athabascan women well informed about current Western medical and psychological theories about women's bodies. The Gwichyaa Zhee university library is well stocked with self-help books in this vein. Occasionally discussions turned to traditional methods of dealing with childbirth (both past and present) and traditional methods of raising children. Other forms of body conditions were frequently discussed in both single-gender and combined-gender groups. Both men and women described their physical ailments in clinical detail to me or whoever happened to be in company at the moment. Curative techniques rather than sympathy seemed to be solicited in these moments. Because this was one of the customs that I inherited from my Koyukon background, I might have unknowingly encouraged this trend in conversation. However, such details of body knowledge also appear in Athabascan oral and written narrative, such as that described later in this chapter. Athabascan oral tradition also delineates aspects of age and gender behaviors.

Women's Roles in Athabascan Oral Traditions

Some Athabascan traditional narratives indicate that many longstanding Athabascan customs lead to the violation, shunning, and eviction of women. One of the most popular traditional narratives involves the kidnapping of an ancestral Athabascan woman, Łihteerahdyaati, who was later called Ch'atthan Vee (White Shell). Émile Petitot (1976) transcribes the name as "Latpatsandia," as told to him by Canadian Athabascans, and he translates it as "She Who Is Ravished." Petitot also translates the name as "She Who Delights" and "Desired Woman." Slobodin (1975) uses the translation of "Prize Woman." The translations of the former name, Łihteerahdyaati, by Petitot and Slobodin are interesting as possible representations of how women have been described to Euro-American men during the past century. Athabascan sources suggest that Łihteerahdyaati was intelligent, beautiful, and honorable. The traditional story about her involves her kidnapping and the murder of her husband's brother as well as other people in their extended family by Ch'eekwaii. Her husband, Ko'ehdan, nearly starved to death in his attempt to find help, but he succeeded and later was able to recapture Łihteerahdyaati from the Ch'eekwaii. Almost every version suggests that Łihteerahdyaati was espoused by her Ch'eekwaii (Iñupiat or Inuit) kidnapper, and Slobodin (1975) theorizes that this was a traditional custom in Athabascan–Ch'eekwaii (Inuit) relations at one time. When Itree's mother told this story she remarked that Łihteerahdyaati had to be careful not to say anything about her sexual relationship with the Ch'eekwaii man to Ko'ehdan, her Athabascan husband, or he might kill her. Models of women's behavior are encoded in several ways through this narrative and others like it, and the stories give evidence of the primary aspirations of Athabascan women to be strong, intelligent, socially independent, and willing to share this mental base with others.

Another concept from Athabascan traditions, discussed in the previous chapter, that is pertinent regarding women's roles in Athabascan culture is dat'aii, which conveys the notion of accomplishment as it conforms to public service. Because the idea of achievement is linked with mental, physical, and metaphysical strength, even the smallest deeds serving an ultimate goal of dat'aii are valued. As a consequence of the potential valuation of everyday actions, the tendency to rank occupations by prestige value is suppressed. Because group survival through independent action is a dominant ideal in Athabascan culture, the traditional Athabascans did not forefront gender status as a cultural theme in survival situations. Both men and women were expected to use their intelligence and physical strength to come to the aid of their people, a theme that dictates much of the action in the Ko'ehdan narrative. Unfortunately, with exposure to Western culture, a present-day, almost exclusive use of the English language, and numerous social problems, contemporary gender relations are not often harmonious even in that respect. Earlier in this chapter I describe the way in which Athabascan mothers teach their young to encircle themselves in a mental barrier of aloofness as a first-level defense against molestation. Themes of rape and kidnapping appear in some of the traditional tales, such as the tale of Ko'ehdan, and carry over into contemporary life.

In 1993 a novel based on a traditional Athabascan tale appeared that displays many of these same themes. The author, Velma Wallis, was born in Gwichyaa Zhee and lives there off and on. The story is about two old women who have become somewhat dependent on their younger companions but who still have services to offer their people. The young men would pitch their camps for them, and younger women helped them pull their gear. The story begins when the band is facing starvation because the hunters have not been successful. The two old women represent a liability to their band because they have become a drain on the energy resources. At the beginning of the story the chief and the rest of the band decide that the time had come to go on without their relations, and they do so without much consultation with the women.

After a very short period of shocked inactivity, the women draw on their mutual knowledge and the few resources left with them to survive that winter and the following summer. Wallis dramatizes the emotions that might have attended the women: "So I say if we are going to die, my friend, let us die trying, not sitting" (1993:15–16). When the band members return to the area, they find the women restored to usable levels of strength and productivity and invite them to rejoin the group. They do so, and the story ends.

Vat'aii and dat'aii are both present and not present in the novel. They are present to those who have an understanding of the traditional concepts. They are not visible as anything but strength and accomplishment to those who do not. Nonetheless, educated Athabascans can perceive the presence and nature of both vat'aii and dat'aii in the novel. The tale involves the details of recovery of vat'aii in physical as well as mental ways. Both of the two women had become accustomed to having someone else do the more strenuous physical chores involved in traditional Athabascan life. Wallis describes them as arthritic and weak. It had been so long since either had hunted that they had to relearn some survival techniques of setting snares and fishing when summer came. As it happened they remembered and could implement most of the crafts needed to find, catch, and prepare food, shelter, and clothing. They could depend on each other for company and sympathy. In short, they recuperated many of the basic elements of their youthful vat'aii, and by traditional Athabascan standards they did it with the conscious effort known as dat'aii.

A significant difference between *Two Old Women* and the Ko'ehdan tale is that the motif of implacable revenge that calls for the death of an enemy is not present in the novel. Wallis includes a theme of revenge, but the traditional revenge as in the Ko'ehdan tale or the Inuit murder trials is not a part of this tale. It could be that too many brutal encounters with Western law have caused Athabascans to modify their customs to exclude outright murder. Western influence has not caused them to exclude violence and deportation of offenders, as in the case of the Langfield family and others. Wallis brings themes of trust and mistrust, the behaviors of trust and mistrust, and the logic of mistrust to her novel. For instance, when the band members are discussing their strategies of survival at the beginning of the saga, they also have to think about danger, particularly the danger represented by other people. Paranoia about the dangers that a stranger might present carry through to the present day in Athabascan lands.

The following passage from Wallis's novel illustrates such sentiment. At the end of the tale, when members of the larger group search for the two old women, there is a moment of tension as the larger group tries to establish credibility: "Suddenly, out of the stillness, the women heard their names called. . . . The man's voice became loud, and he identified himself. The women knew the old guide. Perhaps they could trust him. But what of the others? It was Ch'idzigyaak who spoke first. 'Even if we do not answer, they will find us' '' (Wallis 1993:108). The women's response is not the joy of meeting an old friend, which the old guide had been, or the pleasure of visiting company for the first time in more than a year. They are unwilling to open themselves to the threat of spatial and personal invasion by other human beings. The women do respond and talk to the visitors, and they slowly come to an understanding of each other. The old women accept the invitation to rejoin the band, but unlike the case in a Hollywood happy ending, the women do not throw their arms around their relations in gratitude. They hold themselves aloof until they are sure of a safe reception.

Harmony represents a thwarted or tarnished ideal in the Athabascan novel *Two Old Women*. In the novel survival of the group enacted by a tribal decision clashes with the harmony of the band. The expelled women were not part of the decision and did not agree with the judgment passed on them. At the heart of Athabascan *t'eeteraa'in* (their way of life) is the concept of survival: survival as a people, survival as individuals, survival against the challenges of life in the Arctic. Survival is the primary justification for the commission of acts that are harmful to another person, whether the person is part of the group or not. Athabascans live in a region where traditionally extra food or even enough food during the winter months is a hope and not a reliable reality. The presence of noncontributing members who also take energy away from food production or gathering jeopardizes the welfare of the entire community. In the context of *Two Old Women*, *yinjih* reflects common, albeit dispassionate, sense in the face of starvation. What is not present in the story is awareness of the term *yinjih*. Wallis describes the process by which all members of the band knew that the two old women were to be left behind on the first occasion and how they came to be welcomed back by the entire group on the second occasion. She simply does not say it in Gwich'in. Because the term *yinjih* is not often verbalized, there is no great loss to Athabascan t'eeteraa'in that is not iterated in the novel. Yinjih does not require language to convey meaning, and no expression in English adequately explains the complexity of Athabascan silent communication behavior. It is both ironic and logical that Athabascans have such a vocabulary item, implement the process that it denotes, and have little need to verbalize the concept.

This section has explored the many ways in which women refine and redefine Athabascan society through social censure, parenting, and serving as role models. The primary thrust of this section has been to indicate the severe way in which Athabascans interpret the rules of intergender behavior. The pilot's widow, for example, was able to garner significant public support for her right to grieve publicly without the presence of her deceased husband's mistress at his funeral. The support she obtained was partially in display of familial solidarity and partially in display of moral disapproval of the marital disruption caused by the mistress. Women, by virtue of their roles as mothers and in their roles as daughters who are trying to act out the rules enjoined on them by their mothers, mete out public policy regarding social misdemeanors by shunning and inclusion. Shunning often leads to evictions, though not necessarily. In this respect, women are primary instruments of shaping Athabascan social identity and solidarity. The next section describes two of the women who have taken their roles as social shapers to a more active political level.

Athabascan Women as Political Activists

There are several Athabascan women in Alaska and Canada who have taken political roles on behalf of Athabascan people. I have already mentioned Shreevyaa, who has worked primarily in her village in leadership roles pertaining to tribal business and education. Another Athabascan woman has traveled the world as an officially designated spokesperson for the Gwich'in Steering Committee centered in Vashraii K'oo. I have given her the pseudonym of Sarah James (a distant cousin of Shreevyaa). In her capacity as Athabascan spokesperson, James advocates for environmental protection of regions surrounding every Athabascan village. Because her position has become so visible, she has also been asked to lobby on behalf of other Native issues throughout Alaska. In 1995 she traveled to Europe to speak before one of the United Nations nongovernmental organizations on behalf of indigenous peoples. She has testified in Congress several times on various issues. To a certain extent her life story identifies her age (51 in 1993) because of the educational strategy that her parents arranged for her. She first was taught by her parents and then by grandparents, and then she entered into an Indian boarding school at the age of 13 in 1956 — three years before Alaska became the 49th state. After statehood in 1959, the state education administration went through a number of challenges and changes. Now all Alaskan children begin their public school education by the time they are five, if not sooner. The following is a statement by James about her life. It is pertinent here in the context of the public life that has been constructed for her to note the topics she includes (environmental issues and education) and those she excludes (Athabascan social or economic problems):

> I grew up out in the country where we help each other to survive, and we live there year round. It's about 50 miles from the nearest neighbor. There I learned lots about respect and responsibility. So when I got into high school when I was 13 years old, those are the two points that's very important everybody learn is respect and responsibility, which helped me to get my high school diploma within six years, even though I was 13 years, barely

talking English. Took me six years, two summers, and one summer job to
finish high school. What I learned out there living in the country helped me
more than what I see and what was taught to me out there. Because out there
[beyond Athabascan land] there's greed and waste, and which I don't . . .
that's one thing that my parents and what we did out in the country is to
respect the land and in return it will take care of you. Those are the things
that are very important that we teach to our kids. I can see that there's —
what are the risks of the oil development to the Porcupine Caribou Herd?
[personal communication, Vashraii K'oo, November 7, 1993]

As a political activist Sarah James has few role models, makes little or
no money, and risks criticism by other Athabascans constantly. Nonetheless, she uses every opportunity to speak on behalf of Athabascans in
public meetings and uses the telephone to make conscientious contact
with me and others she has met to inform of us of progress made by her
tribe in its political endeavors or by the Steering Committee on environmental issues. She used the 1993 forum of the "People, Science, and
Caribou" Conference to inform the audience of some of the ongoing effects of colonialism that have become the basic issues that she brings to
nearly every public meeting:

Another thing, somebody was talking about we go out with researchers, peo-
ple, scientists, and biologists, and we always available for scouting to show
them around. Talking about our knowledge. But we never got credit for it.
The people that put it down on the paper, the scientists is the one that got
credit for it. I even think that Indian is the one that climbed Mount McKinley
first, but you know, it's even in the record that he was the scout, but the non-
Indian got the credit for it. You have [to] include Native knowledge along
with your report. This has to stop. All we're asking for is respect. We never
gave up anything. We never gave up our education, law, or anything like

that. *The intruder or the Western people came in. They assumed they have
it. They assume it's rightfully theirs. But we never gave it up. We never gave
up our land, we never gave up anything.* [Vashraii K'oo, November 7,
1993][1]

Unlike Sarah James, her distant cousin Shreevyaa has a much more
inwardly focused agenda, although some of their concerns are the
same. During the time I spent in Gwichyaa Zhee, Shreevyaa was concerned with the education of Athabascan youths. However, where James
emphasizes external relations between global societies and Athabascans, Shreevyaa brings up the currently debated internal social problems within Athabascan territory. In 1993 she invited me to the Youth
Survivor's camp. It was an old fish camp about six miles away from the
village by river. There were six of us: Shreevyaa, her mother, two boys,
the man who owned the boat, and me. Shreevyaa wanted to see how
much work would be required to get the camp ready for summer. There
were two cabins, several lean-tos, a couple of large fire pits, and a couple of rough wooden tables. It was cold and still very damp from the not
quite melted snow of winter. Wild crocuses (kii choodaii) were still
blooming in the woods. Shreevyaa's mother walked around the perimeter of the camp, examining spruce trees. She collected the yellowed
pitch seeping out of some of the trunks. "It's chewing gum," she told
me. "Good for the gums." She put clumps of the resin into a small paper sack for later use. Shreevyaa wanted to make tea and have a snack
while we were there, so we chatted in a desultory fashion, each of us
exploring how to make conversation across age and gender barriers.
Shreevyaa's mother was in her late seventies and suffered from severe

1. Walter Harper, a Koyukon Athabascan, was the first man in recorded history
to ascend Mount McKinley (also known as Mount Denali) in 1913. He was the
Native guide for the Hudson Stuck party and was also my great-uncle.

heart trouble. She had several children, and Shreevyaa was a middle child. After we drank tea, ate some fish, and tidied the camp a bit, we walked back to the boat. Shreevyaa walked ahead of her mother. Looking back, I noticed that Shreevyaa's mother was moving with some difficulty, and I asked if we should help. Shreevyaa glanced back and said, "No, she's okay." Nonetheless, we both walked more slowly, and soon Shreevyaa found something fascinating in the woods to one side, leaving me to walk ahead. When I reached the riverbank, I saw that Shreevyaa was behind her mother by several feet. We got into the boat and were soon back in Gwichyaa Zhee.

Native peoples all over North America are using the idea of outdoor camp to educate their youth about what it means to be Native American. It is patterned after the Western models provided by Boy Scouts of America and other similar organizations. There were no similar organizations in Gwichyaa Zhee prior to Youth Survivors. Athabascan youths could and still can attend summer educational camps in urban centers; these are occasionally centered on Alaska Native customs, but more often they are not. Between 1993 and 1995 the camp programs was a struggling endeavor that relied almost entirely on the energy of Shreevyaa to keep it going. When she was ill for a few months during 1993, few of the camp programs occurred. When she was participating, however, there were many who joined into the events.

6 What Does the Future Hold? Prognosis in Question

They tell me that 80 to 90 percent of Indian women in alcohol treatment centers in Canada have been sexually abused. They are saying that 80 percent of the men in alcohol treatment centers have been sexually abused. We've learned these behaviors. They are not here before the white man came in the 1800s. We learned much physical abuse and sexual abuse in the Christian boarding schools. How could you not learn to inflict violence on others when it was inflicted on you for so long?

Cecilia Fire Thunder, LAKOTA (1992:13)

Discourses related to social pathology are culturally potentiated to provide terms that fit mainstream American ideas of Native Americans. Health and death statistical reports are laden with terminology that is infused with U.S. conceptions of health, race, and ethnicity. These terms do not fit in the spectrum of Native American, Alaska Native, or Northern Athabascan healing theories. Because of this, the present chapter discusses the state of the academic discourse regarding symptoms of social pathology, starting with the concept of social pathology. The term indicates that some form of disease has harmed or is eroding a society.

Everyone agrees that the entire Northern Athabascan social system is in peril when alcoholism is a routine part of life. However, does the term *alcoholism* suggest a single cohort of behaviors or many? I used to think that I could tell, almost to the amount of alcohol consumed, how drunk someone might be and, therefore, what that individual would be likely to do. Imagine my surprise, then, when a non-Native friend confided in me that her father was finally seeking help for his alcoholism. I had known her father for a few years and had seen him drinking liquor without recognizing that he ever became drunk. According to his daughter, he was "always drunk." I had been reading mainstream literatures about alcoholism to understand my own family, and many of the theories I read made sense. However, when I realized that I did not know what a white drunk looked or acted like, I was shocked into wondering whether there could be a common bond between alcoholics of one culture and those of another. If alcoholism has a cultural component, it seems likely that alcohol treatment should likewise have a cultural component. Moreover, if alcoholism is a diagnosable disease, by which cultural standards is one to be judged ill from alcoholism and, later, well or rid of alcoholism? These and other questions are posed in this chapter, but they are not answered.

In the previous chapters I have discussed the addiction-related hardships endured by Northern Athabascan people in Alaska. In chapters 2 and 3 I suggest that the origins of these pathologies are historical and perpetuated by economic as well as political hegemonies because of colonialism. Chapters 4 and 5 analyze some of the Athabascan methods of dealing with social problems, the former regarding matters of public leadership and decision making, and the latter delineating some of the daily experiences of Athabascan women in raising families and coping with their own traumas in the face of addiction. In this chapter I present a broader picture of Athabascans in comparison with other Native Americans, as well as other Alaska Natives, in terms of the process of recovery.

Athabascan life in the context of addictive turmoil leaves an impression of bleak hopelessness unless it is viewed with the awareness that those living out these lives are not settling for continued oppression. They have been making efforts to effect survival techniques for social healing by using every device and form of assistance offered. At close range, their success is not easy to see, and for some it is impossible to see. When I first began this project in 1992 I became aware of the low suicide rate among some Athabascans as compared with that in other parts of Alaska. This remained a statistical fact in 1998. Statistics, as one would expect, are harshly dissonant with the visceral pain of dealing with the suicides of Athabascan children. The very dissonance between individual trauma and analytic theories of social pathology leads to a major question that this chapter addresses: Do Athabascans perceive the same linkage between addiction and suicide that is postulated in the social sciences, which is, sketching broadly, psychological, individual, and biological? I suggest that the answer is no: the Athabascans whom I interviewed generally attributed social pathology to political and economic hegemony. This corresponds in a thematic way to analysis proposed by other research in Native American communities.

This chapter is divided into three general sections. The first challenges statistical information about Native American health care usage patterns as categorized and reported by mainstream medical sources. Health care usage by Alaska Natives in general and Northern Athabascans in particular is included in this section. The second section confronts information about violent death in the United States, Alaska, and Northern Athabascan territory. The third section offers theories of social pathologies, starting at a global level, and finally ends with Northern Athabascan theories and solutions to these problems.

Health Care Facilities Usage

In this section I discuss the reported usage of mainstream health care facilities in Alaska by Athabascan people and dispute the cultural categories imposed on Athabascans by some researchers. From a quick glance at the table titles, however, it appears to be primarily about death, for most of the statistics about how people relate to health care are taken from studies about how people die — a statement more about the intensity of socially constructed meanings regarding human death in North America. Many deaths are categorized into structured meanings in which blame is assigned to either the social body surrounding the individual or the individual physical or mental condition. Death by alcoholism is such an example. Alcoholism is listed as a cause of death in many studies, and the question arises, How does an alcoholic actually die? Is there but one expression of this form of illness in death? Even to ask such a question suggests how intricately tangled the webs of meaning regarding death are.

Despite these evidentiary obstacles, this form of analysis is often attributed to the larger Native American population of the United States. These statistics are reported on a segregated population: those who report symptoms of illness or malaise to U.S. Indian Health Service (IHS) personnel or contractors. Those Athabascans or Native Americans who seek treatment by alternative medical practitioners, whether they be of the mainstream medical force, traditional healers, or others, are not included in these statistics. O'Connor, summarizing the research of several others, reports that "the majority of health-related actions in any population are undertaken outside the sphere of the conventional health care system, even by those actively considering themselves to be sick or in compromised health" (1995:25). Many Native Americans likewise use a variety of "helping strategies," as Ronald Niezen (1993) phrases it (including over-the-counter pharmaceuticals and herbal remedies).

Niezen, in "Telling a Message: Cree Perceptions of Custom and Administration" (1993), analyzes the way James Bay Cree have conceptualized problems of violence and suicide, as well as customary methods of overcoming them. Niezen suggests that the bureaucratic apparatuses of Canadian social services and health care agencies are inconsistent with traditional forest lifestyles, particularly with respect to violence. In contrast to the often punitive, legalistic measures prescribed by Canadian law in these instances, Niezen reports that "many Cree people seem to be looking for healing and reconciliation, qualities they hope will be found in the way elders once handled social and individual crises before the recent era of administrative formalization" (1993:235). Niezen (1997) elaborates on these issues of cultural logic or intolerance on the part of medical administrators, which is related to a fundamental underpinning in Christian evangelism. In a 1997 article that describes an incipient collaboration between local Cree leaders and the Canadian government regarding health care, Niezen argues that Western biomedicine, which is founded on monotheism, leads to an elimination of medical pluralism "first by serving as an instrument of Christian conversion, then with its own administrative and technological apparatus," which eventually encourages "dependency on formal agencies and outside expertise" (1997:485).

Many of the Athabascans I met seemed to use such a hodgepodge of resources by asking parents, other family members, and friends for advice. I learned a lot of practical Arctic environment first aid tips by listening to these conversations, as well as occasional tidbits about Athabascan theories of spirit intervention. Many Athabascans have some form of health insurance and use it along with the IHS as a routine aspect of IHS fiscal strategies. Those who have health insurance also make use of private physicians, and in fact, many prefer to do so to avoid public exposure of their private dilemmas. There is no privacy in the villages as most people soon discover, and that includes privileged information about illness or physical problems.

As an example, in villages of 750 or less, such as Gwichyaa Zhee, information about women's medical conditions becomes a public issue, as a matter of course. The very nature of the IHS bureaucracy works against standards of privacy. When the IHS gynecologist comes to the village on infrequently but routinely scheduled visits, notices about the visits are posted around the village, and some of the residential women are called or can make appointments, while others are reminded (usually in public) by well-meaning relatives or friends. Thus, by the time the day of the appointment arrives, most people in town know about their female neighbors' medical concerns. Men, by contrast, suffer a little less unwanted public exposure. If they have prostate problems, they are referred to doctors in Fairbanks by the resident physician assistants. Women in need of non-emergency but nonetheless time-sensitive medical attention for venereal diseases that can be treated in greater privacy in urban centers can do one of four things in the villages: (1) they can ignore the problem and thereby infect their partners; (2) they can go to the local clinic (staffed by relatives and other people they know) for preliminary diagnoses and referral to doctors in Fairbanks; (3) they can spend their own money on airfare ($150 round trip from Gwichyaa Zhee to Fairbanks during 1993–95) to go to a private doctor; or (4) they can try to find a traditional healer for assistance. However, local healers are limited to midwifing, easing menstrual cramps, and rebalancing hormones through herbs.

The statistical information in this section and the one to follow has been compiled by a number of researchers at uneven intervals for many decades, and each numerical construct depicts a slightly different segment of issues. Thus, with this considerable, complex caveat in mind, the statistics presented represent a percentage of a much larger population of health care users and helping strategies for which there are no composite statistics available in Alaska. Table 5 lists the ten leading causes of death among Native Americans in the United States in 1990 in contrast to those among the general U.S. population. Cardiovascular disease caused more than double the number of deaths in both the general and the Native American populations according to this study. Obesity is usually targeted as the primary cause for cardiovascular disease,

Table 5. Leading Causes of Death among Native Americans in the United States, 1990 *(Rates per 100,000)*

Cause of Death	All Native Americans	United States
Cardiovascular disease	163.7	189.8
Malignant neoplasms	94.5	135.0
Accidents	86.0	32.5
Chronic liver disease	30.3	8.6
Diabetes mellitus	29.7	11.7
Influenza, pneumonia	20.5	14.0
Suicide	16.5	11.5
Homicide	15.3	10.2
Chronic obstructive pulmonary disease	13.8	19.7
Tuberculosis, all forms	2.7	0.5

Source: Based on data compiled by the U.S. Department of Health and Human Services (1994).

along with high-fat diets, nicotine usage, and stress. Chronic liver disease, ranked fourth in the Native American population, is listed as ninth in the general population. Alcoholism is often linked to many liver diseases, such as cirrhosis, and such data are probably used as corroboration of that theory.

In contrast to the information in Table 5, the leading cause of death in the general Alaska Native population (again keeping in mind the absence of complete information in this respect) is not cardiovascular disease but accidents, as demonstrated in Table 6. Accidents in 1970 caused

Table 6. Leading Causes of Death among Alaska Natives in Alaska and Other States, 1970 (*Rates per 100,000*)

Cause of Death	Alaska Natives	Alaska Total	United States
Accidents	199.4	116.9	56.4
Cardiovascular disease	73.0	87.4	362.0
Malignant neoplasms	67.1	61.6	162.8
Influenza, pneumonia	49.3	61.6	162.8
Alchoholism	41.4	10.9	—
Vascular lesions of the central nervous system	35.5	26.2	101.9
Diseases of early infancy	29.6	25.5	21.3
Suicide	29.6	13.2	11.6
Homicide	27.6	10.6	8.3

Source: Based on data compiled by Kraus and Buffler (1977:91).

well over twice the number of deaths among Alaska Natives than any other factor, and, at least in 1970, cardiovascular disease was not a significantly greater cause of death than malignant neoplasms were; meanwhile, in the general U.S. population, heart disease in 1970, like in 1990, was the leading cause of death.

The low rate of cardiovascular disease among Alaska Natives may be attributable to three factors: village life usually entails a good deal of walking, they eat less fast food (hence, less contaminated fat), and genetic luck. To add to the confusion, it is possible that Alaska Native people have not been diagnosed as often as others for heart disease, particularly if they do not report it. "I just feel bum" is a common, totalizing statement of otherwise unverbalized malaise made by many elderly Native people. Such an ambivalent statement can cover a wide range of symptoms of heart failure or other cardiovascular illnesses. It is also interesting to note that in 1970 alcoholism was not reported as a cause of death among any group in the United States but Alaska Natives. Considering the vast machinery of governmental research, not to mention funding resources, that has been allocated to the study of alcoholism in the United States for many decades, I find it remarkable that it was not reported in the death certificates of a statistically measurable population. I also take exception to the framing of studies, such as that from which Table 6 is derived, that emphasize violence. The implication made by Kraus and Buffler (1974, 1977) is that there is a functional or thematic link among homicide, suicide, and accidental death. Such may well be the case; however, the researchers have failed to analyze the types of accidents, such as car accidents (was the victim a driver, a passenger, considered to be at fault, etc.?), boating drownings, plane crashes, or hunting accidents, to name a few. One would, of course, expect there to be suicide involved in some accidents, just as some accidents must simply be accidents and are not necessarily linked to a meaningful explication of culturally or racially marked existence.

Besides examining death certificates, there are some indirect ways of conjecturing the persistence of some form of traditional theories of strength and endurance. The use of the public health facilities in the Northern Athabascan area shows that Athabascans' use of the health facilities and community health aid services declined in volume usage between 1992 and 1993, possibly indicating better health. Like the statistics on violent death rates discussed previously, with respect to health care needs, the Gwich'in appear to fare better than other Athabascans do. In Gwichyaa Zhee, population 750, they averaged approximately four appointments per person per year, which seems reasonable considering the environment. Even though the clinic provides free medical

Table 7. Indian Health Service Outpatient Activity in Interior Alaska, 1992–93

Area	Total Outpatient Visits			Primary Care Provider Visits		
	Fiscal Year 1993	Fiscal Year 1992	% change	Fiscal Year 1993	Fiscal Year 1992	% change
Gwichyaa Zhee	4,097	4,643	-11.8	4,061	4,452	-8.8
Tanana	5,448	4,887	11.5	5,448	4,887	11.5
Chief Andrew Isaac in Fairbanks	60,190	44,127	36.4	27,763	26,263	5.7
McGrath	1,338	1,427	-6.2	1,232	1,427	-13.7
Total	71,124	55,084	29.1	38,543	37,029	4.1

Source: Data derived from Alaska Area Native Health Service 1993:table 3.

care as well as dental care, the figures in Table 7 give an indication of patient visits in the five largest regional health care facilities in the interior of Alaska. Tanana Chiefs Conference employs community health aides in the smaller villages, and all of the clinics and community health aides have the authority to send patients to the Chief Andrew Isaac Health Center in Fairbanks. The health center in Fairbanks sends patients in need of in-patient care to the Fairbanks Memorial Hospital or to the Alaska Native Health Services Hospital in Anchorage. Patients diagnosed to be in need of more complex medical care are referred to the other hospitals in Anchorage or in Seattle, Washington.

With reference to patients who seek other forms of help, there is only anecdotal information. Much of what Niezen (1993, 1997) has written about the way in which Canadian health care bureaucracies impede interaction or information exchange between traditional or alternative medical solutions may also be true in Alaska. In a few situations, however, there may not be so much a refusal to acknowledge alternative medicines as a misapprehension of meaning. As Edith Turner found in her research among the Iñupiat in northern Alaska, "healing was an inseparable part of a wider phenomenon within the village — spirit perception and action" (1996:xix–xx). Among Northern Athabascans the concepts of malaise and healing are part of wider categories of meaning. The usual phrase for expressing malaise, "I just feel bum," pulls in a network of signs regarding physical aspect, emotional affect, and ineffable sources of energy, only some of which fall within categories of mainstream illness theory. Athabascan healing theories also involve pragmatic concepts of body energy, spatial or environmental healing (a range of conceptions regarding psychic ability, spiritual intrusion or presence, and the use of traditional plants and animals), herbal therapy, Western medicine, and political awareness. I include the evictions mentioned in earlier chapters as a method of healing. Just as piercing a boil can cleanse an infection, so too does removing unwanted people. By the same token, the violence attending evictions is a token of something out of harmony, something that they might call *shen* in their own language. Hence, the evictions are indicative of both pathology and a means of purification.

Table 8 contains some data on Northern Athabascan villages, and Table 9 contains data on the neighboring Koyukon villages. The data in Table 10 refer to the number of times that either patients went to the smaller village clinics or the community health aides went to the homes of the villagers. The smaller Koyukon villages appear to use their in-village health care facilities at approximately the same rate as their upriver Athabascan neighbors do. The residents of the two Gwich'in villages of Beaver and Viihtaii tend to use the facilities more frequently than those in the smaller villages do, and this may be because the community

Table 8. Community Health Aide Outpatient Encounters Compared with Deaths by Accident and Suicide, by Village, within the Northern Athabascan Region, 1993

Village	Total Outpatient Encounters	Deaths by Accident	Deaths by Suicide	Population
Vashraii K'oo	592	2	0	113
Beaver	960	4	0	103
Jałk'iitsik	535	1	1	83
Danzhit Hanlii	242	0	0	95
Gwichyaa Zhee	4,097	10	2	729
Dinyee	555	5	1	93
Viihtaii	1,863	5	0	231

Source: Data derived from Alaska Area Native Health Service 1993:table 5.

health aides in those areas are paid as full-time employees. They may also have received more training than those in the smaller villages. The health aide in Viihtaii, for example, had many years of experience in the village and was widely respected for her skill.

There does seem to be a correlation between the number of health care encounters per person per year and a reduction in the number of accidental deaths. Where there are fewer encounters, there appears to be a higher risk of death by accident, and this seems to be particularly true of the villages in the Koyukon region. Whether there is a significant correlation remains to be investigated, but there is a logical connection between the availability of help and whether or not a life can be saved. One must also consider that because health care is provided equally in

Table 9. Community Health Aide Outpatient Encounters Compared with Deaths by Accident and Suicide, by Village, within the Koyukon Region, 1993

Village	Total Outpatient Encounters	Deaths by Accident	Deaths by Suicide	Population
Galena	1,252	7	3	831
Hughes	360	5	1	54
Huslia	1,771	2	4	207
Koyukuk	876	9	2	715
Nulato	1,694	11	5	359
Rampart	469	1	0	68
Ruby	1,296	3	1	170
Tanana	5,448	4	1	345

Source: Data derived from Alaska Area Native Health Service 1993:table 5.

all villages, and each villager knows how to reach his or her community health aide at any time of the day, there may be a simple reluctance to do that which could sustain one's life longer than desired.

A comparison of data from the villages of Tanana and Gwichyaa Zhee is worthy of note. Each of these villages contains health center facilities of superior quality to that of the other villages in their regions. According to the 1990 census data Tanana is half the size of Gwichyaa Zhee, yet its health center featured twice the number of outpatient counters per person during 1993. In that year there were comparatively few accidental deaths in Tanana as compared with the number in other villages. There are obviously too few data to make generalizations about health trends, but it does seem to me that the data within these tables

Table 10. Suicide Deaths in the United States, 1974–91

Year	Alaska Natives and American Indians	All Races
1991 (projected)	184	—
1990	195	30,906
1989	192	30,232
1988	185	30,407
1987	187	30,407
1986	158	30,904
1985	172	29,453
1984	148	29,286
1983	161	28,295
1982	154	28,242
1981	157	27,596
1980	146	26,869
1979	162	27,204
1978	117	27,294
1977	161	28,681
1976	143	26,832
1975	139	27,063
1974	122	25,683
1973	116	25,118
1972	113	25,004
1955	39	16,760

Source: Based on data compiled by the U.S. Department of Health and Human Services (1994).

suggest a need for further study about the correlation between frequency of health care visits and violent death rates.

I was unable to obtain comparable information about the Canadian health care services or violent death rates. Health care is one of the few services provided to Native peoples of Canada. Health care is provided to all Canadian citizens; however, I understand that indigenous health care is funded separately from that of the mainstream society. I know of two Gwich'in women who married Gwich'in men of Vuntut. Both appeared distrustful of the health care provided to Canadian Natives, and one of them was indicted for using Alaskan health care facilities no longer legally available to her upon her marriage to a Canadian man. The other has avoided using the Canadian health care for several years despite serious medical problems.

In 1994 the Council of Athabascan Tribal Governments (CATG) went from two to seven employees, and in 1995 it expanded to 35 employees working in four locations in two villages. CATG, which is discussed more fully in chapters 2 and 4, now operates the local clinics in nine villages.

As a final comment about trends in health statistics, I looked to these figures with an eye toward the possibility that Northern Athabascans are now healthier and less prone to become victims of violent death than they used to be. Regional data by village on these issues are limited, for such studies are relatively new, and modes of collecting information vary from individual to individual; hence, I was unable to support that hypothesis. The next section explores issues of homicide, suicide, and trends in other forms of unexpected death.

Death by Suicide, Death by Violence

Suicide among Native American peoples has been studied intensely for several decades, and yet, as I discuss in this chapter, the information seems both inaccurate and exaggerated. Lester suggests two reasons for the interest. The first is that suicide has been taken as an indicator of social pathologies since Durkheim's inquiries. The second reason is that policy makers are concerned about the welfare of American Indians (Lester 1997:1–2). I suggest a third, which is that because a large segment of Native Americans is registered from birth with the federal governments of either Canada or the United States, that population is controlled not only politically and economically but also scientifically. Like laboratory animals, Native Americans with a certificate of blood quantum can be observed from birth to death in a scientific manner. Both the U.S. IHS and the Canadian Health Service keep medical information on Native Americans by individual, by race, and, where fiscally appropriate, by tribe.

As I mentioned in the previous section, the data are incomplete. Native Americans seek help from a variety of sources for bodily, emotional, and spiritual needs, only some of which is through the IHS. However, only the IHS records are available. In addition, as Lester (1997:12–13) has discovered, methods of compiling information about cause of death are incomplete or inaccurate, and suicide is underreported, even when the coroners' reports clearly identify the death cause as such. I further challenge the accuracy of cause of death data for the simple reason that few autopsies are conducted by which to verify analysis of cause of death. Thus, the line items in Tables 5 and 6 are debatable. Why was alcoholism selected as a cause of death? Was the individual inebriated at the moment of death? Was each deceased person so listed under a physician's care for alcoholism? Were any so listed untested or unchallenged assumptions? Because there is cause to be suspicious of the death data listed on these tables, I suggest that they be analyzed from the standpoint of what is gained from categorizing death in the ways defined in the tables in this chapter. Because suicide is such a common theme, one question persists: What constitutes suicide and from whose point of view? All of the tables were fabricated using mainstream categories rather than Native American categories.

While I lived in Gwichyaa Zhee and during the three years since then five Athabascan people died by what was publicly termed suicide, and there were others about which there was speculation in the gossip circles. The first of the five acknowledged suicides occurred in 1993 when a man in his sixties, who had been diagnosed with brain cancer, shot himself. In 1994 a man in his thirties killed his girlfriend and then himself at a lonely spot on the Yukon River. They were found a few days later and assessed as having been drunk at the time of death. The other three were teenagers whose deaths occurred after I left Gwichyaa Zhee. In February 1996 a 16-year-old Gwichyaa Zhee man reportedly shot himself while intoxicated. Four months later another teenager hung himself in Gwichyaa Zhee in an event that was said to be related both to heavy intoxication and to the February death. In April 1998 another Gwich'in teenager hung herself in Fairbanks. Her death is likewise associated with the February 1996 death of her friend. In each of these events the individuals controlled the moment and means of their deaths. The intoxicated youths may not have been in clear command of their awareness at the time of death, but there is no doubt that they accomplished goals that they established themselves.

Suicide in Athabascan traditions is normally linked to informed choices controlled by the individual and is usually related to the survival of others. In meaning-laden narrative tradition, disabled people, for instance, supposedly announced that they would stay behind so that the rest of the group could continue a journey unburdened. There are no traditional categories for alcoholism or death related to intoxication. Such deaths are postcolonial events. Additionally, there are no traditional stories about people who hang themselves. In other words, of these five deaths, only one can be related to a traditional Athabascan meaning code for suicide. The other four deaths are not codified by Athabascan traditions, leaving those who mourn the loss to explain the deaths in two discursive realms. The first of these is mainstream, a rhetoric that dominates and is attended by counselors who bring into the events an array of blame and prejudice regarding the bodies and minds of the deceased and the social system surrounding them. The second is a more or less pan-Indian discourse that blames the political and economic hegemonies occurring in the society of the deceased.

These discourses are intertwined, and together they create an even thicker web of meaning about such deaths. However, do these theories explain the death of each of the deceased Athabascans described previously? Did any of them kill themselves because they were Indians suffering economic or political oppression? Can these deaths be converted to evidence supporting political statements without regard to the sentiments, personalities, or thoughts and social discourse of the deceased and their immediate cohort at the moment of death? *Suicide* is a term laden with socially constructed implications about the form of death, not to mention the mental stability, strength, and coherence of the deceased. The traditional Athabascan form of voluntary suicide accords ultimate agency in intention and execution to the deceased, whereas death by drowning implies some sort of mental, physical, or emotional frailty on the part of the individual that leads to the death. Many people who live along the Yukon and other rivers in Alaska have died by drowning while intoxicated. Of late some of these deaths have been included in the category of suicide, as have deaths by drug or alcohol overdose. I raise all of these questions in order to render suspect and dangerous the assumptions made by the researchers who prepared the tabulated data and suggest that future studies about so-called suicide need to include full awareness of the cultural, financial, and political implications that motivate the investigation of suicide.

To return to the arguments raised with respect to the machinery involved in the addictive economic system in Athabascan villages (as well as other regions), those who are the primary financial beneficiaries of such research are the researchers themselves. They are prompted to prove and promote the merit of their work by reporting significant numerical correlations between events. They are also encouraged to make dramatic or at least original discoveries as part and parcel of academic standards. Hence, findings such as those in Table 11, which lists drug overdoses as a leading means of suicide, reflect semiotic choices that are not necessarily meaningful to the population involved. With these caveats made, I suggest that the tables in these pages be viewed with caution.

Table 10 lists suicide rates throughout the United States, dividing the population into Native Americans and all others. According to Table 10 nearly four decades of putative Native American suicides constituted less than 1 percent of the suicides reported in the "U.S. All Races" category since 1955. According to the 1990 census, this indicates that the rate of Native American suicides is lower than that of other people, an unstated finding that disagrees with every analysis I have read about suicide in the United States. The inaccuracies of this information are further compounded by the questions raised in the 1990 census regarding who is a Native American. What is the population base for the figures listed here? Like many Native Americans, I do not carry my certificate of blood quantum card on my person at all times; would anyone report my death as that of a Native American? I am of mixed descent; the issue might never arise, especially if I am not in Alaska at the time. Information collected regionally is likewise subject to question.

In a study querying the deaths of New Mexico Indian youths, May and Van Winkle (1994) provide data showing a marked increase after 1972 (less than 100 per 100,000 prior to 1972 as compared with 162 per 100,000 in 1978 — the highest volume of suicides reported). The increase found by May and Van Winkle may simply be related to global population growth trends, perhaps in combination with the national

Table 11. Suicides and Suicide Attempts among Iñupiaq Men in Kotzebue, Northwestern Alaska, 1977–80

Characteristics	Men	Women
Median age	23.2	22.0
Number of years of education achieved	10.5	9.5
% unemployed	75	82
% never married	92	77
% with annual household income < $10,000	77	88
Means employed in suicide		
% drug overdose	39	77
% gunshot	20	3
% cut/stabbing	22	11
% other	19	8
Number of cases	51	68

Source: U.S. Public Health Service Medical and Counseling records, 1977–80; Kotzebue Police records, 1977–80. Based on research done by Robert Travis (1983).

social problems associated with the end of the Vietnam War. In any event, the population of federally registered Native Americans in New Mexico is much higher than it is in Alaska and thus provides a larger basis for statistical reportage. The study provides statistics that imply a serious increase in Native American suicide. However, it omits several important issues. A breakdown by specific cause of death would be helpful to determine how suicide is defined differently from death by other causes, such as accident or drug overdose. Also, as New Mexico is populated by people of many Indian nations, a breakdown by tribal identity should have been easily obtained. Furthermore, the data are limited to suicide reported in the State of New Mexico. What of those New Mexico Indian youths whose deaths occurred outside of New Mexico? Once again, while these data are highly suggestive, they lead to more questions, questions that may not be answered in the data as they are collected in the first place.

The researchers who compiled this data attempt to correlate their information with employment figures, which are highly inconclusive, suggesting that well over one-half of those who died were employed, another one-third were students, and the rest were unemployed or "unclassifiable" (May and Van Winkle 1994:12–13). Similar studies have been conducted in Alaska. Table 12 provides some information about general death rates in Alaska in a useful but already meaning-charged analysis that assumes that there are meaningful relationships between the categories of accident and violence.

Data from yet another study give an indication of suicide rates among Alaska Natives around the state (Travis 1986). According to Travis's data, Bristol Bay Corporation (Alutiiq and Yup'ik peoples), NANA Corporation (Iñupiat people), and Koniag Corporation (made up mostly of Alutiiq people) have experienced the highest increases in suicide. In the years 1971–76 Bristol Bay Corporation reported 9.5 suicides, and it reported 84.1 for the years 1977–82. NANA Corporation reported 62.7 suicides for the years 1971–76 and 101.9 for 1977–82. Koniag Corporation reported 9.3 suicides for the years 1971–76 and 35.5 for the years 1977–82. In the same study, Travis reports that Doyon, representing interior Athabascans, and the largest Alaska Native Claims Settlement Act (ANCSA) corporation, by contrast, reported a significant drop (64.7 suicides in the years 1971–76, a number that dropped to 31.5 for the years 1977–82). The two other Northern Athabascan ANCSA corporations (Ahtna and CIRI) also reported fewer or minor changes in the rates of suicide among their shareholders (-26 percent for Ahtna and 7 percent

Table 12. Annual Average Violent Death Rates in Alaska by Sex and Ethnicity, 1980–90 (*Rates per 100,000*)

Ethnicity	Men	Women
Alaska Native		
Accident rates	214.2	65.5
Suicide rates	85.0	12.3
Homicide rates	44.7	19.1
Non-Native		
Accident rates	82.9	23.0
Suicide rates	26.3	5.7
Homicide rates	12.5	6.2

Source: Data derived from Berman and Leask 1994:5, table 2.

for CIRI). Each of the corporations has a different history in terms of economic success. Bering Straits and Doyon have both faced bankruptcy since the passage of ANCSA in 1971, and between them Doyon has made a more successful recovery. Travis's data are important from the standpoint of providing geographic guidance regarding social problems in Alaska. Nonetheless, he and others point out that these figures are statistically meaningless because of the low state population figures (less than 700,000 in the entire state in 2000, according to the U.S. census). Moreover, some researchers suspect that suicide statistics are prone to error. David Lester (1997), for instance, has found inconsistencies between the number of deaths reported as suicide on coroners' reports and the number of deaths by suicide reported on police and other agency documents, suggesting that future suicide research requires a good deal more awareness of all potential factors.

NANA, whose rates appear to be the worst, is one of the more successful in terms of annual revenue. Its collaboration with Cominco, a mining corporation, has reportedly been very lucrative for Cominco and less so for NANA. Table 11 provides some information about the NANA situation for the period 1977–80, during which approximately 1.5 percent of the population died in a category called "drug overdose." Over one-half of the 119 deceased were young, unemployed, unmarried women who died by drug overdose. Most of them earned less than $10,000 per year (approximately 60 percent of the average household earnings in Gwichyaa Zhee in 1990).

While these statistics are alarming, and are certainly cause for investigation, I suggest that the researchers have made a serious error in analysis by lumping drug overdosing with death by self-inflicted gunshots and stab wounds. Nonetheless, 119 people of the Kotzebue region died during the time of this study by self-inflicted gunshots, self-inflicted stab wounds, "other," and drug overdose. Unless there is clear evidence that excessive drugs were taken to induce death, then applying the term *suicide* to such deaths is making unverifiable assumptions about the psychological inner state of the individuals. Generally speaking, suicide refers to a certain degree of agency or choice on the part the social actors involved. In labeling 72 (60 percent) of the 119 deaths that occurred in Kotzebue between 1977 and 1980 as caused by drug overdose as suicide (see Table 11), the researcher has interpreted the information beyond the empirical evidence in a number of ways. He has presumed that suicidal tendency is functionally linked with the use of lethal drugs. In addition, he has presumed that each of the 72 deceased listed in the survey intended to die by drug usage. One effect of these presumptions is that by including in the survey 72 deaths that are not empirically suicide, the researcher has doubled the figures that signal suicide, giving a misleading indication that suicide in Kotzebue made a sudden jump from 0.9 percent (in a population of approximately 5,200 in the Kotzebue region) to 2.2 percent. Again, these facts are an alarming indication of social pathology.

What are the potential problems that might stem from this misnomenclature? One possibility is that by calling all of the deaths "suicide," the researcher attributes choice to the individual, however invisible it may have been to those in the community of the deceased. By doing so, the researcher has located all responsibility for the deaths within the mind of the deceased and thereby has removed accountability from other individuals or the social milieu of the deceased. It is a way of saying that these people, especially the women, are mentally unstable or weak.

The tables show the grim ratios of suicide by age and ethnic group in Alaska. Statistics show that until the mid-1960s suicide was rare among Alaska Natives — 13 per 100,000 (Kettle and Bixler 1993:34). The rate of suicide has climbed steadily to more than five times that rate. The suicide rate among Alaska Natives in 1986 was 67.6 per 100,000 (Kettle and Bixler 1993:35). Most analysts associate high suicide with alcoholism, but I consider the fact that natural resources were discovered and exploited (oil and hydroelectric energy) beginning in the 1960s to be the fundamental source of turmoil. ANCSA and all of the changes in Native lifestyles because of it may have more to with causing suicide than anything else.

Tables 13 and 14 contain comparative death rates from accidents, suicides, and homicides in the United States and Alaska. Matthew Berman (1995; Berman and Leask 1994) has used these figures to ascertain that violent death rates among Alaska Native people as a whole are far greater than they are nationally and that the rates are much worse for Alaska Native men than they are for Alaska Native women. In 1988 Berman found that Alaska Native people are four times more likely to die by suicide than any other ethnicity. Northern Athabascans were appalled by the total number of deaths that occurred in their communities dur-

Table 13. Violent Deaths in Athabascan Villages, 1990

Village	Native Accidents	Native Suicides	Native Homicides	Native Population	Non-Native Population
Vashraii K'oo	2	—	—	90	6
Beaver	4	—	—	98	5
Deenduu	1	—	—	38	4
Jałk'iitsik	1	1	—	83	7
Central	—	—	—	1	51
Danzhit Hanlii	—	—	—	63	10
Gwichyaa Zhee	10	2	4	493	87
Dinyee	5	1	—	93	9
Viihtaii	5	—	—	171	11
Total	28	4	4	1,130	190

Source: Berman 1995.

ing the short time I lived there. In view of their underlying values of endurance and strength, my opinion is that suicide death rates among the Alaskan Gwich'in are usually low, but it is statistically difficult to ascertain this because the populations are so small. These figures derive from information supplied by Matthew Berman (1995) of the Institute of Social and Economic Research, University of Alaska Anchorage. The population figures used in Table 13 are significantly lower than those presented by the Alaska Department of Community and Regional Affairs (1994) from the same database: the U.S. Bureau of the Census for 1990. See Table 14 for comparative information.

The figures in Tables 13 and 14 are taken from statewide and nation-

Table 14. Violent Deaths in Koyukon Villages, 1990

Village	Native Accidents	Native Suicides	Native Homicides	Native Population	Non-Native Population
Allakaket	3	4	—	160	10
Galena	7	3	1	377	456
Hughes	5	1	—	50	4
Huslia	2	4	2	188	19
Koyukuk	9	2	1	191	524
Nulato	11	5	3	348	11
Tanana	4	1	1	270	75
Rampart	1	—	—	64	4
Ruby	3	1	—	126	44
Total	45	21	8	1,774	1,147

Source: Figures derived from information supplied by Matthew Berman, Institute of Social and Economic Research, University of Alaska Anchorage, 1995.

wide averages. The raw numbers of violent deaths among Northern Athabascans are at least one-half the number for the Alaska Natives who live farther down the Yukon River, the Koyukon Athabascans. The rate of violent deaths among Northern Athabascans during the year 1990 was lower than the statewide averages, and the rates among the Koyukon were higher than the statewide averages.

My purpose for presenting this information is to indicate that there is a trend among Northern Athabascans toward a positive mental outlook on life, which I relate to *vaťaii* and *yinjih* through *daťaii*. Cultural support for this tendency comes from such common expressions as "We suffer, we endure, but we continue on."

Earlier in this chapter I present information from studies on violent death because there is an indication that there have been comparatively fewer deaths by suicide, accident, and homicide in Athabascan communities than there are in other Alaska Native villages. In my opinion this is an indication that Northern Athabascans have increasing confidence in themselves as human beings to know who they are, be what they can be, and make changes within their communities that are what they understand as improvement. There appears to be a correlation between more frequent visits to the clinics and fewer accidental deaths, possibly another indication that Northern Athabascan people perceive themselves individually as strong people and that, therefore, they are doing that which is necessary to preserve their own lives. In my opinion this is an attitude that stems directly from their own metaphysical traditions regarding survival, sacred strength, and harmony.

Discourses on Cultural Depression

In 1990 Terry O'Nell was narrating her ideas for a dissertation that has since been published as *Disciplined Hearts: History, Identity, and Depression in an American Indian Community* (1996). She described going to the Flathead Indian Reservation of Montana to ask if people there were interested in research on depression. The Flathead encouraged her to come. They said that 80 percent of their people were depressed. When O'Nell started working with them she discovered that they did not mean psychological depression. They were talking about tribal consciousness, knowledge of the Flathead's loss of freedom, lands, and dignity ever since they were confined to their reservation in the 19th century.

Shreevyaa of Gwichyaa Zhee linked the Flathead theory of depression to Native American loss of self-esteem. In her analysis the white man's tendency to locate depression within the individual fails to identify one of the leading causes of depression among her people: loss of identity.

She considered that, with respect to Gwich'in, depression should be studied as "cultural depression." Shreevyaa was referring to the many ways in which her people neglect themselves and seem unaware of the concepts of vat'aii and yinjih. She was by no means the only Athabascan person to voice such a concern.

In Alaska, noted Yup'ik scholar Harold Napoleon of Hooper Bay talks about yuut tu'qur'pat'rrat'ne, "the Great Death," which through disease and starvation took up to 60 percent of the Yup'ik people in the 19th century. Napoleon describes the abandonment of yuuya'raq (the Yup'ik "way of being a human being"). He argues that "with the Yup'ik people and most of Alaska Native tribes, the case can be made that resistance collapsed because of mass death, the result of famine, illness, and the trauma that accompanied these" (1991:17). Even more devastating to the Yup'ik was that they lost contact with their sacred traditions, that body of knowledge and thought that gives the Yup'ik an understanding at all levels of what it takes to be Yup'ik. Napoleon maintains that the Yup'ik people who survived this loss have "receded with their tattered lives and unbearable emotions into a deep silence" (1991:19). The Yup'ik rates of death by suicide are among the highest in Alaska. Napoleon asks Yup'ik people to end the suffering of future generations by talking openly about themselves, "leaving nothing out, to see what was causing these disturbances in their lives" (1991:25). Napoleon himself talks openly about his alcoholism and the fact that he murdered his son because of it. Napoleon uses the post-traumatic stress syndrome usually associated with veterans of the Vietnam War as a metaphor to explain his theory of dysfunction among the Yup'ik.

Larry Merculieff of Saint Paul Island, an Aleut, has responded to Napoleon's work by suggesting that it takes more than talk to solve problems of this magnitude. He has opined that the rituals that were abandoned because of Christian influence played important roles in traditional indigenous societies (Merculieff, personal communication,

1994). Many have criticized the missionary dogma that prohibits Native Americans from expressing their traditional beliefs in any way. Christians of various denominations dominate the spiritual landscape of Athabascan communities. Other ideologies are mentioned and practiced privately, even secretly, especially the indigenous Athabascan religious traditions. So forceful is the Christian presence in Athabascan land that people are very guarded in their speech about alternative beliefs, although many of the Northern Athabascan people I have met are aware of and incorporate into their daily lives elements of the old practices. Inés Talamantez (1995) states that Native American religious traditions are usually so fully integrated into all aspects of indigenous culture that it is not easy to isolate them as purely religious features. Likewise, it is not always clear when a habit, practice, or idea may be part of a sacred process. For these and other reasons Athabascan people cannot be considered completely disconnected from their sacred traditions, but they may have great difficulty in perceiving the original philosophy that guided them. Without their traditional language they may lose contact with that philosophy altogether unless they begin to translate and articulate it in another language.

Napoleon's post-traumatic stress syndrome theory has value in explaining what has happened to Native Americans, but it is rigid in the sense of freeze-framing the condition of Natives into one mode of being and one way of having reached that point. Napoleon thinks of violence, alcoholism, drug abuse, and depression as caused by the Great Death, but they can also be caused by other forms of trauma. The strength of his theory rests in the healing power that comes with channeling all pain to one point in order to make it easier to analyze and remove. This is what the Flathead have done in isolating social pain around the fact of their relocation onto their reservation. Other aspects of my research led me farther afield to areas of the world where there is ethnic conflict, par-

ticularly where the conflict emerges in social dysfunction attending colonial presence.

Loss and Change by Peter Marris (1974) delineates a theory about African tribal peoples whose colonial experience is similar to that of Native
Americans up to a certain point. The main difference lies in population
ratios. There are fewer white people in Africa than there are in the
United States. Marris's analysis did not totally satisfy my search for a
theory of social survival as Northern Athabascans experience it, but it is
worth mentioning in some detail in order to understand Northern Athabascans as victims of colonialization. Marris identifies certain kinds of
social change as resulting from traumatic irretrievable loss that requires
the healing powers of formal public mourning. Marris talks about three
stages of change that are specific to grief. He lists the patterns of grief
starting with shock and denial, followed by acute distress, and then
ending with reintegration (1974:27). Although his labels are different,
there is a similarity to Van Gennep's theory of the rites of passage. The
Native American reaction to colonialism in the United States has been
different from what Marris found in Africa. Rather than cycles of grief
as Marris describes them, Native Americans experience continual epi-
sodes of denial mixed with suppressed anger that sometimes turns to
violence and, more often than not, to substance abuse or related psychological and social dysfunctions. There do not appear to be predictable
cycles of behavior.

Marris narrows his focus to situations involving public loss, such as
the mass eviction and removal of urban slum residents from familiar
surroundings to new locations. Because they usually were not moved as
a group to a single new setting, the slum residents did not have an opportunity to complete what Marris considers to be an essential part of
healing through sharing their feelings and thoughts. As a result they
tended to behave apathetically, displaying many behaviors common to

individuals in deep grief— indeed, many behaviors in common with Native Americans. He observes the following conditions about grief: "The typical signs of grief can be summarized, then, as physical distress and worse health; an inability to surrender the past — expressed, for instance, by brooding over memories, sensing the presence of the dead, clinging to possessions, being unable to comprehend the loss, feelings of unreality; withdrawal into apathy; and hostility against others, against fate, or turned in upon oneself" (1974:26).

Except for the fact that they are not cyclical, these and other aspects of Marris's theory resonate with what I know of Athabascan experiences. Marris's description of grief also conforms to addictive behaviors as described by Anne Wilson Schaef (1987). According to Schaef, addictive behaviors work to distract their victims from being present to and aware of their immediate situation. Marris emphasizes the role of consensus in a social process. The transitional stage as Marris views it is a long period of ambivalence and indecisiveness, a period of waiting to see what the others will do. Another potential link between Northern Athabascan and African efforts includes an interest in sovereignty. Marris states, "The desire for complete autonomy seems a natural temptation of innovators. Absolute power gives the illusion of absolute certainty: if everything depends on you, nothing will happen which you have not foreseen" (1974:113).

This also represents a peculiar sort of forced consensus in which participants are encouraged, possibly even coerced into agreeing with the dominant agenda of more powerful personalities. The Native experience usually finds that it is the white man, rather than one of their own, who wants absolute authority. Athabascan people speak nostalgically about a time before 1970 when their chiefs and tribal council members held coercive authority over their communities. The coincidence of ANCSA in 1971, which profoundly affected the lives of all Alaska Natives, the rising rates of suicide among Alaska Natives since the mid-1960s, and the loss of power of the village chiefs tells a different story from that which Marris presents about Africans. Northern Athabascans' desire for sovereignty emerges from the complex relationship of litigation between Native American tribes and the U.S. government. Marris's theory provides an explanation for many of the behaviors and attitudes I have encountered among Athabascan people. Many of the people with whom I have discussed this idea were equally attracted to it, but some people voiced doubts, including Shreevyaa of Gwichyaa Zhee and Yeendaa (a pseudonym) of Vashraii K'oo. For Yeendaa the word *grieving* involves loss of pride; it cuts to the heart of Northern Athabascan people. Shreevyaa argued that I was overemphasizing death. These objections once again elicited discussions about Northern Athabascans as survivors. A metaphor in use by Northern Athabascans themselves would be far more likely to explain their attitudes and history than an idea imported from another continent.

A review of Marris's concept with Clarence Alexander of Gwichyaa Zhee led to consideration of the concept of consensus — yinjih. Alexander criticized the grief analogy because it tends to miscue or misdirect one's thoughts. He observed that the idea of grieving has become popular within the past decade or so, especially among those who like to grieve. However, his elders taught him that tears were precious, part of one's soul, and not to be wasted. This is a key statement about Gwich'in reliance on vat'aii as a means to achieve a cultural ideal of stoicism or as proof of one's stamina while suffering. Nonetheless, Alexander acknowledged that denial, one of the phases of the grieving cycle described by Marris and others, is present among Athabascan people in a variety of forms.

Denial is often considered to be part of the recovery from any trauma and is not particular to grief, although here again is a culturally constructed category of thought that conflicts with Athabascan formulations of grief or denial. Some people, for instance, deny being Native because of personal experiences of racism. They prefer to highlight their other ethnic or national roots instead. Another, perhaps more pervasive, form of denial is "the denial that Native people can do things for ourselves" (Alexander, personal communication, March 1995). Alexander and other Athabascan leaders are challenging the latter form of denial through the development of such agencies as the Council of Athabascan Tribal Governments. CATG was organized several years ago when a chief in Tsee, Alaska, asked Alexander how he thought Native people were going to stop putting their hands out, waiting for help from outsiders. Their subsequent debate led to the formation of CATG, a nonprofit organization that includes several Athabascan communities in the Yukon Flats area. By creating CATG, Alexander and his colleagues drew on the logic of vat'aii, dat'aii, and yinjih to begin a process that could emerge as a larger social movement. Marris's theory juxtaposed with the discussions I have mentioned reveal my Gwichyaa Zhee experience: a mind full of theory coupled with action that relates to theory much as any cousin would. The uncanny resemblance disappears as soon as one gets into an argument with it. There is no shortage of Gwich'in metaphors about themselves: "Dinjii Zhuh" (little people, humble people), "the Caribou People," and "poor people" are a sample. Any one of these yields useful insight into Gwich'in society, but I sought a metaphor that also expresses the idea of survival in the midst of chaos.

Many Athabascans endorsed the idea of survival in my writings: Itree, Wally Peter, Sarah James, and Gideon James are just a few of them. Slobodin states, "Survival is a subject of particular interest to the Kutchin [a synonym for *Gwich'in* used until the 1980s]" (1975:284). Slobodin provides a detailed, annotated version of a Northern Athabascan traditional tale, "Without Fire" (as the tale of Ko'ehdan), which illustrates aspects of vat'aii as well as yinjih. The story is about a legendary

Gwich'in hero who survived an enemy raid and the theft of his outer clothing and food. He walked for days in midwinter to the nearest neighboring campsite. For Northern Athabascans the story epitomizes their core values: survival and strength. Personal strength is obviously a basic element of survival, but what causes Northern Athabascans or any society to remain a cultural unit?

Trimble Gilbert of Vashraii K'oo offered me one of the most complete theories about Gwich'in survival. He suggested that the actions of Athabascan people can be compared with the behavior of a herd of caribou when wolves attack, causing them to scatter. Gilbert remarked that it takes a long time for the individual animals to get back together, but they always make the effort. He further explained that drugs and alcohol are like wolves, scattering the continuity of Athabascan society. Alexander preferred Gilbert's analogy to Marris's grieving metaphor, although he noted that the caribou image best suits northern communities such as Vashraii K'oo, where the caribou predominate. Gilbert's metaphor holds with my observations about Northern Athabascans both in their own territory and in other places. They find each other and keep up with each other's foibles almost on a daily basis, no matter where they are. They accept each other despite ravages of alcoholism and other abuses. In their conversations and actions they express a unity that usually overrides personal enmities. In short, they stick together more than most people I know.

Rather than spotlighting the negative effects of loss, Alexander suggested a broader metaphor to emphasize the sources of continuity that bind Northern Athabascans together in the first place — their kinship affiliations among villages. He said that in former times people knew exactly who they were by their relations in every Northern Athabascan village. He considered that since approximately 1950 Athabascan people have become less familiar with their kinship connections. Most of the elders are well versed in their family affiliations. Several Athabascans are researching their genealogies and devising methods of archiving the material as their collections grow. Alexander thought that the post–World War II era marked the time of greatest change for Northern Athabascans. Alaska witnessed a third wave of immigrants to the territory in less than a century at that time, and a number of them came to Gwichyaa Zhee. Most people see the exploitation efforts of the 1960s as the point of greatest impact. Chapter 2 discusses this topic.

At the 1994 Gwich'in Gathering in Vuntut nearly every speaker talked of his or her desires, plans, experiences, and hopes for healing Athabascan people. The chief of the Vuntut Gwich'in, Robert Bruce, talked with me about the use of the word *healing* there. He said that the band council in an effort to control substance abuse had passed an ordinance to prohibit the importation of alcohol. Many people objected and seemed particularly to resent the word *prohibition*. Bruce then introduced the word *healing*, asking people if they would prefer to use that concept instead of prohibition. The word itself seemed to have some palliative effect on the community, helping people overcome their resistance to the idea.

The present-day emphasis on positive words such as *healing* may reflect popular television culture. Those who were born after World War II tend to use such terms, while those who are older favor words reflecting endurance and suffering. In comparison to people's economic and physical conditions prior to World War II, the present-day Athabascans are healthy and relatively well off economically (see chapter 3 for additional information on this topic). They do not suffer in the way that the traditional tales describe Athabascans as suffering, although they certainly suffer the trials of social dysfunction. Nonetheless, healing and suffering are two sides of the same issue: When there were no options Northern Athabascans suffered and expressed a certain pride in doing so without breaking. Now they have more options, among which are physical recuperation and emotional growth. Counseling and group discussions about their problems have become common. As Gilbert Stevens of Gwichyaa Zhee remarked, it implies the need to examine the past and to envision a future. The question remains: From what are they healing? Is it the loss of population or loss of a body of sacred knowledge as Harold Napoleon writes? Is it the loss of identity as Shreevyaa speculated? Is it the loss of community as Trimble Gilbert suggested? It helps to put these questions in the context of those who are trying to heal from personal addictions.

In 1993 Dadzaii (a pseudonym) of Vashraii K'oo asked if she could stay with me during the fall teacher's conference in Gwichyaa Zhee, and I agreed. She told me that she had been sober for 14 years, and she was afraid of walking alone in Gwichyaa Zhee because she considered the village to be dangerous. Although I had been walking around the village for months by that time with no discomfort, I was happy to offer escort services to and from the school. During her subsequent visits Dadzaii became more relaxed about Gwichyaa Zhee and began to walk around more independently. Her initial fears, however, are indicative of a significant difference between personal attempts to heal from addiction and the recovery environment. Until Dadzaii gained some measure of confidence that she could trust the villagers of Gwichyaa Zhee to respect her and her attempts to be sober, she was intensely uncomfortable. As so many counselors have advocated in healing situations, not only does the individual have to learn new habits, but so does the community around that individual. With the help of such trained professionals, the people of Gwichyaa Zhee are active beginners in developing new community behaviors about addiction. I have mentioned the Youth Survivors drug and alcohol conference in earlier chapters, and it is useful to revisit some of the substance of that conference one more time.

On February 1, 1993, the village tribal government (Native Village of Gwichyaa Zhee) and one of its subordinate entities, the Gwichyaa Zhee

Youth Survivors, hosted a two-day conference on substance abuse. They had invited chiefs from three other Athabascan villages plus an Alaska Native alcohol counselor from Anchorage, Ernie Turner. Because of bad weather, only the chief and Episcopal minister from Vashraii K'oo, Trimble Gilbert, was able to make it, and he arrived late on the second day of the conference. His joke about the pilot, who refused to turn off the engines while the chief deplaned, reminded everyone that only fools chose to be out in that weather. According to my field notes, the day started with temperatures at -30 degrees Fahrenheit with thick ice fog. Most trucks, cars, and snow machines were too frozen to start at that temperature. The uninsulated log building that housed the village Tribal Council and this conference was heated, although most people remained in their outer gear throughout the day. I was comfortable with my heavy parka unzipped and the hood down. The room was filled with approximately 60 high school and upper elementary school students and 30 adults, almost meeting room capacity. Students and elders filled the seats in long rows of folding metal chairs, while most of the adults stood or sat beside the walls. The conference coordinator and director of the Youth Survivors program introduced each speaker. Speaking in the clipped, strident accent of Northern Athabascans, she told the young people that she was presenting role models and that they needed to make up their own minds about what to do in their lives: "Once you do that, you can get help from people in town."

All of the speakers had been instructed to address the conference theme, which was drug and alcohol dependence, and all of them had been chosen because of their success in recovery. The first speaker, a man in his late sixties, was the most effective elder in Gwichyaa Zhee with respect to directing the large flow of money coming through Gwichyaa Zhee through three or four elder's agencies. I refer to him as "the Elder," although by Athabascan standards he was still a young man.

During the 1960s and 1970s he had been one of the most active leaders in the community with respect to stopping the Rampart Dam project (see chapter 2) and creating village bureaucratic structures to enable ANCSA. His speech began at 11:30, just when the school district had arranged to bring the students back to school for their lunch. One of the teachers apologized.

As the youths clattered out of the building, the Elder complained that even though this was a Gwich'in meeting for Gwich'in students they were still subject to Western ways of dealing with schedules. He felt that the students should have stayed there during the entire meeting. He started his life story by saying that he was an alcoholic and that he lived in Fairbanks for a while. His wife got sick, and they could not live together anymore because she needed heat and he needed a cooler environment, especially to sleep. He told us that he was moving out when she became even more ill, and he had to stay to make arrangements for long-term care of her in Fairbanks while he moved back to Gwichyaa Zhee. He had been sober for two years, which he attributed to help from God. While the Elder was disappointed in the noisy departure of the students, the mere fact that he was imparting his experience about alcohol abuse and recovery to younger people is significant. I was told that there had been other such conferences in the past decade, so his words were not unusual to the community.

There is a good deal of interest among Northern Athabascans in healing methods for personal addiction through models such as Alcoholics Anonymous. The 12-step program began in 1908 through a nondenominational Christian organization called the Oxford Group. The Oxford Group started with four steps, which became six steps in 1934. Bill Wilson, an alcoholic, and Dr. Bob Smith created the first 12-step program between 1938 and 1939 and also originated the name Alcoholics Anonymous (Kasl 1992:139–141). In earlier chapters, particularly chapter 3, I mention some of the efforts Northern Athabascans have made in bringing professional counselors from many backgrounds to their region. As researchers (Mellody and Miller 1989; Miller and Hester 1989; Schaef 1987, 1988) in this area indicate, there are many techniques suggested for treatment, some that locate all effort in the individual and others that address the individual and his or her social network.

Anne Wilson Schaef (1986, 1987, 1988) has introduced the study of a paradigm shift away from investiture in the individual to the societal situation. She uses the theory of codependence as the rationale and mechanical formula for explaining alcoholism as a social phenomenon. Schaef distinguishes between two terms in codependency theory. The first is *enabler*, which is a term "used in chemical dependency circles to describe the person — usually the spouse — who subtly helps support the drinking" (Schaef 1988:5). The other term is *codependent*, used in these circles to define all persons who (1) are in a love or marriage relationship with an alcoholic, (2) have one or more alcoholic parents or grandparents, or (3) grew up in an emotionally repressive family (Schaef 1988:14). By Schaef's definition of *codependency*, 96 percent of the U.S. population are codependent and therefore act out behaviors associated with alcoholism, such as irrational unexpected flashes of anger or rage, obsessive behaviors, and methods of avoiding emotional rapport with another. There is no empirical evidence for this figure, which seems ludicrous in terms of developing a meaningful theory about alcoholism. However, creating such a ubiquitous image of society as suffering the same behavioral turmoil as their clients might elevate comfort levels and communicative rapport between counselors and those who go to them. By enlarging her paradigm to include the entire social system of any given alcoholic, Schaef suggests that systematic methods of analyzing any given social setting for solutions to alcoholic behavior might exist within the group itself.

I discovered Schaef's materials through discussions with other Alaska Native people, found that they were understood and used in Gwichyaa Zhee, and consider that Northern Athabascans are actively striving toward finding social-based solutions within their own context. While others may disagree, I think that the frequent evictions in Athabascan villages are both a manifestation of alcoholic behaviors and a potential source of socially based solutions to alcoholism in Athabascan territory. Through this mechanism of efficiently and socially expressing effective antipathy toward specific behaviors and specific individuals, Northern Athabascans demonstrate that they are effective and efficient in acting out social solidarity.

With respect to healing methods, Northern Athabascans are determined to find solutions and have said so in private and in public for a number of years. There has been no cessation of alcoholism or other addictions. Young Athabascan children get drunk, and Athabascan teenagers kill themselves. The determination to find healing methods has not yet been met by an agreement among Northern Athabascans, first, about what needs healing and, second, about how to perform such healing techniques. Once they take command of their own ideas of what social pathology means, I think they will find that the healing techniques are present, viable, and Athabascan. Of note is that in nearly every discussion about healing, Northern Athabascan people who testified in public meetings or in private conversations always brought in some element of political or economic hegemony. The conference on healing during the Northern Athabascans' Gwich'in Gathering of 1994, for instance, featured elders who spoke (some for the first time) about the hardships they endured through enforced separation from their families at Canadian residential or U.S. Bureau of Indian Affairs boarding schools. In terms of social pathology, Northern Athabascans usually refer to the effects of colonialization on their communities, their families, or themselves. Healing, therefore, must perforce include attention to the social problems inherent in the economic and political imbalances presented by the dominant force of the U.S. federal government and other entities within mainstream society with respect to education, health, and economic enterprises.

7 Final Comments

This study has explored Northern Athabascan ontologies and epistemologies with respect to theories of gender, history, wellness, and social relations with outsiders. All Athabascan indigenous theories have
come in conflict with Euro-Americans, resulting in economic, religious,
and political hegemony in Alaska. Resentment is ever present, as any
visitor to Athabascan villages will affirm, and while its expression has
evolved into a consensual, often violent expulsion of the unwanted,
there is as yet no formalization of these movements into a rhetoric of
ethnic ethos or a mobilization into the formation of an autonomous
Athabascan state. To a certain extent they have used music (country music, fiddle music, and some rock music) to develop and express a collective sentiment about dealing with life's daily hegemonies. Because music is so much a part of the quotidian pattern of Athabascan life, I have
used their music metaphors to explain the indeterminacies of contemporary Athabascan social rules and practices. Throughout these pages I
have examined three central and mutually supportive issues that I consider to have contributed the most to informing a Northern Athabascan
self-awareness and cultural persistence. They are women's investment
in sobriety efforts and child rearing, Athabascan modes of collective
action, and factors in the local Athabascan economy. Of these, mainstream economic domination in the addictive system has infiltrated
more aspects of Athabascan individual lives than anything else. The
addictive infrastructure in Athabascan communities deforms and im-
poverishes many Athabascan people, and there are few mechanisms
available to provide Athabascan children with a grounding in how to

understand the implications of living brown in a white society or how to cope in an alcoholic home environment.

As I suggest in chapter 5, Northern Athabascan women are weaving new issues into the intimacies of Athabascan family life to compensate for the daily ravages of alcoholism. These familial approaches are pragmatic, related to the specific situation and people involved, and not contextualized in a larger social theory. They are the efforts of the Athabascan bricoleur, rather than of individuals acting out tried and true social policies. For the most part Athabascan women have been ignored in most studies except as figures of a mystical past, yet they tend to be the primary motivators in initiating personal and social changes. Women like Shroodiinyaa know and use skills from both Northern Athabascans' traditional world and that of mainstream America. She attended a Native-run business school before starting her restaurant and also learned how to run a kitchen expediently according to the State of Alaska health regulations. In addition to these Western expectations, Shroodiinyaa was expected to be able to prepare traditional game meat and fish in an appropriate Athabascan style, primarily because she was the wife of the man who brought it home but also because she was a matriarch of some standing in the community. Athabascan matriarchs like Shroodiinyaa are called on in many subtle ways to display the social capital of being Athabascan to outsiders, such as myself, and from Shroodiinyaa I learned most of what it takes to be a modern Athabascan woman in Gwichyaa Zhee. One of Shroodiinyaa's predominant characteristics was her intense religious devotion as a Baptist. Her conversion had occurred a few years before I came to Gwichyaa Zhee and was largely related to the support she received from the Baptist minister in raising her family in a nonalcoholic environment. Shroodiinyaa located a spiritual power in Christianity that has helped her maintain a focus on a collective goal.

Other Athabascan men and women with whom I spoke sought similar spiritual power in other areas, and some had success equal to that of Shroodiinyaa. There are many Athabascans who are trying to educate themselves about Athabascan religious traditions with the same fervor that Shroodiinyaa has learned about Christianity. While Northern Athabascans offered many explanations regarding what spiritual belief actually does or is, one social fact remains constant: most of the people who were trying to draw others together as a collective, whether for social gatherings or for political action, did so with prayer and invocation of the numinous. Given a material world that is destitute in every imaginable way, explaining survival and continuance as a form of success based on the invisible has proven to be viable method to avoid negativities and depression for many people throughout the world.

The 19th-century epidemics left Northern Athabascans with few resources, leaving them vulnerable to systems of economic dependency. Now that they have recovered from the decimating diseases of the first sweep of colonial encounters, they find themselves with only a fraction of the land and wildlife resources that their ancestors had before Euro-American colonialization. The historical process has brought implements of defense toward Northern Athabascans in the form of political allies and informal education about other Native American efforts in the United States and Canada. Northern Athabascans have been negatively impacted by Euro-American colonial process in several areas: population, methods of collective action, and religious philosophy. They have recovered some of their precolonial population and are making strong inroads in finding healing therapies that work on the remaining diseases that continue to destroy them (alcoholism, diabetes, and hepatitis B, among others). Their religious traditions are dominated by the Christian presence of several churches in every village, although most Athabascans have some knowledge about their ancient spiritual traditions. Northern Athabascan people are a society in jeopardy of economic poverty and social disintegration. Most damaging of all is the imposition of an economic infrastructure fomenting addictive products and related enterprises. Many also find themselves ignorant of the customs and skills they once had. As a whole they are aware of these dilemmas and have taken some measures to counter what they perceive as the causes. In many instances they have been helped by others, such as Episcopal Church missionaries Rowe and Stuck at the beginning of the 20th century and environmental groups during the last four decades of the 20th century. Among those measures is a search for political identity, which has been supported and instigated by various political interest groups, particularly environmental action forces. The result is a stronger awareness of their cultural distinctiveness and a growing confidence in the appropriateness of rediscovering their traditional strengths. These ideas have been suppressed since Euro-Americans first arrived, and there is some support from the mainstream bureaucracies in Athabascan territory to revitalize them, as well as a dominant force among environmentalists to unify their public image in concert with those of other North American indigenous groups. Alaska's Athabascans are particularly worthy of study because they are supposedly a people at peace in mainstream America, except for the hostile, individual evictions that they effect with frequency. Northern Athabascans cannot be said to be a rebellious ethnicity because they have no uprisings, collective meetings, riots, or collective demonstrations of ethnic violence.

Nonindigenous entrepreneurs continue to exploit Alaska's resources, and each such project has forced political maneuvering of Alaska Natives into circumcised power relations with each other and larger entities. The Alaska Native Claims Settlement Act (ANCSA) of 1971 represents a culminating hegemony. A large body of Alaska's indigenous peoples has been deprived of any political authority by ANCSA and its primary agent, the Alaska Federation of Natives. Northern Athabascans, whose identity is tied to the rural area from which they derive, have almost no voice in Alaska's political events. Those rural Native peoples, such as Northern Athabascans, who have remained in the villages are dispossessed of the power to claim themselves as Natives. By the same token they are deprived of the authority to make any decisions about their own needs.

Northern Athabascans have taken steps toward political and economic recovery in several directions. One of them is apparent in the work of the Gwich'in pioneer John Fredson, with the Venetie Reserve that united Vashraii K'oo and Viihtaii. Another is a regional coalition of Athabascan people that formed in protest of the proposed hydroelectric Rampart Dam project in the 1960s. A third effort has been with the aid of conservationist groups that are helping several Gwich'in villages to protect the Porcupine Caribou Herd on Alaska's northern coast. Women in Athabascan territory have been active in most of these efforts and have added programs such as the Gwichyaa Zhee Youth Survivors program as a means to teach young people something about their traditions as well as basic outdoor survival skills. While these efforts have consumed energy, time, and money, they have resulted not in a unified effort to resume an autonomous Athabascan state but, rather, in an attempt to negotiate within the parameters of dependent domestic relations with the U.S. federal government. Striving for sovereignty at that level has been resisted at national and state levels with significant force.

In chapter 3, I describe some of the complexities involved in Athabascan economic issues, such as the interference of cash and its meaning webs in the traditional sharing economies. The traditional sharing patterns of Northern Athabascans have been misunderstood, refused, or abused by many outsiders. Nonetheless, Athabascan people persist in using them, often without recognizing that there are alternative modes of thought. In the economic realm, for instance, their trading networks with other indigenous Americans are not as formal as they once were, but they are far more expanded to include Native Americans from many parts of the continent and beyond. One of the central economic issues for Northern Athabascans resides in personal choices that individuals make regarding their investment in the subsistence economy or the cash culture. Most Athabascan villagers maintain their social and personal identities through symbols taken from the subsistence economy. At a minimum this involves eating and otherwise enjoying wildlife in preference to purchased groceries. These personal choices partially define Northern Athabascans as a cultural entity. Far more significant in positioning Northern Athabascans in the global arena are the exploitive aspects of both the cash culture and the Athabascans' economic entrapment within the addictive system. In this respect Northern Athabascans are not viewed in cultural or national terms but, rather, in their utility as defined by the economic objectives of large energy corporations, federal policy makers, and outsiders whose subsistence depends on funding from federal sources.

In discussing local Athabascan economy I have distinguished between revenue in name only (which is designated as for or about Northern Athabascans but rarely, if ever, reaches Athabascan hands) and revenue that enters Athabascan villages as cash. While individual Athabascan people may profess to maintain their lives in a traditional manner, their choices are of no importance to the larger forces that use Northern Athabascans as financial depots. Despite these negative aspects of cash culture, Northern Athabascans in Alaska take hostile measures to gain control over their own economies in order to prevent further exploitation. To a certain extent, their success in this regard can be documented through the material goods and wage-earning jobs they have created and maintained in their villages. The information included in this work testifies that Northern Athabascans of Gwichyaa Zhee have been experiencing a steady increase in cash input during the past two decades. The addictive system that binds Northern Athabascans to many positive and negative institutions in the world is one that, like a cancer, has destroyed many Athabascan lives and traditions by becoming a tradition unto itself. As much as $10 million a year circulates through direct or negative addictive activities in Gwichyaa Zhee (liquor, drugs, and gambling). Nearly $1 million a year comes to Gwichyaa Zhee residents who earn wages working for the positive elements of the addictive system (counselors, health clinicians, and administrators who concern themselves with projects to reduce addictions). Many more millions of dollars circulate in Alaska and elsewhere because of the addictions in Gwichyaa Zhee. These include the air transport companies that take addicts and health care professionals in and out of the villages, the administrators of state and federal grants who are located elsewhere, health care facilities to which addicts are directed for various forms of recovery, and law enforcement personnel who deal with the crimes associated with addictions. Little of these latter forms of revenue enters the Northern Athabascans' economy, but all benefit from it. The addictive system in Gwichyaa Zhee can thus be both lucrative and destructive for those directly involved in it. From a perspective of a larger or global economic milieu, the addictive system is far more lucrative than it is destructive for those who provide both addictive products and addictive healing mechanisms. It is the biggest business in Athabascan territory and one whose prosperity renders impotent ideals about removing it from Gwichyaa Zhee or elsewhere.

Northern Athabascan women have emerged from the household to take prominent positions in Athabascan economic life. Some have become quite successful in personal endeavors, while others have tried and shied away. However, Athabascan women have been no more successful than have Athabascan men in avoiding personal addictions. Teenage alcoholism is linked to issues of entrapment, whereby girls are lured or forced into consuming alcohol in return for sex. Some of the girls ask for help from older women, and sometimes they are lucky in reaching out to someone whose techniques work in their situation. Others are not so lucky. Healing efforts are yet to become community-wide phenomena as they must once have been among Northern Athabascans. Traditional methods of addressing community pathologies are ineffective against the forces of the addictive economy. For instance, the Alkali Lake method suggested in chapter 3 solicits stereotypes of Native American religious traditions as well as practices stemming from modern mainstream spiritualists. These techniques are not unwelcome to some Athabascans, but they have not yet inspired the development of a uniform Athabascan healing theory.

In chapter 4 I discuss some underpinnings of Athabascan collective action and leadership that I generalized into three areas. These include elements of traditional religion that remain in usage, their particular implementation of consensus to direct indeterminate acts of cohesion and violence, and, finally, the complex of signs that are attributed to individual and public strength. With respect to religious traditions, I point out that traditional Athabascan leaders derived their abilities to lead their followers in hunting, seasonal travels, and war expeditions from metaphysical abilities. Contemporary Athabascan leaders hint metaphorically, hopefully, that they might have such skills. In addition, they rely on conventional expectations to negotiate their identities as leaders based on religious theories, such as the ideal of being both great and humble at the same times (*gwintsii veegoo'aii*). Athabascans' everyday behaviors are equally conflicted between an ideal of absolute individualism and an ideal of conforming to what one supposedly knows everyone else is doing or thinking. The paradox between these two concepts is somewhat, but not entirely, resolved or at least signaled in the linguistic union of two concepts of strength: *vat'aii* (personal strength) and *dat'aii* (public strength). In this sense, Northern Athabascans are metaphorically reminded that these two realms of behavior are supposed to coexist harmoniously. One of the accepted modes of collective behavior is violent eviction, which I suggest is evidence of incipient ethnic conflict, for the community often (but not always) evicts non-

Athabascan people. Such evictions have become routinized to include predictable epithets in Gwich'in to denounce *vaanoodlit* (white man) or *oonduk Gwich'in* (outsiders). In addition, I suggest that a parallel exists between the logic of consensual behavior and the logic that motivates traditional sharing behaviors. Both seek to displace accumulated power, authority, or wealth. The same awareness of displacement is evident in the leadership sign of gwintsii veegoo'aii, which requires the individual to behave with force while maintaining a humble demeanor. To be a Northern Athabascan leader requires great sacrifices in time and pride.

As I remark at the beginning of chapter 6, I had hoped to present a full spectrum of ideas about how Northern Athabascans have healed themselves as a society. Instead, I have simply verbalized the indeterminacies regarding contemporary theories of social pathology. The primary source of ambiguity in this area is semiotic, in that researchers begin with a set of assumptions about body, medicine, healing, and death derived from mainstream American theories. Edith Turner (1996) has pointed out that the Iñupiat, for example, consider healing inseparable from spirit perception and activities. Northern Athabascans recognize a similarly broad spectrum of possibilities in healing, as mentioned previously. I also challenge the terms used in defining illness and death among Native Americans, especially with respect to suicide. The death of a teenager by self-inflicted gunshot, stab wound, or hanging is a tragedy that should be considered in isolation from the meanings attached to death by drug overdose or drowning because of drunkenness. I criticize a report of suicidal behavior in an Iñupiat village that conflates these as if all were suicidal. There are connotations of agency and will involved in each of these forms of death that have meaning that is contained in the social system of the deceased. The definitions used by researchers may work in mainstream communities, but I find them unsatisfactory for use in Alaska Native communities.

In sum, with respect to methods of healing, Northern Athabascans continue to make and find solutions, prefer to think in terms of social healing, and have said so publicly for a number of years. Nonetheless, there has been no cessation of alcoholism or other addictions. Northern Athabascan children get drunk at an early age, and many Athabascan people die while still young. The determination to find healing methods has not yet been met by an agreement among Northern Athabascans about what needs healing and how to perform such healing techniques. Once they take command of their own definitions of what social pathology means, they will derive their own methods of understanding what healing is, when it has occurred, and how to identify their own social groups as strong. In their own traditional language, they will find social strength through their own theories of dat'aii. Perforce, Athabascan women have been struggling to develop methods to preserve their children and to train their daughters in how to cope with the abusive behaviors of people in their families (including themselves) as well as people from the larger Athabascan social system. While their methods have been focused on short-term individual survival, they have also become something of a predictable collective Athabascan phenomenon. Like the evictions, they are primarily routinized measures taken against immediate, although generally not discursively defined, danger represented by others. Except in the case of Shreeyvaa's Youth Survivors, most of the measures taken by women are not routinized behaviors that have collectively recognized, positive goals. The Youth Survivors group takes the long-term philosophical approach of the Boy Scouts of America, in that it is focused on empowering future Athabascan adults with Athabascan ideals of strength and skill.

Counterbalancing their efforts to effect positive change in their communities are the ever present pressures of economic instability and dilemmas presented by inconsistent interpersonal habits and behaviors because of alcoholism or other addictions. In many cases their traditional culture offers them solutions along with conflicts, particularly in the case of whether to be self-effacing or brash in dealing with others. These continuous sources of indeterminacy are a significant aspect of the problems that Northern Athabascans face in resolving the social, economic, political, and personal pathological obstacles in their communities.

Alaska Department of Community and Regional Affairs

1994   Community Profile of Arctic Village, Beaver, Birch Creek, Central, Chalkyitsik, Circle, Circle Hot Springs, Fort Yukon, Rampart, Venetie, and Stevens Village. Juneau: Alaska Department of Community and Regional Affairs.

Alaska Federation of Natives

1991   ANCSA: Twenty Years Later. 1991 Annual Report. Anchorage: Alaska Federation of Natives.

Alaska Native Review Commission

1984   Transcript of Proceedings, Overview Roundtable Discussions, vol. 4. ANCSA Institutions and Legal Regimes. Anchorage: Alaska Native Review Commission.

Alaska Rural Development Board

1959   Alaska Village Census — 1958: A Cooperative Project. Juneau: Alaska Rural Development Board.

Alaska Vital Signs

1996   Youth Mortality in Alaska. Alaska Vital Signs 6(1) February.

Albers, Patricia

1983   Sioux Women in Transition: A Study of Their Changing Status in a Domestic and Capitalist Sector of Production. In The Hidden Half: Studies of Plains Indian Women. Patricia Albers and Beatrice Medicine, eds. Pp. 175–236. Washington DC: University Press of America.

Albers, Patricia, and Beatrice Medicine, eds.

1983   The Hidden Half: Studies of Plains Indian Women. Washington DC: University Press of America.

Alderete, Wara, Gina Pacaldo, Xihuanel Huerta, and Lucilene Whitesell

    1992   Daughters of Abya Yala: Native American Women Regaining Control. Summertown TN: Book Publishing Co.

Battaille, Gretchen M.

    1991   American Indian Women: A Guide to Research. New York: Garland.

Battaille, Gretchen M., and Kathleen Mullen Sands

    1984   American Indian Women Telling Their Lives. Lincoln: University of Nebraska Press.

Bellah, Robert, Richard Madsen, William M. Sullivan, Ann Swidler, and Steven M. Tipton

    1985   Habits of the Heart: Individualism and Commitment in American Life. New York: Harper and Row.

Berger, Thomas R.

    1985   Village Journey: The Report of the Alaska Native Review Commission. New York: Hill and Wang.

Berman, Matthew D.

    1995   Total Violent Deaths, Yukon Census Area, Alaska by Community, 1980–1990. Unpublished MS, Anchorage.

Berman, Matthew D., and Linda Leask

    1994   Violent Death in Alaska: Who Is Most Likely to Die? Alaska Review of Social and Economic Conditions 29(1):1–12.

Bissett, Don

    1967   The Lower MacKenzie Region: An Area Economic Survey. Ottawa: Industrial Division, DIAND.

Bourdieu, Pierre

    1977[1972]   Outline of a Theory of Practice. Richard Nice, trans. Cambridge: Cambridge University Press.

Brant, Beth

    1994   Writing as Witness. Toronto: Women's Press.

Brightman, Robert A.

    1993   Grateful Prey: Rock Cree Human–Animal Relationships. Los Angeles: University of California Press.

Brumbach, Hetty Jo, and Robert Jarvenpa

1997   Woman the Hunter: Ethnoarchaeological Lessons from Chipewyan Life-Cycle Dynamics. In Women in Prehistory: North America and Meso-america. Cheryl Claassen and Rosemary A. Joyce, eds. Pp. 17–32. Philadel-phia: University of Pennsylvania Press.

Burke, Clara Heintz (as told to Adele Comandini)

1961   Doctor Hap: The Fresh and Appealing Love Story of a Dedicated Cou-ple in the Alaskan Wilderness. New York: Coward-McCann, Inc.

Cambell, Maria

1973   Half-Breed. Halifax, Canada: Goodread Biographies.

Campisi, Jack

1991   Report on the Neets'aii Gwich'in Tribe of Indians of the Chandalar Reservation (Preliminary). Unpublished MS.

Carlo, Poldine

1978   Nulato, an Indian Life on the Yukon. Fairbanks: Poldine Carlo.

Champagne, Joseph-Etienne

1949   Les Missions Catholiques dans l'Ouest Canadien (1818–1875). Ottawa: Editions des Etudes Oblates Scolasticat Saint Joseph.

Childers, Robert A.

1994   Cultural Protection: A Link to Tradition. Forum for Applied Research and Public Policy 9(4):79–83.

Childers, Robert A., and Mary Kancewick

N.d.[c. 1992]   The Gwich'in (Kutchin): Conservation and Cultural Protec-tion in the Arctic Borderlands. Unpublished MS, Gwich'in Steering Commit-tee, Anchorage.

Christian, Jane, and Peter M. Gardner

1977   The Individual in Northern Dene Thought and Communication: A Study in Sharing and Diversity. Mercury Series, Canadian Ethnology Service Paper, 35. Ottawa: National Museum of Man.

Claassen, Cheryl, and Rosemary A. Joyce, eds.

1997   Women in Prehistory: North America and Mesoamerica. Philadel-phia: University of Pennsylvania Press.

Cobb, James C.

1992   From Rocky Top to Detroit City: Country Music and the Economic Transformation of the South. In You Wrote My Life: Lyrical Themes in Country Music. Melton McLaurin and Richard A. Peterson, eds. Pp. 63–80. Philadelphia: Gordon and Breach.

Cook Inlet Tribal Council

1993   What You've Often Needed to Know — But Didn't Know Where to Look. Anchorage: Cook Inlet Tribal Council.

Dean, David M.

1988   Breaking Trail: Hudson Stuck of Texas and Alaska. Athens: Ohio University Press.

De Laguna, Frederica

1975   Matrilineal Kin Groups in Northwestern North America. In Proceedings: Northern Athapaskan Conference, 2 vols. A. McFadyen Clark, ed. Pp. 17–145. Mercury Series, Canadian Ethnology Service Paper, 27. Ottawa: National Museum of Man.

De Mers, Pierre, and Judy Erick

N.d.   Luke. Western Gwich'in Translation. Venetie AK: Wycliffe Bible Translators.

Dobyns, Henry F.

1991[1983]   An Outline of Florida Epidemiology. In The Spanish Borderlands Sourcebooks, vol. 2. Clark Spencer Larsen, ed. Pp. 81–129. New York: Garland Publishing, Inc.

Dove, Michael R.

1988   The Real and Imagined Role of Culture in Development: Case Studies from Indonesia. Honolulu: University of Hawaii Press.

Durkheim, Émile

1965[1915]   The Elementary Forms of the Religious Life. Joseph Ward Swain, trans. New York: Free Press; and London: Collier Macmillan Publishers.

Episcopal Church Center

1991   Steve Charleston Consecrated Sixth Bishop of Alaska. Ikhana: The Newsletter of American Indian/Alaska Native Ministry of the Episcopal Church (spring):12–14.

1992   The Phoenix Nine: Resolutions of 70th General Convention Specifically Significant to Native Americans. New York: Episcopal Church Center.

Fast, Phyllis

1990   Naatsiłanei and Ko'ehdan: A Semiotic Analysis of Two Alaska Native Myths. M.A. thesis, University of Alaska Anchorage.

Fire Thunder, Cecilia

1992   I Get My Courage and Strength from Being an Indian. In Daughters of Abya Yala: Native American Women Regaining Control. Wara Alderete, Gina Pacaldo, Xihuanel Huerta, and Lucilene Whitesell. Pp. 13–16. Summertown TN: Book Publishing Co.

Fischer, Douglas, and Kristian Kelly

1996   Alcohol, Suicide Pose Daunting Problems: Alaska's Political Candidates Offer Solutions for Bush Villages. Fairbanks Daily News–Miner, July 7: A1, A6.

Fredson, John

1982   John Fredson Edward Sapier Hàa Googwandak: Stories Told by John Fredson to Edward Sapir. Katherine Peter, transcriber; Jane McGary, ed. and trans. Fairbanks: Alaska Native Language Center, University of Alaska.

Goulet, Jean-Guy

1982   Religious Dualism among Athapaskan Catholics. Canadian Journal of Anthropology 3(1):1–17.

1994   Rècit de Rêves et de Vision chez les Dénés Tha Contemporains: Vision du monde et principes épistémologiques sous-jacents. Anthropologie et Sociétés 18(2):59–74.

Green, Rayna

1983   Native American Women: A Contextual Bibliography. Bloomington: Indiana University Press.

Gridley, Marion E.

   1974   American Indian Women. New York: Hawthorne Books, Inc.

Guédon, Marie-Françoise

   1994   La Pratique du Rêve chez les Dénés Septentrionaux. Anthropologie et Sociétés 18(2):75–89.

Gwich'in Niintsyaa

   1988   Resolution to Prohibit Development in the Calving and Post-Calving Grounds of the Porcupine Caribou Herd. Resolution Passed 10 June. Arctic Village AK: Gwich'in Gathering.

Hara, Hiroko Sue

   1980   The Hare Indians and Their World. Canadian Ethnology Service Paper, 63. Ottawa: National Museum of Man.

Havighurst, R. J., and B. L. Neugarten

   1969   American Indian and White Children: A Sociopsychological Investigation. Chicago: University of Chicago Press.

Herbert, Belle

   1988   Shandaa: In My Lifetime. Bill Pfisterer with Alice Moses, recorder and ed.; Katherine Peter, transcriber and trans. Fairbanks: Alaska Native Language Center, University of Alaska Press.

Hertzberg, Hazel W.

   1971   The Search for an American Indian Identity: Modern Pan-American Movements. Syracuse: Syracuse University Press.

Herzfeld, Michael

   1992   The Social Production of Indifference. New York: Berg Publications.

Hylson-Smith, Kenneth

   1988   Evangelicals in the Church of England: 1734–1984. Edinburgh: T&T Clark.

Indigenous Survival International

   1988   Resolution No. 1. Unpublished MS, Fort Yukon AK.

James, Caroline

   1996   Nez Perce Women in Transition, 1877–1990. Moscow: University of Idaho Press.

Jakobson, Roman

1971 Shifters, Verbal Categories and the Russian Verb. In Roman Jakobson: Selected Writings, vol. 2. Word and Language. Pp. 130–147. The Hague: Mouton.

John, Peter

1996 The Gospel according to Peter John. David J. Krupa, ed. Fairbanks: Alaska Native Knowledge Network.

Joyce, Rosemary A., and Cheryl Claassen

1997 Women in the Ancient Americas: Archaeologists, Gender, and the Making of Prehistory. In Women in Prehistory: North America and Meso-america. Cheryl Claassen and Rosemary A. Joyce, eds. Pp. 1–14. Philadelphia: University of Pennsylvania Press.

Karamanski, Theodore J.

1983 Fur Trade and Exploration: Opening the Far Northwest, 1821–1852. Vancouver: University of British Columbia Press.

Kari, James

1990 Ahtna Athabaskan Dictionary. Fairbanks: Alaska Native Language Center.

Kasl, Charlotte Davis

1992 Many Roads, One Journey: Moving beyond the Twelve Steps. New York: Harper Perennial.

Kassi, Norma

1996 A Legacy of Maldevelopment. In Defending Mother Earth: Native American Perspectives on Environmental Justice. Jace Weaver, ed. Pp. 72–84. Maryknoll NY: Orbis Books.

Katz, Jane

1995 Messengers of the Wind: Native American Women Tell Their Life Stories. New York: Ballantine Books.

Kearney, J. M. Patrick

1962 Au Pays des Peaux-de-Lièvres: Héros ignoré de l'Arctique. Edmonton: Arthur Douville.

Kettle, Paul, and Edward O. Bixler

1993 Alcohol and Suicide in Alaska Natives. American Indian and Alaska Native Health Research 5(3):34–45.

Kidwell, Clara Sue

1979 American Indian Women — Problems of Communicating a Cultural/Sexual Identity. The Creative Woman 2(3):33–38.

1992 Indian Women as Cultural Mediators. Ethnohistory 39 (spring): 97–107.

Kraus, Robert, and Patricia Buffler

1974 Patterns of Mental Illness, Alcohol Abuse, and Drug Abuse among Alaska Natives. Unpublished MS, Alaska Federation of Natives.

1977 Intercultural Variation in Mortality Due to Violence. In Current Perspectives in Cultural Psychiatry. E. F. Foulks, R. M. Wintrob, J. Westermeyer, and A. R. Favazza, eds. Pp. 81–91. New York: Spectrum.

Krech, Shepard, III

1976 The Eastern Kutchin and the Fur Trade, 1800–1860. Ethnohistory 23(3):213–235.

1978a Disease, Starvation, and Northern Athapaskan Social Organization. American Ethnologist 5:710–732.

1978b On the Aboriginal Population of the Kutchin. Arctic Anthropology 15(1):89–104.

1979a Interethnic Relations in the Lower MacKenzie River Region. Arctic Anthropology 16(2):102–122.

1979b The Nakotcho Kutchin: A Tenth Aboriginal Kutchin Band? Journal of Anthropological Research 35:109–121.

1980 Northern Athapaskan Ethnology in the 1970s. Annual Review of Anthropology 9:83–100.

1983 The Beaver Indians and the Hostilities at Fort St. John's. Arctic Anthropology 20(2):35–45.

Krech, Shepard, III, ed.

1980 Indians, Animals, and the Fur Trade: A Critique of Keepers of the Game. Athens: University of Georgia Press.

Leechman, Douglas

    1954   The Vanta Kutchin. Anthropological Series, 33, Bulletin, 130. Ottawa: National Museum of Man.

Lester, David

    1997   Suicide in American Indians. New York: Nova Science Publishers, Inc.

Lincoln, Georgianna

    1998   Lack of True American Indian History in Textbooks. In Authentic Alaska: Voices of Its Native Writers. Susan B. Andrews and John Creed, eds. Pp. 91–95. Lincoln: University of Nebraska Press.

Loh, Shirley

    1990a   Projections de la population indienne inscrite, 1986–2001. Ottawa: Demography Division, Statistics Canada.

    1990b   Registered Indian Household and Family Projections 1986 to 2011. Ottawa: Demography Division, Statistics Canada.

MacKenzie, Clara Childs

    1985   Wolf Smeller (Zhoh Gwatsan): A Biography of John Fredson, Native Alaskan. Anchorage: Alaska Pacific University Press.

Mankiller, Wilma, and Michael Wallis

    1993   Mankiller, a Chief and Her People. New York: St. Martin's Press.

Marris, Peter

    1974   Loss and Change. London: Routledge and Kegan Paul, Ltd.

Martin, Calvin

    1978   Keepers of the Game: Indian–Animal Relationships and the Fur Trade. Berkeley: University of California Press.

May, Philip A., and Nancy Westlake Van Winkle

    1994   Indian Adolescent Suicide: The Epidemiologic Picture in New Mexico. In Calling from the Rim: Suicidal Behavior among American Indian and Alaska Native Adolescents. Christine Wilson Duclos and Spero M. Mason, eds. Pp. 2–34. American Indian and Alaska Native Mental Health Research, the Journal of the National Center Monograph Series, 4. Denver CO: The National Center for American Indian and Alaska Native Mental Health Research.

Maybury-Lewis, David

1997   Indigenous Peoples, Ethnic Groups, and the State. Needham Heights MA: Allyn and Bacon.

McDonald, Robert

1898   Thlukwinadhun Sheg akǫ Ketchid Kwitugwatsuį: Takudh Ttshah zit Thleteteitazya. London: British and Foreign Bible Society.

McKennan, Robert A.

1959   The Upper Tanana Indians. New Haven: Yale University Department of Anthropology.

1965   The Chandalar Kutchin. Technical Paper, 17. Toronto: Arctic Institute of North America.

McLaurin, Melton, and Richard A. Peterson, eds.

1992   You Wrote My Life: Lyrical Themes in Country Music. Philadelphia: Gordon and Breach.

Medicine, Bea

1978   The Native American Woman: A Perspective. Austin: National Educational Laboratory Publishers.

1983   Warrior Women. In The Hidden Half: Studies of Plains Indian Women. Patricia Albers and Bea Medicine, eds. Pp. 267–277. Washington DC: University Press of America.

Meister, Cary W.

1991[1976]   Demographic Consequences of Euro-American Contact on Selected American Indian Populations and Their Relationship to the Demographic Transition. In The Spanish Borderlands Sourcebooks, vol. 2. Clark Spencer Larsen, ed. Pp. 371–382. New York: Garland Publishing, Inc.

Mellody, Pia, and Andrea Wells Miller

1989   Breaking Free: A Recovery Workbook for Facing Co-Dependence. New York: Harper and Row.

Miller, William R., and Reid K. Hester

1989   Treating Alcohol Problems: Toward an Informed Eclecticism. In Handbook of Alcoholism Treatment Approaches: Effective Alternatives. Pp. 3–13. New York: Pergamon Press.

Mishler, Craig

1981 Gwich'in Athapaskan Music and Dance: An Ethnography and Ethno-history. Ph.D. dissertation, University of Texas, Austin.

1990 Missionaries in Collision: Anglicans and Oblates among the Gwich'in, 1861–65. Arctic 43(2):121–126.

1993 The Crooked Stovepipe: Athapaskan Fiddle Music and Square Dancing in Northeast Alaska and Northwest Canada. Urbana: University of Illinois Press.

1995 Neerihiinjik: We Traveled from Place to Place, Johnny Sarah Haa Googwandak (the Gwich'in Stories of Johnny and Sarah Frank). Fairbanks: Alaska Native Language Center.

Mooney, James

1928 The Aboriginal Population of America North of Mexico. Smithsonian Institution, Miscellaneous Collection, 80(7). Washington DC: Smithsonian Institution.

Morice, A. G.

1923 L'Abbé Émile Petitot et les découvertes géographiques au Canada étude géographic-historique. Quebec: Imp. L'Action Sociale.

Murray, Alexander H.

1910 Journal of the Yukon, 1947–48. Publications of the Canadian Archives, 4. Ottawa: Canadian Archives.

Murray, David W.

1992 Self-Sufficiency and the Creation of Dependency: The Case of Chief Isaac, Inc. American Indian Quarterly 16(2):169–188.

Napoleon, Harold

1991 Yuuyaraq: The Way of the Human Being. Eric Madsen, ed. Fairbanks: College of Rural Alaska, University of Alaska Fairbanks, Center for Cross-Cultural Studies.

Niezen, Ronald

1993 Telling a Message: Cree Perceptions of Custom and Administration. Canadian Journal of Native Studies 13(2):221–250.

1997   Healing and Conversion: Medical Evangelism in James Bay Cree Society. Ethnohistory 44(3):463–491.

1998   Defending the Land: Sovereignty and Forest Life in James Bay Cree Society. Needham Heights MA: Allyn and Bacon.

Northern Native Broadcasting Yukon

1989   Gwich'in Niintsyaa: 1988 Arctic Village Gathering. Videotape. George M. Henry and Ruth Carroll, producers. Anchorage: Gwich'in Steering Committee.

O'Connor, Bonnie Blair

1995   Healing Traditions: Alternative Medicine and the Health Professions. Philadelphia: University of Pennsylvania Press.

O'Nell, Theresa DeLeane

1996   Disciplined Hearts: History, Identity, and Depression in an American Indian Community. Berkeley: University of California Press.

Ortner, Sherry B.

1996[1971]   Is Female to Male as Nature Is to Culture? In Making Gender: The Politics and Erotics of Culture. Pp. 21–42. Boston: Beacon Press (originally published in Feminist Studies).

Osgood, Cornelius

1934   Kutchin Tribal Distribution and Synonymy. American Anthropologist 36:168–179.

1936   Contributions to the Ethnography of the Kutchin. Yale University Publications in Anthropology, 14. New Haven: Yale University Press.

1958   Ingalik Social Culture. Yale University Publications in Anthropology, 53. New Haven: Yale University Press.

1959   Ingalik Mental Culture. Yale University Publications in Anthropology, 56. New Haven: Yale University Press.

1966   The Ethnography of the Tanaina. Yale University Publications in Anthropology, 16. New Haven: Yale University Press, reprinted by Human Relations Area Files Press.

1971   The Han Indians, a Compilation of Ethnographic and Historical Data on the Alaska–Yukon Boundary Area. Yale University Publications in Anthropology, 74. New Haven: Yale University Press.

Palkovich, Ann M.

1994 Historic Epidemics of the American Pueblos. In In the Wake of Contact: Biological Responses to Conquest. Clark Spencer Larsen and George R. Milner, eds. Pp. 87–96. New York: Wiley-Liss, Inc.

Parezo, Nancy J., ed.

1993 Hidden Scholars: Women Anthropologists and the Native American Southwest. Albuquerque: University of New Mexico Press.

Peake, F. A.

1975 Robert McDonald (1829–1913): The Great Unknown Missionary of the Northwest. Journal of the Canadian Church Historical Society 17(3): 54–72.

Peter, Julia

1989 Ko'ehdan. Told in Gwich'in to Marilyn Savage and Phyllis Fast. Marilyn Savage, trans. Taped in November, University of Alaska Fairbanks Library.

Peter, Katherine

1979 Dinjii Zhuh Ginjik Nagwan Tr'iltsaii. Gwich'in Junior Dictionary. Katherine Peter, compiler; J. Leslie Boffa, illustrator. Anchorage: National Bilingual Materials Development Center; and Fairbanks: Alaska Native Language Center.

1992 Neets'aii Gwiindaii: Living in the Chandalar Country. Fairbanks: Alaska Native Language Center.

Peterson, Richard A.

1992 Class Consciousness in Country Music. In You Wrote My Life: Lyrical Themes in Country Music. Melton McLaurin and Richard A. Peterson, eds. Pp. 35–62. Philadelphia: Gordon and Breach.

Petitot, Émile

1886 Traditions indiennes du Canada nord-ouest (Les Litteratures polulaires de toutes les nations 23). Paris: Maisonneuve freres et C. LeClerc.

1888   Traditions indiennes du Canada nord-ouest (Textes originaux et traduction littérale). Alençon, France: E. Renaut de Broise.

1889   Quinz Ans Sous le Cercle Polair. D. Dentu, ed. Paris.

1976   The Book of Dene: Containing the Traditions and Beliefs of Chipewyan, Dogrib, Slavey, and Loucheux Peoples. Translated from French and compared with versions in the original tongues. Yellowknife, Canada: Programme Development Division, Department of Education.

Petroff, Ivan

1900   The Population and Resources of Alaska. In Compilation of Narratives of Explorations in Alaska. Pp. 52–281. Washington DC: U.S. Congress, Senate Committee on Military Affairs.

Ramos, Alcida

1988   Indian Voices: Contact Experienced and Expressed. In Rethinking History and Myth: Indigenous South American Perspectives on the Past. Jonathan D. Hill, ed. Pp. 214–234. Urbana: University of Illinois Press.

Rowe, P. T.

1917   Annual Report of the Bishop of the Missionary District of Alaska for the Year 1916–1917. In The Domestic and Foreign Missionary Society of the Protestant Episcopal Church. Pp. 5–12. New York: Church House.

Russell, Frank

1898   Explorations in the Far North: Being the Report of an Expedition under the Auspices of the University of Iowa Dating the Years 1892, '93, and '94. Iowa City: University of Iowa Press.

Sample, Tex

1996   White Soul: Country Music, the Church and Working Americans. Nashville: Abingdon Press.

Sanneh, Lamin

1989   Translating the Message: The Missionary Impact on Culture. American Society of Missiology Series, 13. Maryknoll NY: Orbis Books.

Schaef, Anne Wilson

1986   Co-Dependence Misunderstood-Mistreated. San Francisco: Harper and Row.

1987   When Society Becomes an Addict. New York: HarperCollins Publishers.

1988   The Addictive Organization: New York: Harper and Row.

Schmitter, Ferdinand

1910   Upper Yukon Native Customs and Folk-Lore. Smithsonian Miscellaneous Collections, 56(4). Washington DC: Smithsonian Institution.

Scollon, Ronald, and Suzanne B. Scollon

1979   Linguistic Convergence: An Ethnography of Speaking at Fort Chipewyan, Alberta. New York: Academic Press.

Shoemaker, Nancy, ed.

1995   Negotiators of Change: Historical Perspectives on Native American Women. New York: Routledge.

Slobodin, Richard

1960   Some Social Functions of Kutchin Anxiety. American Anthropologist 62(1):122–133.

1962   Band Organization of the Peel River Kutchin. Anthropological Series, 55, Bulletin, 179. Ottawa: National Museum of Canada.

1970   Kutchin Concepts of Reincarnation. Western Canadian Journal of Anthropology 2(1):67–79.

1975   Without Fire: A Kutchin Tale of Warfare, Survival, and Vengeance. In Proceedings: Northern Athapaskan Conference, 1971, vol. 1. A. McFadyen Clark, ed. Pp. 259–301. Canadian Ethnology Service Paper, 27. Ottawa: National Museum of Man.

1981   Kutchin. In Handbook of North American Indians, vol. 6. The Subarctic. June Helm, ed. Pp. 514–532. Washington DC: Smithsonian Institution Press.

Smith, Marvin T.

1991[1987]   The Demographic Collapse. In The Spanish Borderlands
Sourcebooks, vol. 2. Clark Spencer Larsen, ed. Pp. 22–58. New York: Garland
Publishing, Inc.

Stiffarm, Lenore A., and Phil Lane Jr.

1992   The Demography of Native North America: A Question of American
Indian Survival. In The State of Native America: Genocide, Colonization,
and Resistance. M. Annette Jaimes, ed. Pp. 23–53. Boston: South End
Press.

Szasz, Margaret Connell

1988   Indian Women between Two Worlds: Moor's School and Coeducation
in 1760s. In Indian Education in the American Colonies. Pp. 218–231. Albuquerque: University of New Mexico Press.

Talamantez, Inés

1995   Seeing Red: American Indian Women Speaking about Their Religious and Political Perspectives. In In Our Own Voices: Four Centuries of
American Women's Religious Writing. Rosemary Skinner Keller and Rosemary Radford Ruether, eds. Pp. 383–424. San Francisco: HarperSan-
Francisco.

Tambiah, Stanley

1996   Leveling Crowds: Ethnonationalist Conflicts and Collective Violence
in South Asia. Berkeley: University of California Press.

Travis, Robert

1983   Suicide in Northwest Alaska. White Cloud Journal 3(1):23–30.

1986   Suicide since Statehood. Alaska Native Magazine 4(5):38–40.

Turner, Edith

1996   The Hands Feel It: Healing and Spirit Presence among a Northern
Alaskan People. DeKalb: Northern Illinois University Press.

United States and Canada

1987   Agreement between the Government of the United States of America
and the Government of Canada on the Conservation of the Porcupine Cari-

bou Herd. Agreement signed in July by Donald Paul Hodel for the United States and Tom McMillan for Canada.

Wallis, Velma

1993   Two Old Women. Fairbanks: Epicenter Press.

1996   Bird Girl and the Man Who Followed the Sun. Fairbanks: Epicenter Press.

Waring, Marilyn

1988   If Women Counted: A New Feminist Economics. Gloria Steinem, intro. San Francisco: Harper and Row.

Weaver, Jace

1997   That the People Might Live: Native American Literatures and Native American Community. New York: Oxford University Press.

Weaver, Jace, ed.

1996   Defending Mother Earth: Native American Perspectives on Environmental Justice. Maryknoll NY: Orbis Books.

Wescott, Masako Cordray

1995   Voice from the North: The Gwich'in People and the Arctic National Wildlife Refuge. Videotape. Maui Video Co.

Wright, Miranda

1995   The Last Great Indian War, Nulato 1851. M.A. thesis, Department of Anthropology, University of Alaska Fairbanks.